Allen, Margaret,
1933-

Selling dreams

Also by Margaret Allen

THE TIMES 1000
THE MONEY BOOK
BOOK OF MONEY

MARGARET ALLEN

SELLING DREAMS

Inside the Beauty Business

SIMON AND SCHUSTER

NEW YORK

SIMON AND SCHUSTER and colophon are trademarks of Simon & Schuster
Designed by Eve Kirch
Picture Editor: Vincent Virga
Manufactured in the United States of America

1   3   5   7   9   10   8   6   4   2

Library of Congress Cataloging in Publication Data

Allen, Margaret, date
Selling dreams.

Includes index.
1. Cosmetics industry—History.   2.   Cosmetics
industry—United States—History.   I.   Title.
HD9970.5.C672A44   338.4'766855'09   81-1038
AACR2

ISBN 0-671-41143-8

The author is grateful for permission to reprint excerpts from the following:

The "merger madness" quote (Oct. 1963) © 1963 *Beauty Fashion.*
The "Bernard Mitchell formula" (Apr. 1975) © 1975 *Beauty Fashion.*
Article about Michel Bergerac (June, 1978) © 1978 *Beauty Fashion.*

(Continued after Index)

ACKNOWLEDGMENTS

It is impossible, when writing about the cosmetics industry, to mention all the companies in the business around the world, or even all the items sold by a particular company, let alone all the products on the market. In writing this book I have done my best to portray an overall view of the industry in its international aspects. To do that, I have called on friends and colleagues all over the world; they have given me much information and advice, and if I have missed anyone who thinks he should figure in these pages, my apologies.

I have to thank Charlotte Hughes for all her assistance in getting together the scientific and industrial base of the industry, Olga Leapman for her support and help in watching trends in the industry over the past two years in North America, and Debra Kasouf of the Washington Office of the London *Times* for her help on legal aspects of the business in the United States. Jennifer Newton, my secretary, was always ready to check and assist me when it seemed difficult to get information and, in typing out the manuscript, pointed out statements that seemed unclear or misleading.

I also have to thank many people in the industry who, without exception, willingly answered my questions and thus helped bring the book to life. The Max Factor, Elizabeth Arden, Helena Rubinstein, Avon, Revlon and Estée Lauder companies, and many of the smaller ones, were especially helpful in the U.S.A. Shiseido, the American subsidiary of the Japanese concern, the Cosmetic, Toiletry and Fragrance Association, Inc., and BAT Industries of the United Kingdom filled other gaps.

In particular, in the United States, I must thank Mr. Joseph Ronchetti of Elizabeth Arden; Carol Walters of Max Factor; Frank Johnson, Jr., of Revlon; Andrew Philip of Shiseido, Inc.; James Nixon of Cosmair, Inc.; Leonard Lauder of Estée Lauder; Margaret Hayes of Saks Fifth Avenue; Sam Kallish; Hazel Bishop of Evans and Company, the New York brokers; Shirley Lord and Joe Mann of Helena Rubinstein; Merrill James Gray of Avon Products; and Suzy Parker Dillman and Baroness Fiona Thyssen. In San Diego, Bill Randall and Zetta Castle were a fund of stories about the industry from their La Costa health farm base. I had been led to them by Nadja Avalle, a leading cosmetics chemist based in Switzerland, who explained to me just what was and was not possible in cosmetics. In the United Kingdom, Eric Morgan, managing director of BAT Cosmetics, and Prudence Glynn of *The Times* were of special assistance. In Japan, Peter Hazelhurst of the London *Times* and Mariko Maeda were of great help. Many others who talked to me wished to remain anonymous.

To everyone, sincere thanks. To critics, the opinions expressed in the book are my own.

I am also grateful to several publications and authors for permission to quote from their works. Rosemary Simon gave me permission to quote from her book *The Price of Beauty*. *The New Yorker* allowed me to reprint an excerpt from its profile "Glamour, Inc.," by Margaret Chase Harriman, which was published on April 6, 1935. The London-based *News of the World* permitted me to quote Jean Shrimpton as reported by that publication in 1980. *Forbes* magazine provided me with the quote by David Mahoney in its November 1976 issue; *The Wall Street Journal*, a September

1978 issue on the Yves Saint-Laurent Opium launch; *The New York Times*, an article on Leonard Lauder in 1973; *Newsweek*, material on Jean Shrimpton in its September 23, 1965, issue; the New York *Post*, an article on the Chinese Americans' opposition to the Opium fragrance in 1978. The Bodley Head in London and Simon and Schuster in New York together with the Helena Rubinstein Foundation permitted me to quote from Helena Rubinstein's *My Life for Beauty*. I am grateful to Jessica Mitford for a quotation from her article on Maine Chance beauty farm which appeared in the March 1966 copy of *McCalls Magazine*; to the *Harvard Business Review* for an excerpt from "Second Thoughts on Going Public" by Richard Salomon in the September–October 1977 issue; to *Time* magazine for two quotations, one from December 9, 1935, on Max Factor, and another on Revlon on September 30, 1957; to *Women's Wear Daily* for a quotation by Sam Kallish on August 27, 1976, on joining Max Factor; to Avon Products for material from David McConnell's memoirs; to *Beauty Fashion* for a series of excerpts from many articles; to *The Lancet* on the cancer risk in hair dyes from March 1976; to the Messrs. Kirkland and Venitt, who allowed me to quote from their paper on cancer risks; and, finally, to the Cosmetic, Toiletry and Fragrance Association for material on the effects of cosmetics from a statement made in November 1979.

I have been fortunate, too, in my agent, Michael Sissons, and my publishers in both the United Kingdom and the United States of America. Alice Mayhew of Simon and Schuster in the U.S. could not have been a more creative editor, and at Dent in London, Peter Shellard was encouraging and patient. Thank you both.

for Michael

CONTENTS

PREFACE

Birds do it, bees do it, the Dutch in old Amsterdam most certainly did it*—all animal and human life does it. *It* is self-decoration, the purpose—usually—to entice the opposite sex. Over the centuries all that has distinguished humans from animals in this regard is that people have always taken artificial steps to make themselves look more attractive: most animals get to be that way naturally when the occasion demands.

Yet it's all an illusion. In the past thirty years alone women seem to have changed markedly. Without seeing their birth certificates, it's difficult to believe that some mothers and daughters are even related. In the 1950s, women had large lush-lashed doe eyes with no mouths at all, wearing very little makeup on their faces. Mere illusion. By the 1960s, mouths were back and eyes were less round. Illusion. As the 1980s began, faces were altogether different again, with features sharply defined in garish unnatural colors. Faces that in the 1950s were gently rounded or oval have become sharp and pointed. Illusion. There is no chance in the world that

* With apologies to Cole Porter.

these changes are physical. They owe it all to a single, massive industry based on selling dreams—the cosmetics industry.

Beauty secrets have been handed down through the ages, and not just from woman to woman. Men have always been as concerned about their attractiveness to women as women have to men, sometimes more so. It's all merely a matter of fashion, which has dictated periods when men were the lavishly dressed, extravagantly coiffured and made-up sex, and when women resembled the mundane peahen, leaving the splendor and color to the male.

But basic though the urge may be, cosmetics have come a long way from Cleopatra's fabled bath in asses' milk, the decorative wigs of the seventeenth and eighteenth centuries, the highly colored faces of the courtesans, the paint used by American Indians when they fought their battles—the original war paint—or the touch of rouge on the cheek of the 1920s flapper. Cosmetics today are big business—very big business.

The trick has been to steer customers away from the idea of simply looking good, according to the day's fashion, persuading them—mostly quite erroneously—that cosmetics are good for them. As a result, as has happened in many other fields in the twentieth century, what was previously a simple, harmless human activity for the most part, has developed into a multimillion-dollar trade touching the entire world, making massive fortunes for those few people who have had the knack of setting trends and spotting developments before anyone else. What makes the cosmetics trade unusual, if not unique, is that this gigantic high-technology industry developed first, not only in the industrialized West, but at least as early and quickly in the East, although it must be said that most companies, once they reach a certain size, attack the most lucrative market of all, North America—if they were not set up there in the first place.

Success is based on the simple premise that if it's a question of being attractive and fashionable, you can sell people anything. Wartime governments realized this: they stopped production of many inessentials during the war effort but not lipstick. They understood the psychological boost that her lipstick gave a woman working in a munitions factory, for example. The psychological approach continues. Only two years ago, perhaps the most notable success in cosmetics was Yves Saint-Laurent's almost instant change-of-image—through a single publicity campaign —from couturier to established cosmetics manufacturer. He did it with Opium. Is there a single woman in the world who thinks that Opium is for swallowing or "shooting"? Hardly. Yet sales of Opium perfume soared to many hundreds of thousands of dollars during the week its initial advertising campaign was launched, a campaign that featured an extremely glamorous and beautiful woman looking stoned out of her mind: on a smell? (There was also, of course, a little help from the world press.) So successful was this campaign that Chinese-American organizations said it made narcotics romantic and insulted the Chinese people.

At first glance, few of those who made fortunes from cosmetics in the early years of this century seemed to have obvious credentials for success. A funny little Polish woman, stretching to all of four feet ten inches, apparently unable to speak any language properly and, if not downright ugly, certainly no beauty, went the circuitous route to America via a first salon in Melbourne, Australia, through London and Paris, amassing a fortune, one of the finest collections of art in the world and a title on her way. She was Helena Rubinstein.

Few people have heard of her arch rival, the daughter of a Canadian truck driver, under her real name, Florence Nightingale Graham. Under her adopted name of Elizabeth Arden, however, she prospered even more than Rubinstein. There was none of the gentle touch of her namesake, the saintly lady-of-the-lamp, about *this* lady, who by all accounts had a vicious temper and much preferred horses to people, or at least to her husbands.

A French dress designer, tired of being unable to find lipsticks that matched the clothes she created, decided to make her own and eventually abandoned dress designing to make a full line of cosmetics, later selling out in the late sixties to a multimillion-dollar conglomerate based in the United Kingdom. Today Germaine Monteil lives in luxury at her homes in France and America—while BAT Industries struggles to make a profit on her company.

An aggressive, thrusting New York Jew, with little personal taste, finesse or charm and certainly no respect for the women in his personal life nor for the many millions from whom he made many millions of dollars, based his company for many years on just one product—nail varnish. Charles Revson was such a terrifying employer that executives who survived in the company for more than a year were said to hold a long-server's celebration. Yet when he died, his company, Revlon—a little-known partner, Charles Lachman, having provided the "l"—was selling $605 million worth of cosmetics in a single year. These are just four of the dozens who have made fortunes in cosmetics since the turn of the century.

And it still goes on. New people with new ideas and new dreams to offer constantly enter the business. Many fail after an initial flush. Many succeed in a small way and then sell out to the big (usually) pharmaceutical companies. A few—a very few—go on to build large empires.

And those who succeed have created their wealth on a dream, an insubstantial fantasy, which certainly cannot become reality, not yet anyway. These dreams have added to the age-old human illusion that if a woman uses a little dab of powder here, some cream there, a touch of mascara, a smudge of lipstick or a trace of blush, someone somewhere will find her attractive and, what is more, maybe actually fall in love with her—all as a result of a change that is neither permanent nor skin deep. Cosmetics, claim the manufacturers, no longer merely make you look good according to current fashions but, more important, are good for you, keeping the skin elastic and youthful. Yet it is all a fake. Cosmetics do no more than cover the skin and change the appearance of the surface. They cannot have a permanent effect on the skin. They either simply wear off or wash off. No cream has yet been created that can go through the skin and prevent aging. If it had been, it could not be sold as a cosmetic but only as a drug, subject as such to all kinds of official regulations and conditions. Skin creams may make your skin *feel* good, but they cannot *do* it any good. Cosmetic surgery may help a person look young, but the procedure in fact merely tucks up or cuts away old skin, so that, without it, the face looks younger.

Having said all this, what's wrong with a dream, a make-believe? Three years ago I started to study the cosmetics industry. I then used a variety of creams, usually expensive ones. Now I know that the good they can do is very limited, affecting the surface only; if any physical benefit is derived, it is the result of the cleansing of the skin, the slowing of the loss of moisture and the natural effect of massage. And certainly price has nothing to do with effectiveness. But the creams are still there and they are still pricey ones and I still use them. No fool like an old fool, I suppose, unless you happen to be a Rubinstein, or an Arden, a Monteil or a Revson. They were no fools.

ONE

ENTER THE DRAGONS

Spend all you have for loveliness.
Buy it and never count the cost;
For one white singing hour of peace
Count many a year of strife well lost,
And for a breath of ecstasy,
Give all you have been or could be.
　　　　　　　　　　　—Sara Teasdale

Elizabeth Arden was not a nice woman. Few people found her at all likable, and she had only a handful of friends. Her two husbands obviously did not care for her much: the second one stuck out the marriage for less than a year. People who could find much to forgive in the domineering and eccentric Helena Rubinstein could see few redeeming features in Arden, who was not even originally Elizabeth Arden. Born in Ontario, Canada, on New Year's Eve 1878, the daughter of an immigrant truck driver, she spent the last fifty years of her life trying to live like the lady she was not. There was little in the early days and young adulthood of Florence Nightingale Graham to suggest the latent entrepreneur who would leave a multimillion-dollar empire. Until she descended on New York in 1908, when she was almost thirty, she had a series of ordinary jobs, the last as an office assistant to a dentist.

Her first job in New York was as a treatment girl with Eleanor Adair, then a leading light in the small world of cosmetics. Arden's tips were her salary. A year later she joined Mrs. Elizabeth Hubbard at a new salon on Fifth Avenue. Mrs. Hubbard specialized in the then-famous so-called "Grecian preparations," which had nothing to do with Greece. The arrangement between the two women did not last long. There was a tremendous quarrel about money—the upshot, that Mrs. Hubbard announced she was unimpressed with Miss Graham's treatment technique, and that Miss Graham confessed herself equally unimpressed with Mrs. Hubbard's creams. They set up rival establishments, with Miss Graham remaining on the original premises. It was in 1910 that she formed the embryonic Arden empire, four years before Helena Rubinstein's arrival in the United States. Miss Graham borrowed $6,000 from a cousin, a loan she repaid in six months.

Her first problem was her name. Florence Nightingale Graham was not glamorous enough. She rather liked the name Elizabeth (Elizabeth Hubbard's name was still printed on the windows of the premises, although the lady herself had moved in two doors away), but Elizabeth Graham did not sound right. Rumor had it that the name was taken from two Victorian novels, *Elizabeth and Her German Garden* and *Enoch Arden*. A plausible enough explanation, but there is little in the story of Miss Graham to indicate that she would have known of such novels. It is said that she made the final decision after posting letters to Elizabeth Arden in care of Graham to see what impact the name made on the envelope. She liked it. However it was arrived at, the name proved very successful.

Arden copied Eleanor Adair's massage techniques, eventually putting that lady out of business, and next allied herself with three Ogilvie sisters, well known in New York for their hair treatments and from whom Arden later also stole business.

There is no doubt Arden was good at massage, and her creams were copied from Mrs. Hubbard, whose business failed in 1916. Soon Elizabeth Arden had two salons in New York and was considering locations in other parts of the country. From that 1910 beginning, with homemade products and a capable way with facials, she was establishing a profitable little business, but not, in the early years, towering above her competitors.

Arden was still not completely satisfied with her new name and continued to use Graham in her private life. In 1914, Miss Graham vanished, and from then on it was Mrs. Graham in her private life even after her two marriages and Miss Arden at work (Arden was the Miss, Rubinstein the Madame, and Chanel the Mademoiselle of the cosmetics trade of that era). Although Arden was not married at that time, she felt it was more appropriate to be Mrs. in her private life.

As this transformation was taking place, Miss Arden decided to go to look at how sophisticated French women used beauty products. When she arrived in Europe, Arden went on an orgy of salon visiting. In Paris she went to four different ones each day. During that time it seems likely that she visited the already famous Maison de Beauté Velaze, owned by Helena Rubinstein, although Arden always denied it later. Indeed, both women maintained throughout their lives that they had never met. At that moment, however, Elizabeth Arden had no reason to suspect that Rubinstein was to be her greatest rival, at least until Charles Revson came on the scene in 1932.

The Paris visit was an eye-opener for Arden. She had never seen such a range of perfumes, and she bought every one she saw. She felt that Europe merited a long visit, but the Great War curtailed her efforts, and she returned hurriedly to the United States, although not before she had seen for the first time women wearing eye shadow.

The sight was shocking to her, as Rubinstein also claimed it had been to her. In North America, only women of dubious repute wore any colored makeup at all, but later on, Arden felt able to claim she had been the first to bring eye shadow to the American market and on the basis of this visit thought she could claim to have been trained in France.

It was a fateful visit, too, in other ways. On the boat going home she bumped into Thomas Jenkins Lewis, whom she had met previously—and by whom she had not been impressed—at her bank when she had gone there to borrow money to open her Washington salon. This time, however, she took to him, and they were married in 1915, not successfully, for they ultimately divorced, with Lewis getting a $25,000 payoff, although for many years he had provided the human companionship so lacking in the first thirty-six years of Elizabeth Arden's life.

Although Elizabeth Arden found the 1914–18 war an irritation, particularly because raw materials were in short supply, it was then she began to develop truly new ideas in cosmetics. What she wanted was "a face cream that's light and fluffy, like whipped cream." First of all, she approached Parke Davis, the well-known pharmaceuticals and toiletries firm, which turned down the opportunity to work directly with her, but were good enough to put her on to the smaller company of Stillwell and Gladding. By 1915, Arden had persuaded A. Fabian Swanson, a chemist at Stillwell, to go into a private agreement with her. After a series of experiments, Swanson produced the required "whipped cream," and Arden never looked back. She was prepared to spend: "You've got to spend a little money to make a little money" was her maxim. Generosity was rarely extended to her own staff—Swanson was running around making deliveries for quite a time when he could have been producing more creams—but she was ready to spend to the hilt for her organization.

She wanted a romantic name for the first Arden cosmetics line. Later on, she was to try to get "Arden" into all her trade names, but for the time being, it was to be "Venice." Once Swanson had developed one cream, the others came along quickly. Venetian Cream Amoretta and Ardena Skin Tonic were the start, followed by a whole "Venetian line"—Venetian Cleansing Cream, Venetian Lille-Lotion, Venetian Pore Cream, Venetian Muscle Oil, Venetian Velva Cream and Venetian Adona Cream. Whether it was your face, neck or bust that was falling apart, or you sported freckles or acne, or you just wanted to clean and soften your skin, there was a suitable Venetian cream, or at least extravagant claims were made for them. To top the creams was a set of tinted face powders and rouges. Elizabeth Arden was certainly showing that she had learned the lessons of Paris. In view of American attitudes to color cosmetics, this was bold and innovative marketing.

One cannot deny Elizabeth Arden a series of firsts in the industry. She was spending just as much time on packaging and design as on developing her products. Gradually she changed her advertising technique, and by 1915 was beginning to place as much emphasis on her products as on her salon techniques. She had already realized that bulk sales were where her future profits lay. But she was not to have the market to herself. In 1914 a rival had appeared. Arden, a mere five feet two in height, was to have a four-foot-ten competitor.

Helena Rubinstein never did anything without careful thought, although she was capable of quick decisions. Before she embarked upon building up an American business, she had established a sound footing in Europe. Rubinstein was born on Christmas Day in 1872 in Poland. She was one of eight daughters and later claimed that her education included periods at the universities of Cracow and Zurich, which is doubtful. The romantic "story" of her life suggests that when she was young she went to visit relatives in Australia accompanied by twelve jars of some homemade family face cream. There, shocked by the dry, rough skins of Australian women, she suggested they try her cream. When her supplies ran out, she sent home for more, eventually deciding to set up a salon and manufacture the cream in Australia. The first salon was opened in Melbourne, in 1902; she was then thirty years old, like Elizabeth Arden, a latecomer to business. Rubinstein started off in only one room, but later the salon was extended to six. Then a providential boost befell the business. Her cream, retailing at the time for 25 pence a jar (12 cents at the then exchange rate), was given a flattering mention in a newspaper. That one mention brought 15,000 sales.

This story of easy and almost immediate success is highly suspect. The dates do not always tally; there is certainly a gap in the story of the Australian period; and it has been suggested that, again like Elizabeth Arden in her early years, Rubinstein had a series of ordinary jobs, one of which might have been teaching music. But when several people who claimed to have worked with Rubinstein approached her when she visited Australia in later years, she denied ever having known them.

Rubinstein's "autobiography," *My Life for Beauty*, written with a command of the English language she never mastered, merely repeats the legend. She admitted to living with relatives in the Australian outback for some time until "nothing I did seemed to please my Uncle Louis anymore" and she departed for Melbourne. Her immediate family, too, never revealed what actually happened, if they knew. Anyone who questioned Madame was simply told that her creams were made by a Dr. Lykusky in Poland. Then, using £250 (then worth about $1,000) borrowed from an English friend, whom she had met on the ship going to Australia, she set up business. This money, she boasted, was the only money she ever borrowed, and it was paid back quickly, with interest.

In her autobiography she describes her next move: "With one half of the money I ordered a large stock of the cream in bulk, directly from Dr. Lykusky in Poland, purchased the necessary jars and labels locally and hand-lettered them myself. The rest of the money I spent on the rent and furnishings of a large second-floor room at 274 Collins Street, in the heart of Melbourne. The light in the room was excellent, and immediately I saw the place, I knew it was exactly what I was looking for. I could divide it into three small rooms, paint the walls white and furnish it with light, inexpensive pieces.

"One room would be my 'kitchen.' Even to this day, I think of our immense laboratories, of *all* scientific laboratories, as 'kitchens.' Once I startled the great Mme. Curie by asking her to let me see her *cuisine!*"

The whole tone of this book, which must have been approved by Madame, even if she did not write a word, is one of quite astonishing naïveté. She never appeared to have a nasty thought nor a single enemy—not one who was mentioned in the book, at least, which appeared in 1964, when she had been fighting the good cosmetics fight for fifty years in America alone.

Whatever the truth of her life in the U.S., once the Australian business was established, it thrived. But Helena Rubinstein realized that Australia was not Europe, which was much further advanced in cosmetics and which was then where the profits lay. She knew she had a lot to learn. It was safe, she decided in 1908 —the same year that Elizabeth Arden was leaving Canada for New York—to go back to Europe, leaving the Australian business in the hands of two of her sisters, Ceska and Manka. There is a sneaking suspicion, too, that she did not like Australia—she had not been an immediate success there—and could not wait to return to Europe.

It was not Poland, however, where she made her base this time. She wanted to use doctors and dermatologists, and the best were to be found in London, so that was the market she attacked next. Helena Rubinstein never did anything on the cheap. She already knew that good premises, a good address and splendid décor would bring the customers in—and that they would be prepared to pay. She chose, therefore, the twenty-room Mayfair mansion of Lord Salisbury and transformed it into a beauty salon with every luxury. Her first Maison de Beauté Velaze in Europe was a resounding and immediate success. By the time she opened the next salon, in Paris, the Rubinstein name was all she needed for customers to flood through the door. In 1912 the name was changed to Maison de Beauté Helena Rubinstein.

All this was not enough for Helena Rubinstein, who was rapidly becoming a wealthy woman. She had reached the age of thirty-six when she opened the London salon. It was time to get married, and in the same year Edward William Titus, an American journalist she had met in Australia, became her husband. They had two sons, Roy, born in 1909, and Horace, born in 1912. That marriage was not to last, again just like Arden's—the parallels between the two women, their careers and even their long lives are extraordinary—although there does not seem to have been the same bitterness in the break with Titus that Arden experienced with Lewis. Helena Rubinstein was said to have blamed herself, for neglecting Titus for her business, although it is doubtful that the split particularly upset her.

It might have been because her husband was American that Madame decided that the United States would be the next market for her to conquer. A desire to keep her family safe as war threatened in Europe might have had something to do with it as well. At any rate, in 1914 she sailed to New York to her greatest triumphs and her bitterest competitor, Elizabeth Arden. Before the battle got underway, Rubinstein declared, just as she had in Australia, that she was shocked by the women's complexions, although this time it was American women who were under scrutiny. It seems more likely that one look was all she needed to know that here was a largely untapped market of women who were less sophisticated than their European sisters. She opened her salon at West Forty-ninth Street, New York, in February 1915.

The scene was now set for two headstrong, arrogant women to try to outdo each other in a struggle that, although personally bitter, was not necessary. There was ample room, as time showed, for both of them in the fledgling cosmetics industry; they both made and left vast personal fortunes. Perhaps, however, the battle provided an extra incentive they both needed for success.

Competition was one thing; what made the rivalry so personal and bitter was not the copying of each other's products—both ranges of cosmetics sold well and made a profit—but the behavior of the two women. They never referred to each other by name; it was always "that woman" or "the other one." At one stage Arden hired almost the whole of the Rubinstein executive staff. Rubinstein retaliated by taking on Arden's ex-husband, Thomas Lewis. Lewis agreed to join her, even though his divorce settlement banned him from working for another cosmetics group. Away from Arden, however, he proved to be a poor executive.

Anyone giving a party was careful not to invite both Arden and Rubinstein, just as, later on, hostesses were careful not to have Estée Lauder and Charles Revson at the same gathering. With her early connections in London and Paris, Helena Rubinstein was always much more an international figure than Elizabeth Arden, who confined her social activities mainly to America.

Apart from her horses, Miss Arden—still Mrs. Graham, of course, in private—had very few interests outside business, and very few friends. Shortly after opening her first Maine Chance health farm, she became involved with a notorious group of lesbians, who were led by Elizabeth Marbury, a well-known socialite of gargantuan proportions. There was never any suggestion that Miss Arden herself had any lesbian tendencies, and it was a puzzle to her acquaintances that she mixed so openly with this group. The general view was that she had no sexual feelings at all. There is no doubt, however, that she was very fond of Miss Marbury and was extremely distressed when she died.

Helena Rubinstein's interest ran not to horses, but to the arts. Her collections were impressive, and in 1965, when her autobiography appeared, she claimed she still had 25,000 miniatures, despite several burglaries. She also had a major collection of Greek sculpture and another one of African art. She had a penchant, too, for having her portrait painted. The best known, although perhaps not the best, was by Graham Sutherland. This painting, which was done in 1959, showed her as a formidable figure, with erect bearing and grand Semitic features, with no hint of her diminutive stature. (Despite that stature, Madame seemed not to know the meaning of personal fear. When she was over ninety, burglars tied her up in her New York apartment and demanded the keys to her safe. She claimed to have told them to kill her if they wanted, as she did not have much time to live anyway. They departed empty-handed; she was unharmed.)

With her European and Australian businesses behind her, Helena Rubinstein was already an established businesswoman by the time she reached America. Arden, too, had been running her company very successfully for four years. Within months of Rubinstein's arrival, competition was fierce. Helena Rubinstein took a full-page advertisement in *Vogue* announcing her arrival and extolling the beauties of her salon and the efficacy of her products. Elizabeth Arden's response was to advertise simply that her salon was "the largest and finest in the world." Each in turn claimed to be the leading beauty expert in the world, and for the first five years each could in some ways justify her claim. Arden's range of products on the market was wider than Rubinstein's. Between 1915 and 1920 she was the biggest cosmetics manufacturer in the world—quite a feat for someone who had started in only 1910. Meanwhile, Rubinstein concentrated her efforts principally on salons, although expanding her range of products. Within four years of her arrival in the United States, she had opened salons in San Francisco, Philadelphia, New Orleans, Chicago and Atlantic City. Arden, apart from San Francisco, chose quite different cities—Boston, Washington, Palm Beach and Newport. There was no accident in these choices. Rubinstein, being Jewish, chose those cities where Jews were accepted; Arden, those where Jews were not welcomed. Arden was to exhibit anti-Semitism and anti-Catholicism all her life and is credited with saying: "To be Catholic or Jewish isn't chic; chic is Episcopalian."

In 1916, there was a new entrant to the industry when Dorothy Gray set up her own company. Though never a rival to Arden in the same way as Rubinstein, she was nevertheless an irritant. Arden accused her of copying everything she did, and there is no doubt that when Arden introduced a product, Miss Gray would follow with something remarkably like it, often with a very similar name. This irritation continued for many years. Later, in 1929, Dorothy Gray opened her own building on Fifth Avenue. This upset Arden, who also wanted her own building, but who found it impossible to get financing as the Depression set in. It seemed that backers thought they could make more profit out of a newcomer than from Arden, who was already established and known to be extremely acute in financial matters.

Elizabeth Arden seemed to be maintaining a lead in the United States, but she badly wanted to enter the European market, where Rubinstein was already well established. A trip to London in 1916 with her husband proved a relative failure. The United Kingdom was then selling the Yardley, Floris, Mary Chess and Rubinstein lines as its front-runners, and at first Arden could not persuade any store to take her products. Eventually, however, Harrods bought $200's worth, a beginning from which she was later able to build up sales.

Like Arden, Rubinstein had some firsts to her credit. In Europe, no one before her had put color into foundation and face powder. She also realized before anyone else that not all skins were the same: some were dry, some oily and still others a mixture of both. She was also the first to use silk in her makeup. This helped women to maintain a matte look to their makeup for longer periods than had been possible before, as silk is a hydrolyzed protein that has enormous sticking power. And though not the first to introduce mascara, Helena Rubinstein did claim to have been the first to introduce the waterproof variety. (To be fair, Max Factor makes this claim as well.) Helena Rubinstein made her claim when she devised a mascara for Eleanor Holm, wife of musician-producer Billy Rose, who was swimming in the Aquacade, a water ballet, at the New York World's Fair in 1939. Rubinstein's mascara was put on the open market in the early 1940s.

When Rubinstein launched her perfume Heaven Scent she was making her first attempt to compete with French perfumes, in particular Arpège from Lanvin. She was tired of watching French perfumes claim most of the American market. The perfume was packed with essential oils, and there has been very little change in the formula since it was launched. Arpège was a perfume for mature women and so was Heaven Scent; today, however, Heaven Scent perfume is preferred by the teenage market, which is more sophisticated now than thirty years ago.

Arden's sister Gladys (both Arden and Rubinstein were to use their families to develop their businesses) was running the company successfully in Paris, and by 1920, Elizabeth was able to open a salon in the fashionable Rue St. Honoré in Paris and, later on, another one in Nice. The London salon was opened in 1922 at 25 Old Bond Street, and the Arden company has remained in the same street, though now at No. 20, ever since. The Helena

Rubinstein salon, in contrast, was to vanish from London in the postwar period.

Throughout the 1920s "that woman" and "the other one" built up their businesses and constantly tried to outdo each other. Other competitors were not serious contenders for big business, merely thorns in their flesh. If either Arden or Rubinstein opened a new salon, the other opened a better one. One brought out a range of products, the other produced something similar. They got used to being the leaders in the industry and saw this as their rightful place.

Then, in 1928, Helena Rubinstein did something that seemed —and indeed proved to be—entirely out of character. She sold two-thirds of her business to Lehman Brothers, New York bankers. Madame had decided to "slow down," as she put it; she was, after all, fifty-six years old. The bankers, in turn, wanted to make the Rubinstein line into a mass-marketed low-priced product on sale throughout drugstores in the United States. They paid Helena Rubinstein over $7 million, and she "retired" to Europe. But Lehman Brothers were not cosmetologists, and very soon the business began to go wrong. Perhaps this episode should have provided a warning for the bid-hungry conglomerates in the 1970s. Madame, of course, still owned all the overseas business. Her slowing down lasted only a few months. Now based in Paris she wrote to the small stockholders, particularly women, as "one woman to another." Men, she confided, did not understand the cosmetics business.

She began to buy back stock. Then came the Wall Street crash, and the price of Rubinstein shared dropped from $60 to $3. Lehman Brothers sold a controlling interest in the company back to Rubinstein at a fraction of the cost they had paid her a year previously. She was said to have made a profit of $6 million, a great financial coup considering the 1929 stock market conditions.

Meantime, Elizabeth Arden's New York salon was also a great success. Margaret Chase Harriman visited there, and in *The New Yorker* on April 6, 1935, she reported that each day 394 women visited the salon, many of them for the "costly climax of the Vienna Youth Mask." This was the application of diathermy techniques to the face. Diathermy heats tissues in the body by means of electrical current and has been used to treat arthritis and damaged muscles and nerves. Elizabeth Arden transformed it into a beauty treatment. Miss Chase Harriman explained: "With one Dr. Last of Vienna [Arden] invented the Youth Mask, a device made of papier-mâché and lined with tin foil, which is fitted to the client's face and connected by conducting cords to a diathermy machine. Arden's belief was that electricity so applied replenishes the cells in a woman's face, which, she said, die first under the eyes and next under the chin." There was, of course, no medical evidence to support either the theory that such treatments could be effective or Miss Arden's theories about the death of skin cells. All diathermy does is stimulate the circulation. Nevertheless, nearly 200 of the women were prepared to pay $200 for six treatments even then. The remaining women in the salon attended for exercise, massage or various kinds of baths.

By now, however, a new rival was on the horizon. In 1931, Charles Revson was looking for a job and finally went to work for a cosmetics company in New Jersey named Elka, which made nail varnish. Revson was not impressed with Elka, a rather small company, but he was impressed with its product, opaque nail varnish. All other nail polishes on the market at that time were transparent in three shades of red—light, medium and dark. Revson decided that he could do better away from Elka and set up Revson Brothers in New York, from which he was authorized to sell Elka nail varnish. Meanwhile, he was learning everything he could about nail varnish and what particularly attracted the customers. When he asked Elka to expand his territory and they refused, he decided to find a new association.

This is where Charles Lachman—the man who put the "l" in Revlon—came in. Through marriage, he, with his wife, owned a company called Dresden Brothers, which operated out of New Rochelle, New York. Dresden made nail polish for companies to retail under their own brand names. Who got in touch with whom is uncertain—they both told different stories—but a new company, Revlon Nail Enamel, emerged. Charles Revson was twenty-five. The new company bought its nail polish from Dresden. The Revsons provided $300, and Lachman, the early credit required. Lachman did not survive long in the business; Charles Revson soon persuaded him to "retire," though he continued to draw a salary and bonuses for the rest of his life. Later the capital structure of the company was changed, first giving Joseph Revson a stake and later finding a 10 percent holding for another brother, Martin. But Lachman continued to control half of the votes in the company. In 1937, however, Charles Revson decided to sever his connection with Dresden Brothers and turned the orders over to Maas and Waldstein, a Newark, New Jersey, company, which still provides Revlon the nail varnish it buys in bulk quantities. Eventually, the original Revlon premises on West Forty-fourth Street, New York, proved too small, and in 1938 the factory was moved to 525 West Fifty-second Street. Here the company does the colors, design, packing, etc. Here also the company first developed its gift packs of nail polish, tweezer, emery board and an orange stick.

It was rather surprising that Charles Revson, with his great dislike for women, chose the cosmetics industry. He did not like women in executive positions in his company, and only a few, like the brilliant copywriter Kay Daly, survived for long. He was equally dismissive of the women in his personal life. He claimed not to remember the name of his first wife and behaved appallingly to his long-suffering second wife, Ancky, who finally could stand him no longer and left him. Later on, he perhaps surpassed himself in the way he treated his third wife, Lyn, who was twenty-six years younger than he was. His tenth wedding anniversary present to her of a $30,000 check and five Van Cleef and Arpels bracelets was followed only two days afterward, without any warning, by divorce proceedings. Apparently he had been considering a separation for over a year, and the timing so soon after the celebration party was thought by some mutual acquaintances to be deliberate cruelty. The news was broken to Mrs. Revson, not by Revson himself—he was said to find it very difficult to fire anyone—but by Judge Simon Rifkind, who eventually became executor of the Revson estate. To win the settlement she wanted, Mrs. Revson had to promise not to talk to the press about her marriage, or to write about it herself.

At Revlon, wives, even Revson's, were banned from business trips, and tales of his sexual exploits were common in cosmetics circles. In 1975, after Charles Revson's death, when he could no longer answer back, a biography of him, *Fire and Ice* by Andrew Tobias, appeared. It painted a picture of a man who behaved like Attila the Hun in his professional life and like an alley cat in his personal behavior. If nothing else, however, the book proved that he had some supporters. Tobias was roundly attacked by friends and foes alike, and Shirley Lord, longtime British beauty journalist, said to me: "Charles Revson simply wasn't like the man described in the book. He was tough, all right, but he always behaved like a gentleman."

Revson survived the Great Depression of the 1930s by concentrating his efforts on hair and beauty salons. At that time, permanent waving was booming, and women liked to while away the time under the dryer getting a manicure as well. By 1941 he was selling to around 100,000 salons and almost had a monopoly of this trade. He had started to sell in the stores in 1937, but for many years afterward he still concentrated his main energies on the salons, where he not only sold in bulk to the salon itself, but also directly to customers.

Because of his concentration on salons, Revson stuck to making just nail varnish for some years, and as a result, he did not incur the wrath of Arden and Rubinstein, who were more interested in selling their treatment products and color cosmetics. But quietly the Revlon Company was exploding in size. By 1938, sales had risen to over one million dollars and Revlon was paying himself a salary with bonuses which amounted to almost $40,000. In 1940, before the United States entered World War II, Revson added lipstick to the Revlon range of nail products, and the value of sales almost doubled in a year. He was already using the exciting names for his ranges which were so to capture the public imagination in the late 1940s and 1950s. Two of them, Fatal Apple and Kissing Pink, made their debut in the 1930s.

In their eagerness to outdo each other, neither Arden nor Rubinstein took much notice of Charles Revson. They did not see him as a major competitor for many years, and it was not until 1962 when Revlon launched its first skin cream that the danger became clear. Eterna 27 (the Revlon offices were on the twenty-seventh floor of 666 Fifth Avenue) was a direct competitor to the Rubinstein lines, and what was worse, the Revlon offices were immediately across the street from the Rubinstein headquarters. Madame, then in her nineties—she had still never missed a day from work—is said to have raged and shouted from her third-floor office in one of her characteristic screaming fits about the prospect of even more competition.

Before Revson entered the industry, as the ladies competed fiercely on the East Coast and the twenties drew to a close, a new concern, the Max Factor company, was incorporated out on the West Coast. Max Factor had been in business for some time in a small way, and the new corporation was recognition of the explosive growth of the film industry, with its requirement of professional theatrical makeup. Max Factor was an immigrant from Europe. He was born in Lodz in Russia in 1877. He became an apprentice wig-maker when he was fourteen, and when he was twenty, he was able to open his own makeup and hair goods shop in Lodz. Like many other Europeans of his time, Max Factor saw the United States as a land of plenty, and at the age of twenty-seven he had saved enough to leave Russia, taking along his wife and three children. His first location was St. Louis, where, with a partner, he opened a makeup, perfume and hair-products shop and took a booth at the St. Louis International Exposition of 1904. Within a year, the partner had absconded with most of the profits, though Factor was able to find the finances to open another shop in the center of St. Louis. Here his second son, Max, Junior, was born.

But the lure of Los Angeles proved very strong. Max Factor realized that there was a bright future for the motion picture industry. At that time, no cosmetics manufacturer dominated business there, and he reckoned that with his experience he could get in on the ground floor. In 1908, coincidentally as Elizabeth Arden was leaving Canada for the United States and Helena Rubinstein, Australia for England, Max Factor and his family moved to Los Angeles. It is no accident that these characters were all making their moves about the same time. They all recognized that there was enormous potential growth in the embryonic cosmetics industry.

The first Max Factor studio was in the Pantages Theater at Seventh and Hill streets. In 1909, a third son, Louis, was born, and the original Max Factor company was incorporated. It was to be another twenty years before Max Factor made his mark nationally in the cosmetics world. At the beginning he concentrated on formulating and testing theatrical makeup. As well as selling his own products, Factor was the West Coast agent for both Leichner and Miners, who also made greasepaint and the colorful cosmetics required for theatrical and film performances. Gradually, Max Factor became renowned in the film industry, and leading actors and actresses began to come to him for advice on how to avoid looking pale and wan on the screen. As the 1920s arrived, Max Factor was able to move to larger premises. The "House of Makeup" was set up at 302 South Hill Street, proclaiming its business: "Cosmetics, Theatrical Make-up, Wigs and Toupees Retail." The whole family worked in the business, which soon became a center for the early film stars. Like all the other early entrepreneurs, Max Factor introduced a "revolutionary" concept. This was "color harmony." For the first time, makeup items were produced to harmonize with hair, eyes and skins of blondes, brownettes (a Max Factor term), brunettes and redheads. At first this makeup was used only in films, but later on, actresses began to use it in their normal lives as well. Eventually, of course, non-actresses took up the product, and in 1927 "Color Harmony Make-up" was launched on the market, supported by a full advertising campaign. Max Factor was still confined to the West Coast, however, and caused barely a ripple on the East Coast, where Arden and Rubinstein were battling it out.

During these years, Factor had developed a new type of grease-paint, smooth and creamy and easier to apply than the older varieties. He did not sell it, however, until 1922, after he had visited Europe to call on Leichner, to ask for a better commission on the sales he made for them. At the appointed time for their meeting, however, Leichner kept him waiting unduly, and the meeting never took place. Factor, angered by the slight, started to market his own cream, and it very soon became a market leader, selling more than Leichner and Miners together.

In 1927, talking movies were introduced, an event that brought further growth to Max Factor. Films became more sensitive and lighting became much hotter, and new ideas for makeup were necessary. Within six months Max Factor and Max, Junior, had developed Panchromatic Make-up, which provided the right degree of light reflectivity required by the new film. This achievement led to a special award from the Academy of Motion Picture Arts and Sciences. By 1929, Max Factor felt ready to enter the general cosmetics world, and on March 6, Max Factor and Company was founded in Delaware. It incorporated all the assets that Max Factor had spend twenty years building up. Hollywood at that time was fast becoming the world's film capital, and in the same years, the Factor family decided to move again, this time into Hollywood itself, at 1666 North Highland Avenue.

The 1930s were a period of consolidation for the older cosmetics companies. The Great Depression did not, as many had feared it would, destroy the industry, although sales declined quite sharply for a time. (Women, it seemed, were not prepared to go without their lipsticks and face creams altogether; something else had to be sacrificed instead.) This atmosphere would not seem conducive to the setting up of new businesses, but surprisingly, many new cosmetic companies were launched, some of which still exist today. Almay Cosmetics was started in 1931 and was a very early entrant into the field of hypoallergenic products. Revlon, of course, was a 1930s entrant. Clairol, too, was formed in 1932. Its first products were shampoos containing a tint, which came to the United States from Europe, through the United Kingdom. Today,

Clairol is a part of the Bristol-Myers conglomerate and is the market leader in hair products in the U.S. In 1935 the Wella Corporation, also manufacturing hair products, originally in Germany, set up business in New York. Germaine Monteil, mentioned earlier, began to bring out a full range of makeup in 1936. These are but a few of the many companies set up in the decade.

The general economic climate of the 1930s meant that although the older companies managed to trade profitably, they found it difficult to get money for expansion. Elizabeth Arden, still unable to find backing for a building of her own on Fifth Avenue, enterprisingly decided to move ahead with a plan she had for a beauty farm. In 1934 she opened the first Maine Chance farm, in Maine. Fees were high, but the farm was always full, and over the years leading names such as Ava Gardner, Perle Mesta, Clare Boothe Luce and Mamie Eisenhower were regular visitors. Another visitor was Jessica Mitford, a writer from the famous eccentric British family. Jessica, a left-winger in a family of sometimes extreme right-wing views and early supporters of Hitler, was not easily impressed by Maine Chance. In *McCalls Magazine* in March 1966, she was to write: "I had been told the cost was $400 a week. But no; the reservations lady (whose voice, like those of undertakers, exuded controlled inner peace and happiness) explained that this was some years ago. At the present time they have a few rooms with shower only for $600 a week; those with bathtub start at $750." On the first day "I set eyes on my fellow inmates: one and a half tons of female forms in various stages of delapidation each in her little blue number and white terry-cloth robe." In her room, just as the brochure had promised, there were "five breathlessly fresh roses." After being weighed in, customers then settled down to a routine.

"We are doing or being done to (mostly the latter) from nine till five, a full working day, with everything planned to the exact minute, ten-minute intervals between treatments and one hour off for lunch. We glisten alternately with cream and sweat." There were massages, exercises, facials, face masks, wax baths to "draw out all the poisons." The food was low calorie and drink was banned. Miss Mitford guessed: "Maine Chance would not, I think, be a success in England. The aristocratic dowager, nearest equivalent from a class standpoint to the ladies gathered here, is a hardier bloom whose upbringing has endowed her with an intractably matter-of-fact outlook on life. 'Stuff and nonsense!' she would exclaim angrily, if asked to behave like a good child. While she might patronise a Continental health spa for a specific ailment— liver disease, gout, rheumatism are perennial English favourites —she would be unlikely to disburse a small fortune on going into retreat with a group of other women purely for the sake of a sagging waistline and double chin." (Jessica Mitford's words were no prophecy: by the mid-1970s, health farms run on very rigorous lines have become very popular in the United Kingdom, although the cost rarely approaches that of the American farms.) Miss Mitford lost five pounds in her week at Maine Chance, for a cost of $1,000 including tips, or $200 a pound. "The forty of us at Maine Chance represented a total investment of some $40,000 in a one-week effort to jack up sagging muscles and restore the fading roses to aged cheeks. A poignant thought." Indeed. Miss Arden opened a second Maine Chance farm, in Phoenix, in 1947. This second one still operates today, although the first has long gone. Once again, however, Elizabeth Arden had another first in the industry.

Max Factor spent the 1930s developing his business outside Hollywood. His first son, Davis Factor, who had been named general manager, appointed distributors in England, Cuba, Canada and Mexico. Within twenty years Factor was to become the leading American cosmetics company in the international field. In 1935 the retail branch in Bond Street, London, was opened, and the company tackled the French market, a traditionally difficult one but one that also fell to the Factor sales approach. Eventually the concern was represented in 144 markets and had 20 wholly owned subsidiaries around the world.

Max Factor might not have lived on the sophisticated East Coast of America, but he was not a slow learner, and he could see that publicity was the key to success—and he knew that he had the most newsworthy people as his customers. Companies were beginning to organize events that would provide them with good coverage in the newspapers without advertising. An inch or two of editorial in the newspapers and magazines was often far more effective than an expensive advertising campaign, and it was worth spending money to get it. Extravaganzas would become commonplace in the 1950s, but as early as November 26, 1935, Max Factor outdid all his existing rivals at the time with an all-star reception to celebrate the opening of his new makeup studio.

Three thousand invitations were sent out to the elite of Hollywood: the whole evening was run like a film premiere. *Time* magazine wrote: "Great spotlights lighted the sky over Hollywood. Raspberry floodlights bathed the south side, chartreuse beamed the facade of a building near Hollywood Boulevard whose fluted white front bore the architectural devices of Greece, the French Empire, and the U.S. Cinema. Under a marquee passed film folk who had been summoned with great powder-blue and orange cellophane invitations to attend the opening of 'the world's greatest cosmetic factory'—the new $600,000 studio of Max Factor." Actors and actresses signed a "Scroll of Fame." By the end of the evening guests and gate-crashers totaling 9,000 had been gazing at stars like Jean Harlow, who dedicated the powder-blue makeup room "For Blondes Only." Claudette Colbert similarly performed for brunettes in the pink room, Rochelle Hudson for brownettes, and Ginger Rogers for redheads. Everyone who was anyone in Hollywood—and some who were no one—attended the reception. In later years, celebrities were to become more choosy about where they deigned to put in an appearance. But this 1935 reception unquestionably brought the Max Factor name to nationwide attention. Women all over the country suddenly wanted to look like their favorite screen actress. The new cosmetics studio was instantly popular, and more and more film stars insisted that they be made up for the camera by Max Factor and no one else.

The next step for Factor came with color films. The makeup used for black-and-white films showed up red or green in color, and a completely new range had to be developed. "Pancake Makeup" was first used in Walter Wanger's *Vogues of 1938*, and the brand, which had first been trademarked on September 28, 1937, soon became very popular in the industry. It was inevitable that the product would eventually be marketed to the general public. Its launch marked the first time Max Factor used color in advertisements. Those in *Vogue* were all full-page and in two colors, and each one featured a photograph of a well-known film star and a drawing of the product. Within a few months there were sixty-five different imitations of Max Factor Pancake, but the originator led the field, with sales more than those of the sixty-five others together. When Max Factor died in 1938 he left a highly profitable and progressive company in the hands of his sons.

The 1930s, although a decade of considerable growth for cosmetics companies, was also the period when government became more interested in industry, including the cosmetics industry. This interest was focused not only on the efficacy and safety of particular products—Elizabeth Arden was ordered to change the name of her Orange Skin Food to Orange Skin Cream because it was not a "nutrient"—but also on unfair trade practices. One of these was known as "push money," by which representatives of one company would pay a girl originally hired to sell a rival's products, to sell theirs instead. This practice was finally forbidden under the Robinson-Patman Act. Some companies tried to circumvent the legislation, and seven cases were brought against cosmetics manufacturers immediately after the act was passed. The cases dragged on, and the complaints were changed several times. In the end—fourteen yeas later—only one cease and desist order was issued—the one against Elizabeth Arden.

What upset the industry most, however, was the Federal Trade Commission's decision to investigate the industry, in particular those areas in which untrue medical claims were being made. The move for the investigation had come from the American Medical Association, which had established a Board of Standards for cosmetics advertising. This board set up certain requirements. False claims could not be made about the therapeutic properties of a product. It was not unusual at this time for advertisements to claim that skin creams and tonics actually made the skin younger, or that they were allergy-free—nothing can be guaranteed not to cause *anyone* allergies. As a result of the AMA campaign, the Wheeler-Lee Amendment to the Pure Food and Drug Act brought the cosmetics industry under the control of the Food and Drug Administration, and a very sharp eye has been kept on the industry ever since. Elizabeth Arden was furious when told she had to change the name of her Orange Skin Food and stop any advertising of it, and of her Velva Cream Mask and Eight-Hour Cream which made any claim of therapeutic or medicinal benefits, but she was a sensible businesswoman and, after a lot of opposition and abuse of officials, complied with the regulations. Other companies did not do so, with the result that 1937 saw a large number of lawsuits initiated by the FTC and FDA against some well-established companies, including Chanel, Helena Rubinstein, Yardley, Bristol-Myers and Richard Hudnut. In all, it was a troubled time for the cosmetics industry, as companies came to realize that the days of lavish extravagance in competing claims for products were over.

In 1939 a new company emerged. It was derived from a much older concern that had started trading in the nineteenth century as the California Perfume Company. Avon Products, its successor, was to become the biggest cosmetics company in the world, finding a leading place for itself in every country it decided to enter. David H. McConnell, the man who had founded the company in 1886, wrote its story in 1903, a history that was long on sentimentality and short on fact, but, even by this time, he claimed that the California Perfume Company was the largest of its kind, not only in the United States, but also in the world.

Having "through hard work and proper training developed a good, strong, hardy, rugged constitution," McConnell recalls that his first "experience in the business world was as a book agent. I took this up during my school vacation, and developed quite a faculty for talking, which I have since learned is quite essential, and has stood me well in hand many times." The books that

McConnell was selling were bibles, and he soon noticed that the small samples of perfume he gave out with the books were rather more welcome to customers than the bible itself. This gave rise to the idea that success might lie in manufacturing a complete line of products that could be sold through agents, directly from the factory to the consumer, thus cutting out the middleman and also enabling the customer to see and sample the products before buying.

McConnell decided on the perfume business and originally brought out five scents—Lily-of-the-Valley, White Rose, Heliotrope, Violet and Hyacinth. To these were later added a shampoo cream, witch hazel cream, almond cream balm and toothpaste. Within two years business had grown so much that manufacturing was taking up an entire floor of McConnell's premises, and in 1897 he built his own laboratory in Suffern, New York, where he lived. By the time he wrote his little book, the California Perfume Company employed more than 125 people full time and had 48 general agents traveling around training depot managers, of whom there were more than 10,000, all "good, honest, industrious and energetic," and supplied goods to over one million families. Although it was trading very profitably, California Perfume Company was not regarded as a major competitor by the cosmetics entrepreneurs. They were right in a way: the structures of their businesses and McConnell's were very different and their markets completely separate. McConnell's company was not taking trade away from those companies that had several beauty salons and/or sold in prestige stores. It was developing sales in rural and sometimes remote areas with customers who could eventually move over to the prestige lines only as their access to department stores improved. Few people thought, however, that Avon would eventually become the world's leader, operating in thirty markets.

Before the Second World War, activity in the perfume world was confined mainly to Europe, which had centuries of skill behind it. The oldest surviving of twentieth-century perfumes (there are colognes from earlier times), L'Origin, was introduced by Coty in 1909. Chanel No. 5, perhaps the most famous perfume ever produced, was launched in Europe in 1921 and reached the American market in 1925. It has sold steadily ever since and is still the best-selling perfume in the Chanel range. Its sister perfumes, No. 19 and No. 22, followed a few years later, but never caught the imagination in the way that No. 5 has, though they, too, remain on the market. Payot, also in France, launched Pavlova in 1922, and Jean Patou, a clothing designer like Coco Chanel, quickly followed her onto the market in 1925 with Amour Amour. He followed this in 1930 with his most popular perfume, Joy, and in the same year Moment Supreme. Weil, yet another designer, brought out Zibeline in 1928, and by 1930, Coty had added Emeraude and L'Aimant to its range. The perfumes produced in the United States were not yet of the same quality as those from Europe and did not carry the same prestige as far as monied customers were concerned. In the 1930s, however, Fabergé, a small American-based company, brought out three perfumes, Aphrodisia in 1932, Woodhue in 1937 and Tigress in 1938. Elizabeth Arden, too, produced a world-class perfume in 1935. She called it Blue Grass after the grass of the Kentucky hills, where she stabled her horses. It was an immediate success and still sells well today.

Everything began to change in 1939 when war was declared in Europe. At that time total sales of cosmetics in America were just under $40 million. Cosmetics may seem of little relevance in wartime, but they had an important psychological part to play between 1939 and 1945. Governments realized the necessity of keeping up the morale of women as they worked in the munitions factories or were engaged on other war work. Providing cosmetics was one relatively cheap way of making them look good and feel good. Lipstick, which little more than a decade before had been regarded as suitable only for fast women, became a priority product. For a few years the cosmetics companies dropped their competitive thrust against one another and concentrated on supplying lipsticks and other cosmetics cheaply to war workers to help the war effort.

War injuries cause disfigurements, and disguising them gave the cosmetics companies another part to play. Max Factor, in particular, with its long expertise in decorative makeup, was able to teach men and women whose faces had been disfigured how to disguise some of the scars. Plastic surgery, too, which was to play a significant role in the cosmetics world of today, attained new importance in the repair of severe disfigurements. It was from new techniques developed during the war that the increasingly popular cosmetic surgery industry, an industry with very ancient origins, was to grow in the next thirty-five years.

TWO

INTO THE BIG TIME

A *mere copier of nature can never produce any-thing great.*
—Sir Joshua Reynolds
Discourses 3

As the Second World War ended in 1945, the cosmetics industry found itself in a new industrial situation, far different from what it had been when the war effort started. Prospects for growth were much greater, but so, too, was competition. Even the war years had seen a few new companies entering the field. One of them, founded in 1944, was to become very successful. It was the Toni company, the first to offer home permanent waving. The "Which twin has the Toni?" slogan was a big puller worldwide, but Toni did not remain independent for long: in 1948 it became part of the Gillette Company.

Germaine Monteil, a "thoroughly French woman," according to Eric Morgan of BAT Industries, which has owned her company since 1969, also emerged as a cosmetics manufacturer during the war years. She had started out as an *haute couture* dress designer and began making lipstick in 1936 when she found that she could not get existing makers to supply the right shades for the clothes she designed. In 1942 she gave up fashion altogether to concentrate on cosmetics, when she marketed Rose Skin Cream, a product that is still on the market. Since then her lines have been "super"—Super-Glow, Super-Moist and Super-Sheen. The company, under BAT, also makes perfumes and in 1976 introduced a men's line called Realm, which did not do well and was withdrawn in 1978. Germaine Monteil is a company with a good reputation, but it, like Rubinstein, has had problems in recent years. Although it is doing well in some countries, some observers believe it has been losing money in the United States at the rate of $600,000 a year. Germaine Monteil herself, now a very old lady, lives in retirement at her homes in France and the U.S.

If the industry had appeared attractive in the 1930s, it was infinitely more so at the beginning of the post-war era. America and Europe were about to begin a period of sustained and rapid economic growth. Greater numbers of people, including women—who had not been a major element in the work force until the war, but who did not retire to their homes once the hostilities had ended—were earning more money, and had more of it to spend, than ever before.

No one had to be a genius in the early postwar period to see the possibilities. The established companies made their plans, and new entrepreneurs appeared on the scene. The one who was to make the biggest impact was Estée Lauder, who burst into the cosmetics market in 1946. Her battles during the fifties, sixties and early seventies with Charles Revson were to provide new meat for the gossip writers who had faithfully been reporting all the real—and sometimes the imagined—skirmishes between Arden and Rubinstein, who of course did not cease their private hostilities even though by the end of the war Rubinstein was over seventy, with Arden only six years younger.

It comes as no surprise to find that Estée Lauder, like the earlier entrepreneurs, according to her hagiographers, also had romantic beginnings. She is still very active in the company, which remains family-owned and is in fact the largest private cosmetics firm in the world. That privacy is carefully guarded and no one ever knows her age. Her family originated in Vienna, and reference books sometimes give that city as her birthplace. She was born, however, not in Vienna, but in America. But she was raised and educated in the Austrian capital. Even so, her background was far more conventional than that of either Arden or Rubinstein; indeed, her whole life has been far more prosaic than theirs. No scandal has ever attached to Mrs. Lauder. She has led an exemplary private life, and her employees are expected to as well. She has not been beyond fighting for her market share, however, as certain events have proved.

This is how her company tells of her entry into the cosmetics world: "Estée Lauder's beauty career began right in her own backyard. As a girl she dreamed of becoming a skin doctor, a dream whetted by her dermatologically minded, beauty-conscious Viennese family. But fate stepped in with marriage to handsome Joseph Lauder and the subsequent birth of two sons, Leonard and Ronald. So a next-best career for Estée was developing beauty creams for women." Well, the next-best it might have been, but cosmetics have made far more money for the Lauder family than dermatology ever would have. No one tells exactly how old Mrs. Lauder is, but she must be in her seventies by now.

Estée and Joseph Lauder formed their company in 1946, when Mrs. Lauder decided to sell to a small group of clients four treatment products she had developed. Two years later, Saks Fifth Avenue, always on the lookout for products in which it can lead the field, started to sell the Lauder line of All-Purpose Cream, Cleansing Oil, Creme Pack and Skin Lotion. Thus the Lauder family entered the industry with skin treatments only.

What is striking about Estée Lauder's success is that she did not use the "salon route" as earlier entrants to the cosmetics industry had. Arden and Rubinstein and many other smaller businesses had been built from small beginnings in one salon. Revson, it is true, did not own salons, but he certainly sold to them exclusively until he was well established. In effect, he went one better than the ladies and made profits from the salons without having to be involved in any capital expenditure on them. A single salon meant that a business could be built up until there were enough assets to open another establishment, and the business would grow slowly and steadily. In contrast, anyone trying to place a line of products in the retail stores not only faced intense competition from those who were already established there and who could bring out a new line very quickly, but also had to get substantial financial backing if sufficient quantities were to be manufactured to justify the advertising and distributing costs involved.

The experience of Hazel Bishop, one of those who did not succeed at the time Estée Lauder was building up her business, is typical. Miss Bishop, a small, busy-looking woman, is still deeply interested in the cosmetics business—but from a distance: she is an investment analyst with Evans and Company, New York stock-brokers, where she specializes in cosmetics companies. In 1950, however, she was in the center of the industry, and her company showed all signs of success. She looks back on her career with amused nostalgia and readily acknowledges that her path into the industry was fraught with more dangers than those who took the "salon route."

In 1929, Hazel Bishop had paid one term's medical school fees and was set to become a doctor. The slump in September 1929 ended these ambitions, and she found herself looking for work. The entrepreneurial spirit was already strong within her, and, a sufferer from sinus, she touted around the idea of a mentholated paper handkerchief. But, she recalls, "it's difficult to interest any-one in a product like that unless they too are suffering from a cold or sinus."

Eventually, in 1935, she settled down as an assistant to a der-matologist. At that time she began to learn about cosmetics and understand the problems and possibilities in the industry. She saw that skin products created allergies in some people—and that the forms of the allergies differed from person to person. Some victims were allergic to fragrances, some to dyes and some even to the natural products in the cosmetics. She noted these allergies, and her entrepreneurial spirit quickened. She left the dermatologist in 1942 and tried to launch a pimple stick designed to cure spots. She hit the same problems as before. No interest could be aroused in persons without pimples. And she found again, as she had with the mentholated handkerchief, that she could not raise money: "The problem was—and it still is today—to get someone to sponsor you on an untried product. They want to see some sort of sales record and you can't get that unless you can promote your product and you need money to do that. It's a chicken-and-egg situation."

Undeterred, Miss Bishop decided on another product. She had read that in the United States, 98 percent of the women used lipstick but only 96 percent cleaned their teeth, and she had noted the vast array of dentifrices available. She had also noted the skimpy assortment of lipsticks and decided—and rightly, as it turned out—that therein lay a potential market. She went to the cosmetics buyer at Saks Fifth Avenue with her lipstick and was quickly warned away from trying to sell there. The buyer pointed out that it was highly unwise for her to attempt to sell a lipstick in a chic department store. At that time, virtually all the cosmetics salespeople in the stores were employed by the manufacturers and she—with only a single product—could not afford a salesgirl. To succeed, she realized, she had to get her product into the less-sophisticated stores, particularly the cheaper chains of drugstores, which were just beginning to emerge. The mass market in cosmetics was in its infancy, and if a company sold in drugstores, it could afford the necessary advertising. Memory is very short, so the products had to be nearby if the customer was to see and recognize them even a short time after seeing an advertisement.

At this point Miss Bishop asked herself whether she should start a lipstick business at all. She had managed to raise some money, but there were still problems. Because she had so little cash herself, she would not be able to retain control of her company, and although no one would be a bigger investor than she would be, the others would hold a majority investment.

Then she had the "lucky break" that comes to most successful entrepreneurs: Hecht and Company, the Washington-based store, took on her lipstick, marketing it under the slogan "Stays on you, not on him." That made it a new—and desirable—product: no one had ever claimed that before. As a result, 600 lipsticks were sold in the first day alone. And Hazel Bishop felt she was on her way. She went into television sponsorship and now claims she was the first cosmetics maker to do so. TV, she felt, had a wonderful advantage over any other form of advertising: it was the equivalent to a one-to-one beauty demonstration to the customer. She sponsored a fifteenth of the Kate Bush show, which was first seen in several cities and eventually went national, and sales soared. By now Bishop was feeling confident and thought that nothing could go wrong if she kept ahead of the market. She stuck to her indelibility slogan. Different lipsticks were shown in her TV advertisements, and Hazel Bishop's appeared not to rub off as easily as the others. Later on, she sponsored the "This Is Your Life" show— and sales continued to rise.

Overtly, all was going well. By the end of 1950, Bishop had sold one million lipsticks; the figure for 1951 was 3 million; for fifty-two, 4 million; and for fifty-three, an amazing 10 million—25 percent of the market. But where it mattered, within the internal structure of the company, things were beginning to go wrong. Hazel Bishop explained:

"Anytime you come into the cosmetics industry with a product which is a success, it will be copied very quickly. You can't keep your exclusivity for long. You must have something new and fresh to offer your customer as the competition comes in, so that you can keep one step ahead. If you change your products constantly, you can create built-in obsolescence in the industry. Change the color of your nail varnish range and whatever women have left in a bottle at home is obsolete. This characteristic is built into the industry."

Before she had time to develop anything new in 1952, Bishop

was in trouble with her co-shareholders. Her advertising agency had bought up 20 percent of the company stock when the business started. As sales rocketed, the attractions of the company became obvious, and the agency, deciding that they rather than Miss Bishop might as well make the profits, bought out all the other small shareholders for very little more, according to Hazel Bishop, than they had put in to begin with. "Then," she records, "the bite came on me." She went into litigation with the majority shareholders, finally settling—and out of the company which bore her name—in 1954. This was not quite the end of Hazel Bishop, or of her company, but neither was to stay long in cosmetics.

She started over in 1956, trying to sell solid perfume. Her old company quickly stepped in, claiming that under their agreement with her she could never operate in the cosmetics industry again and that they, after all, might bring out a solid perfume one day. This time Hazel Bishop did give up. She joined a stockbroking firm, but it was not until many years later, in 1970, when she joined Evans, that she started to analyze the cosmetics industry. "It would not have set well before," she said. By this time her old company was bankrupt, killed off partly by inefficiency and failure to understand its markets, but just as much—as we will see—by the Revlon initial genius and later sharp practices by the company in beating all opposition in the lipstick field through sponsoring "The $64,000 Question," the television quiz show.

Hazel Bishop and her successors were not the only ones to fail at this time. But it was becoming clear that, overall, the industry had a growing and profitable future. In Paris, the couturiers began to challenge the old names in perfumes, and before 1950, Dior, Balenciaga, Balmain, Carven, Ricci, Rochas and Piquet all had well-established lines. Later on, Fath, Hermes, Grès, Givenchy and Laroche were also to luanch perfumes, a lucrative development that the newer couturiers of the 1960s and 1970s joined in. Some of these couturiers were to disappear into larger companies, and, even later still, some of the American companies were to buy up the names of couturiers to produce French-sounding but American-developed perfumes and cosmetic lines. One example is Revlon, which bought the Balmain name in the 1970s and pays the couturier house a royalty each year. Its latest perfume, Ivoire, launched in 1979, is one of the most expensive in the world; it retails at $125 an ounce in America. It has now been introduced in other markets.

Back in 1948, the American Medical Association set up a Committee on Cosmetics to monitor the industry and to help people to a better understanding of the products they used and the possible dangers in them. The early postwar period, too, saw a growing interest in hormone creams. High hormone levels produced by the body during childhood and young adulthood help to keep the skin youthful, and it is the natural decrease in their level which is partly responsible for the aging of the skin. (Another cause, of course, is exposure to wind and weather.) It was inevitable that cosmetics companies would investigate to see if the application of creams containing hormones would also help to keep the skin young. The early creams were not a success, and research in this area is by no means completed, but eventually the Department of Dermatology at the New York University College of Medicine established, following experiments on humans, not animals, that creams containing hormones had no adverse effect on the system when used regularly and appeared to improve the surface of the skin where they were applied. The money for the research had been provided by James G. Bell, president of the Bonne Bell Company, a Chicago-based group. The company had been selling a hormone cream for some time and wished to know whether it was dangerous to use. The research established that hormone creams appeared to slow down the aging of the surface of the skin. Further research has found out what level of hormone dosage is effective on the skin's surface. In the use of hormones the borderline between cosmetics and drugs is becoming blurred, and the authorities have become vigilant in this matter. The European Economic Community directive on cosmetics ignores hormones altogether, leaving them for the drugs committee to deal with.

The early postwar period also saw the beginning of the interest in cosmetics for men. At first there was an adverse reaction from both men and women on the ground that no "real" man would use cosmetics (ignoring the fact that in different periods of history men have used cosmetics as much as women). The companies were not to be gainsaid: they knew that the growth in women's cosmetics would finally taper off and that they would need a new market if their growth in profitability was to be maintained. Sound marketing techniques gradually broke down public resistance. Men still do not use decorative color cosmetics, but a wide range of treatment products and toiletries are available to them. It is a rare man indeed who does not use at least a deodorant or a shampoo. In an unusual display of humor in 1961, Charles Revson named his new men's line That Man, the only words Helena Rubinstein ever used to describe him.

For the cosmetics companies, life was fun in the 1940s and fifties. By 1950 the cosmetics industry in America was retailing at a total of $40,100,000, and two years later it had joined the ranks of the billion-dollar-a-year industries. There were close to 1,000 manufacturing units employing 30,000 people; another 25,000 were employed in sales and promotion and a further 150,000 in retail stores or house-to-house selling.

Elizabeth Arden and Helena Rubinstein might have been getting old, but they had lost none of their fire, although they had turned increasingly to other activities. They had not, in the meantime, allowed their old rivalry to die down: when Helena Rubinstein was told by journalists that a horse had bitten off the tip of Elizabeth Arden's finger, Rubinstein was reported to have asked: "Is the horse all right?" Elizabeth Arden, who had been the cover story in *Time* magazine on May 6, 1946, then a rare distinction for a woman and a business woman at that, had become a well-known and very successful racehorse owner. In 1945 she had been the top money-winner in U.S. racing. In 1947 her horse Jet Pilot won the Kentucky Derby.

Arden adored horses—her stables were decorated in her crimson and blue racing colors with all the taste she had decreed in her homes—but she did not care for the smell of the liniment they were rubbed down with, and she ordered that the fragrantly scented Ardena skin tonic be used instead. A trainer who protested that this treatment might not suit horses was replaced, and the stable lads, not slow themselves, quickly began helping themselves to the tonic for their wives and girl friends. Miss Arden promptly scotched that by having the tonic for the horses made without perfume.

Helena Rubinstein, meanwhile, continued to lead a peripatetic existence, rushing from one country to another where she had interests and at the same time building up one of the best art collections in the world. The picture that comes down of Helena Rubinstein in these years is of a small, dynamic woman, given to extravagant modes of expression. She never spoke any language properly, had never lost her Polish accent, and her speech was peppered with eccentric phrases. Jewish people were "nebbishy-looking"; anything she did not like was "dreck"; she would be there "in a jiffy"; and when she was angry—as she often was—things "got on her pip." Her behavior was eccentric too. In later years she often fell down, and no matter where she was—at home, shopping or in her office—she would lie where she had fallen, taking quite a time to "catch her breath." She always wore a bowler like a man and an enormous amount of jewelry, and carried an endless variety of paper bags containing bits of fruit and other food. In the early 1950s her business was grossing $22 million a year. Theoretically it was publicly owned, although she held a controlling interest, 52 percent (worth $30 million), of the American business. Madame herself owned all the foreign subsidiaries except the company in the United Kingdom and its subsidiaries in South Africa and the Far East. The original Australian business had been partitioned between her sons, Roy and Horace, and one of her sisters, Mrs. Ceska Cooper.

Rich though she might have been, Madame was extremely careful with money. She cut the Paris household staff allowance by half after deciding that too much was being spent. There was no arguing with her; they were to be cut by that amount, and that was that. It seems she refused to listen to anyone. No arguments could prevail once she had made up her mind. On one of her trips to Europe she made a special journey to Vienna to see her mascara supplier; the sole purpose was to save her company money and she did: future orders cost 3 percent less. But she could also be very generous and quite impulsively gave rings and other jewelry to her staff, after losing her temper with them, as she frequently did.

Helena Rubinstein and Elizabeth Arden, as so often in their lives, had again done the same thing: they had both married princes. Arden had married Prince Michael Evlanoff in 1942, a gentleman whose true manliness was in some doubt: it was rumored that she had spent her honeymoon with her financial advisers and he with a man friend. It was not long before she first locked the refrigerator so that he was unable to eat from it, and then locked him out of the house. They were divorced two years after the wedding.

Rubinstein seems to have fared somewhat better in her emotional affairs, though many doubted whether her second marriage was ever more than a friendly affair. She had married Prince Gourielli in 1938. He was treated rather better by Rubinstein than Evlanoff was by Arden, and he and Madame were together for more than twenty years, until his death. She missed that event, being away in Paris on business at the time, and managed to have herself sedated for a month, after weeping and wailing until the nasty business of the funeral was well over. Rubinstein had formed the House of Gourielli, which for many years ran a line of preparations for men, although Elizabeth Arden was actually the first to bring out a male line. The Gourielli line prospered for a time, but shortly after the death of the Prince, by which time it had been losing money, the Princess discontinued it.

Neither Arden nor Rubinstein saw Revson as quite the competitor they considered each other, or at least they did not view him with such personal loathing. They were wrong if they underestimated him, for he was then building up a cosmetics company that was eventually to become the second largest in America. Rubinstein always claimed that Revlon and Estée Lauder were copying her products: *her* Youth Dew, she claimed, copied Rubinstein's Skin Dew, *his* Ultima line, her Ultra Feminine. She was probably right: they all copied one another to some degree. Nevertheless, Helena Rubinstein seems to have had some admiration for Revson himself. She is said to have bought some Revlon stock with the express purpose of complaining at the shareholders' meeting about his extravagance. Dissuaded from this course, she decided to keep the stock, on the ground that it would be a good investment. She met him only once after which her single comment was that he had "bad skin."

As far as the public was concerned, however, the real rivalries of the 1950s and 1960s according to the media were between Revson and Estée Lauder. From her small beginnings, Lauder was becoming a force in the market. When she was too small to afford large-scale advertising, she invented the "gift-with-purchase" scheme and employed it to such effect that the others all followed. Although Estée Lauder started this trend in the 1950s, Avon might possibly rightly claim that its founder, David McConnell, had the idea first, when he discovered that it was easier to sell a bible with a little gift of perfume than to try to sell it on its own.

The idea eventually proved to be something of a mixed blessing. It pushed companies into more and more expensive promotions. The gift is geared to the amount the customer pays or the number of items bought, and the way the gift is merchandised can vary as well. There is the well-known two-for-the-price-of-one gimmick where the customer will be offered either a much larger jar at a relatively cheaper price, or even an additional jar. Alternatively, there is a small parcel of a quite different product in a sample size which goes with the purchase. The idea behind the gifts is sometimes to unload slow-moving old stock so that a new line can be brought in, or sometimes to bring other products in a range to the attention of the customer. After she has tried the sample, there is always the chance that she will come back and buy that item at its usual price.

Gifts-with-purchase have much more appeal in the higher-priced ranges. Estée Lauder's products are expensive, so the customer seems to be getting more from her little extra parcel than she would if the product she buys costs only a dollar or two. There is sound psychological reasoning behind the free gift in the expensive ranges, too. Although there is actually little to choose between products, a woman feels she is getting better value the more she pays. If she can be persuaded to buy one product from a range on this ground, there is a fair chance she will be attracted to the full range after her "free" gift. A trial of this kind is often quite enough to persuade a woman that it is worth doing without something else to buy a full product range.

Later on, Lauder's idea—of a cosmetics gift with a cosmetics purchase—was adapted by Revlon into P-with-P: purchase-with-purchase. This was strictly for the big companies, and Revlon pursued it actively for some time. One product was sold at its regular price together with a second one, which went at cost-price, or very little above it. The aim was to make the cost-price product look like a very big bargain at about 25 percent of its normal price. At the time when all the bigger companies were using the purchase-with-purchase plan, it had the effect of destroying brand loyalty. Unlike gift-with-purchase, the practice has now largely died out.

The gossip columns were full of stories about the Lauder-Revson rivalry. For all her ladylike ways, Estée Lauder can be as sharp as anyone when she chooses, although since Charles Revson died and the less colorful corporation men have come in to run the cosmetic companies, a great deal of the spark has gone out of the business of upstaging rivals. Friends tell, however, of a famous incident in Venice when a ball was held in aid of flood relief for the city. Earl Blackwell, of *Celebrity Register* fame, had organized the affair, and because he was using Charles Revson's yacht *Ultima II* as a base in Venice, Revson received an invitation. Mrs. Lauder, used to being with royalty and famous personalities, initially did not. Presumably, this was Mr. Revson's doing since it was he who was usually left out in the social cold. But it would take more than that to keep Mrs. Lauder out if she wanted to be in. Eventually, both Mr. and Mrs. Lauder attended the ball—and with an invitation.

A highly unlikely perennial rumor was that Mr. and Mrs. Lauder were pursuing Charles Revson around the Mediterranean bugging his extremely luxurious yacht and listening in to his conversations on the radio, hoping to pick up Revlon secrets. He took (a probably unnecessary) defensive action. What is believed is that somehow the Lauder organization secured a Revson memorandum—at a rumored price of $5,000—containing details of the proposed advertising campaign for the new Revlon Etherea cream, code-named "New Jersey" by the company. They promptly used more or less the exact wording from it in their advertising so that he would be sure to know that they had access to his office. The pattern of the 1930s was being repeated.

Estée Lauder had gone into men's cosmetics with one of the most successful after-shaves ever, Aramis, in 1965. Revlon had replied with Braggi in 1966. Lauder brought out Clinique, the first full allergy-tested fragrance-free line of cosmetics, in September 1968. The Revlon response was rapid, and eight months later, in April 1969, a very short time in development terms for a cosmetics line, Etherea hit the market. It was on this occasion that Lauder used the Revlon phrasings for her Clinique advertising.

Until the Etherea launch, Clinique had not been widely advertised, but in March 1969, just before Etherea came out, advertisements began in *Women's Wear Daily* and other journals using such phrases as "personal skin index," "biologically correct," and "essence of a leading dermatologist's belief." Meanwhile, the Revlon people were not letting on that they had produced their range so quickly. They claimed in their advertisements that it had taken three years to turn the "purest idea into reality."

On May 2, 1969, Lauder advertised in *Women's Wear Daily* that Clinique had brought about a revolution in makeup in eight months. It had "changed a basic trait." This was a reference to women's fickleness in their choice of makeup and implied that Clinique had changed all that. Revlon followed four days later with an announcement that it had achieved a "major break-through in cosmetic science" and that "hypoallergenics were a drag." Two days after that, on May 8, the public was told that Etherea begins "where hypoallergenics end." On May 12, Etherea "stands alone" and a day later "an Etherea first."

This battle was typical of many. When the Ultima II range came out, Charles Revson was increasingly insinuating his viewpoint into his advertisements, that of a man telling women how to make themselves desirable to men. Over at Lauder, however, the emphasis was all on the efforts of one woman creating cosmetics and perfumes for other women. In establishing her market, particularly in the international field, Estée Lauder proceeded cautiously. She had moved backward in the fragrance field anyway: her Youth Dew had originally been a bath oil, but it was marketed as a perfume in 1953 in the United States. In addition, it was not sold as such on the British market until 1960. By 1968, when Lauder's name was well established internationally and the fragrance Estée was introduced, it was on the British market by the following year. Azurée came out in both America and Europe in 1969, but Private Collection, alleged to be Estée's "own" perfume, was on the American market for four years before being introduced to Europe.

Much as he wanted to and hard as he tried, Charles Revson was not able to sell more than Estée Lauder in the lines she carried. Revlon's traditional strength was in the drugstores with their middle-priced ranges, but it also did very well in the department stores with their higher-priced lines. These lines lent a prestige to the cheaper ranges, and because of this, together with extremely good advertising, Revlon products, whatever their price, were all thought to be fashionable. But there was really no shifting of Estée Lauder in the prestige stores. Her lines, whether Lauder, Clinique or her man's range, Aramis, still dominate the top end of the trade. There is no doubt she won the battle between Clinique and Etherea: the latter is thought never to have made a profit and sells only about $5 million worth a year, against a figure approaching $30 million for Clinique. The Ultima II line, first launched in 1964, did not begin to show a profit until 1973, two years before Revson died. Even today the Lauder company is thought to take twice as much out of the prestige stores as Revlon, despite the progress made at Revlon under Michel Bergerac, chosen by Charles Revson to succeed him.

Revson's defeat in his battle with Lauder in the male cosmetics market is not easy to explain. She wins in all her lines, but Revlon carries a much greater price range of cosmetics and is bigger. Perhaps it is true, as Revson always maintained, that he understood exactly what women wanted. Equally, he might not have understood men. It seems likely he failed where Estée Lauder succeeded, in not concentrating his efforts. Lauder found that she had a very successful line when she brought out Aramis in 1965. It was more than a decade before she introduced another one, Devin. Aramis still sells and—the Lauder company does not give details of its sales—is still thought to be a best-seller. Charles Revson first replied with Braggi, then followed it up with several other lines, including That Man, Pub, Bill Blass and Top Brass. Perhaps men are less fickle in their taste for toiletries and cosmetics, or maybe when women are buying for men they are more conservative than when buying for themselves. Whatever the reason, Aramis today outsells Braggi by about five times, or nearly as much as Clinique outsells Etherea.

In another way the companies did not follow the same path. Whereas Revlon went public in 1955, Estée Lauder has remained a private company in family hands, with the whole family, including daughters-in-law, involved in public relations and product planning. No one outside the family has a single share in the company. In 1973, the Lauders' son Leonard, now president of the company, told *The New York Times* that the family "look upon ourselves as winders of the clock and directors of the symphony orchestra who try to stimulate our group of talented and brilliant people to do the best we can." Although it is a private company,

Lauder is run as though it were public, with statements by outside auditors, and quarterly reports, but the company keeps to itself the exact level of profits. Were the family to decide to go public, the stock issue would undoubtedly be one of the most popular seen in many years.

In a testament to her business acumen, Estée Lauder was named by *Harper's Bazaar* as one of the 100 Women of Achievement in 1967. The next year came the Spirit of Achievement Award from the Women's Division of the Albert Einstein College of Medicine. In 1970 she was voted one of the Top Ten Outstanding Women in Business and in 1974 was awarded the first Special Recognition Award by the Fragrance Foundation. Recognition of her work is not confined to the United States. She is a Chevalier of the Legion of Honor in France and has also received that country's "gold medal," the Vermeil Medal of the City of Paris, given to persons held in high esteem for their achievements.

Charles Revson, the first of the great cosmetics entrepreneurs to hire a full-time qualified dermatologist, would not market a product that did not meet his own exacting standards. This led to the elaborate research centers that every major cosmetic company has today. On one occasion, when his company was developing a skimmed-milk treatment line, Revson held back the launch until the product was refined to the point of being absolutely free of fat.

In 1960, Revson decided that his company was tying itself too closely to the upper middle classes, where the market was a limited one. He wanted his company to have a full range and to be run like General Motors, each product being produced separately with its own distinct price and image. This concept was developed, and today Revlon differs from other cosmetic companies in that it has distinct and separate houses, all run autonomously.

Michel Bergerac has retained Revson's structure with some modifications. The various houses are now divided into three groups, each with its own separate marketing and sales organization. Group I is made up of Revlon, Moon Drops, Natural Wonder and Charlie. Group II consists of Flex, Colorsilk, Mitchum, Milk Plus 6 and nail-care implements and other toiletries. Group

III comprises the high-priced lines, such as Princess Marcella Borghese (so you thought she was an Italian?), Ultima II and Etherea/Fine Fragrances, which include Norell, Ciara, Cerissa, Bill Blass for Women and Di Borghese. In addition to these three, Revlon has a Professional Products Group, which serves the beauty salons. All these sections of the company work independently of one another, with the result that although Revlon's total sales are very large, the individual sections have the experience of appearing to work for a much smaller group and thereby achieving a better rate of growth. Another advantage is that they do not compete directly against one another. This technique has meant that Revlon is represented in far more outlets than any other company. Its lines are sold in more than 10,000 stores worldwide, or "doors" as the industry calls them.

Although the cosmetics manufacturers frequently tried to steal one another's secrets to keep a step ahead of their rivals, industrial espionage in the 1950s was not simply an intercompany affair: some organizations were having the phones of their own staff tapped. This curious fact emerged during the battle for the lipstick market. In November 1955 the New York State Joint Legislative Committee met to study "the illegal interception of communications." The meeting followed several complaints by cosmetics companies against one another. Some quite simply stated that other companies copied their products—Helena Rubinstein, for example, made frequent accusations, although she never took legal action. In 1954, the Hazel Bishop company had accused the Toni people of copying its original dome-shaped gold-colored-metal lipstick cases. In March 1955, Revlon had announced the introduction of a "lanolite" lipstick, with the claim that it was the only "non-smear type" available. Hazel Bishop, of course, had already come out with her famous slogan "stays on you, not on him." In truth, as we have said, there is very little difference between one lipstick and another, so Revlon merely found a different slogan. Wearing his lipstick meant that a woman would "wake up beautiful." Lanolite (a lanolin derivative), it turned out, might not even be new. Within a few weeks of the appearance of the Revlon lipstick, Coty, Inc., an old-established company, now part of Pfizer, Inc., commenced an action in the New York Federal District Court, alleging that Revlon had stolen its advertising copy when launching its lipstick. It was Coty's own 24 lipstick that used the new formula, it alleged, not Revlon's. The charge read that Revlon had "appropriated and used for its own purposes much of the advertising material used by Coty." In other words, it was more important to the company that its words had been stolen, rather than its product. In an industry where a brilliant advertising campaign rather than the quality of a product guarantees sales, its concern was understandable. The matter was eventually settled—as prudence generally demands—out of court.

The case that led to the study by the New York court suggested that someone had been spying on the Hazel Bishop company, which was then being run by Raymond Spector, an executive of the advertising agency that had recently ousted Hazel Bishop herself from the company. In November 1954 his agency noticed that there was a series of strange similarities in other people's advertising which, it was felt, could not occur merely by coincidence. As the months passed, the similarities continued and increased in number. Then, in February 1955, a newsletter printed details of a request for a loan by the company. These details had originally been discussed over the telephone. In all the other cases in which Hazel Bishop advertising slogans had been printed by someone else, the slogans had just been discussed over the telephone.

Spector consulted his lawyers and then called in a private detective and a wiretapping expert, Charles B. Gris. After a search, it was revealed that phones of Hazel Bishop's executives were being tapped, including Spector's. He was naturally furious. Gris then offered to tap the phones in the Hazel Bishop offices for Spector's benefit, revealing that this was common practice at Revlon. At the court hearing, Spector reported that his response to the suggestion was: "I wouldn't do a thing like that. I said it may be legal, but it is a dirty business and I wouldn't get down into the gutter."

Announcement of the discovery by Gris did not stop the wire-

tapping, and eventually Spector approached the district attorney
with his story. Who was doing the tapping was never revealed, but
no one was ever prosecuted. Revlon did reveal at the hearing,
however, that the Bell Telephone Company had been tapping
phones in Revlon's own offices on behalf of the company for six
years. William D. Heller, then secretary-treasurer of Revlon, told
the court that the practice had helped the company. Indeed, it
was "extremely beneficial," had "tremendously improved performances" and led to greater "efficiency, service and courtesy"
among employees. Heller also told the court that, like Spector,
Revlon regarded the tapping of a rival's phone as "outrageous and
unlawful."

Later on in the hearing Bernard Spindel, who was in business
making wiretapping equipment, gave evidence. He was asked:

> "To clarify the record, Mr. Spindel, do you know of any other
> instance of tapping insofar as Revlon is concerned, other than the
> tapping by themselves within their own company?
> *Mr. Spindel:* Are you referring to . . .?
> *The Court:* In other words, a yes or no answer. Can you answer it
> yes or no?
> *Mr. Spindel:* I can't answer that yes or no for this reason. If you
> are referring to what might be termed as hearsay evidence, or com-
> petent legal evidence—whichever you want, I will be glad to answer
> that question.
> *The Court:* Let's not go into speculation. Let's have it as competent
> evidence as you call it.
> *Mr. Spindel:* Unfortunately, I am at a point right now that so far as
> legal competent evidence is concerned, I will say I have no further
> information.

The hearings concluded without any really satisfactory answers,
but they served to show that companies were extremely concerned
about keeping their own advertising and marketing plans as secret
as possible, but were very anxious to know what others in the field
were doing.

In the end, however, as we have seen, it was Revlon who won
the lipstick war, quite decisively in 1955.

By this time television sponsorship by cosmetics companies was well underway, and Revlon executives knew that the Hazel Bishop program "This Is Your Life" was hitting Revlon sales. So the company decided to sponsor a new CBS-TV quiz program, "The $64,000 Question." Charles Revson was said to be reluctant about the whole project. He watched the first show and was not impressed. "It's a turkey," he told his executives. He was wrong. The program was phenomenally successful for four years and was to quadruple Revlon's sales to $125 million and increase its earnings by as much as eight times. (Helena Rubinstein, in the interim, had turned down the opportunity to sponsor the show.)

Within four weeks after its premiere, the program was number one in viewer ratings. Already some Revlon products were showing between 300 and 500 percentage increases in sales. Soon 55 million people were watching the show every week on Tuesday night at ten. Revlon sales, which had been rising by between 10 and 20 percent a year, suddenly rose by 54 percent, after the program had been running for only half of the year. In 1956, the advance was even better, with 66 percent added to total sales and doubled profits. What was also attractive was that the program was not expensive to produce: at $27,800, including prize money, it cost about half of what of "This Is Your Life" cost Hazel Bishop. For part of the program's life, Revson insisted on running Revlon commercials live, so that he could decide at a very late stage which of his products he wanted to project on a particular night.

Then, in 1959, disaster suddenly struck: Revlon was accused of rigging "The $64,000 Question." The whole program, it was alleged, was a fraud. Contestants admitted that they had been primed before the quiz show, and Revlon found itself facing a congressional hearing.

The evidence was formidable. Not only did many ordinary contestants confess to being briefed about questions, but celebrities did too. John Ross, for instance, manager of child actress Patty Duke, then aged twelve, stated that she had been given the answers to questions immediately before the program by the assistant producer, Shirley Bernstein. As a result, she was able to tie for the $64,000 prize with another young contestant. She was not the only show business person to appear on the show. Some showed incredible naiveté when questioned. Xavier Cugat, the bandleader, thought the whole thing was simply entertainment, testifying that the answers had come to him in advance from Merton Koplin, the producer. He thought he was making a "good show." He won $16,000.

The spectacle of Charles Revson, his brother and other assorted Revlon executives giving evidence during the congressional hearing, held in 1959, was not an edifying one. Testimony was taken in public by the House Interstate and Foreign Commerce Subcommittee. Among those in attendance for the government on the subcommittee were Representatives Steven B. Derounian of New York, Walter Rogers of Texas and John B. Bennett of Michigan. They were not easy to fool.

As the hearings proceeded, it was clear that there would be disagreement among those giving testimony. By this time, Martin Revson, previously vice president and director of Revlon, had had enough and had left the company on April 30, 1958, after twenty-three years of service with the company his brother had founded. There seems no doubt, however, that he was the senior executive at Revlon responsible for "The $64,000 Question" and its spin-off, "The $64,000 Challenge." Charles refused to give any reason for his brother's departure from the company. "It was a business matter between me and my brother," was all he said. (Martin was later to sue Charles on charges of fraud, misrepresentation and breach of agreement on a stock deal. The case, alleged to be for a sum over $600,000, was settled out of court, for $300,000, and it was not until after the death of Joseph Revson that Martin and Charles came together again. They were said to be very close during Charles's last years.)

As the hearings proceeded, it emerged that Revlon had held regular weekly meetings to discuss each show. Martin Revson, George Abrams, Revlon's vice-president in charge of advertising, some representatives from C. J. Larouche, the advertising agency that handled the Revlon account, and the show's producers attended these meetings. In addition, Revlon conducted their own telephone survey each week. They would bring ratings charts with them to the meetings with information on the various contestants on the show and how the audience rated and felt about them. Charles Revson himself was rarely present; when he was, it was merely a brief appearance at the end, and it was clear that Martin was in overall charge.

During the period of sponsorship, as the company's sales rose sharply, Revlon was spending between seven and eight million dollars on television advertising in America, a figure reckoned to be 60 to 65 percent of the total advertising budget for the company.

As the hearings commenced in April 1959, Martin Revson protested his innocence of any rigging: "We believed we had bought an honest show and we were convinced we had one. Frankly, we would have been foolish to have had anything to do with a show that was not completely honest. After all, Revlon's reputation was staked on the integrity of our programs. We were spending millions of dollars yearly to build that reputation and to build consumer good will. . . .

"EPI's [Entertainment Products, Inc.] people made it clear that they did not need Revlon. They told us constantly that we were lucky to have the show, that other sponsors were lined up at the door. . . .

"My suggestions ranged from the broadest possible policy matters to the narrowest details. I constantly asked that the show be fast-paced and of high dramatic value. I criticized the lighting, the way the contestants were dressed, the conversation that the MC had with contestants before the questioning began. We discussed every detail, large and small.

"But I never once suggested that a particular contestant win or lose. . . ."

Congressman Derounian said Martin Revson was quibbling: "You have been telling us that you did not know a thing about contestants and then you flip-flop and say 'We knew some things about the contestants; we discussed certain things; but as to control of them, I knew absolutely nothing.' To me that seems impossible for a man of your business ingenuity and business acumen.

"You are a pretty sharp fellow in business. To prove it, your sales went up to $110 million [sic]. The dope does not do that. You are no dope. You plead ignorance of every fact that has to do with controlling a contestant, but acknowledge that you discussed every other detail of a contestant. It seems suddenly, when it came to the questions and answers in your discussions, you jumped over them. You say now, 'Gee, I don't know.' "

Later on George Abrams stated in his affidavit: ". . . the primary purpose of the meeting was to keep the ratings high, or raise them, and so . . . a great deal of time was devoted to discussing the destiny of a contestant. . . .

"We understood that the technique used for controlling the destiny of a contestant was to employ questions ranging from tough to easy. . . .

"If a contestant or match did not come out as we had suggested, the sponsor and agency representatives would be upset and express displeasure—often in a very heated fashion."

James D. Webb, president of C. J. Larouche, was asked whether it was customary for the sponsor to supervise so closely the shows he sponsors as Revlon did. "I think probably the best way to answer that for you, sir," he said, "is to say that Revlon, because advertising is so important to them and takes up such a large part of their sales dollar, are much more concerned than would other types of advertisers be where advertising is less important in the eventual sales. . . .

". . . among our clients, Revlon gives their advertising of all descriptions a greater combing over before it ever appears than any other client we have."

Charles Revson might, as he said, have been "flabbergasted" by the riggings, but he was not intimidated at the hearing and put his views forcefully: "I was head of a company that made good cosmetics, and its reputation meant as much to me as my own. Our sales had been growing from the first year the company was founded, and they are still growing at a nice rate now. . . . I thought the shows were honest. If I had had any suspicion that they were not, we never would have taken them in the first place. . . .

"We pay close attention to our advertising, as we do every other phase of our operations. We have always worked closely with our advertising agencies, and we wanted to work closely with the producers of the show. So Revlon did make suggestions to the producers. . . .

"It was my responsibility and Revlon's responsibility to help make this show as attractive and entertaining as possible. We wanted it to continue to be something that the people of America could look forward to every week. It was our obligation to offer suggestions so that the show fits in with the character of our company. We wanted the producers to provide interesting contestants and interesting [quiz] categories."

Congressman Rogers did not seem impressed: "You and your brother come up here and say you were victims of fraud, too, but you were the kind of victims of the fraud that some of the winners on these contests were—that is, you profited very well by being a victim . . . you were the one who profited the most by the deceitful practices that were played upon the American people. I am wondering what is in your mind and the mind of Revlon, Inc., to try to make restitution or correction of a wrong which you admit occurred."

Revson attempted to justify the company. ". . . it is the same as any other commercial company that would earn something because of something—a network or producer or contestant . . . it is part of the business experience . . . we paid for the show. We paid for the time. We paid for the contestants. So therefore in turn we made a profit on it.

"I do feel that a sponsor should and can have the right to work with the producer of a show. Our name is there and everything else is there."

Congressman Bennett joined in: "You got this all secondhand. You were sitting up in an ivory tower, apparently, letting these things go on and doing nothing about them. Your own people, one of your important officers, knew that your firm was involved with this thing. . . ."

At a further hearing, Abrams more or less admitted that the company had put pressure on the producers of the show: "When the rating charts reflected that the dull contestants were resulting in a loss of program popularity, we suggested to the producers that they find a really tough question to terminate the contestant's appearance. They generally were successful . . . but not always. . . .

". . . those of us present at these weekly meetings knew the popularity status of contestants as determined by rating and publicity and expressed to the producers our desires for the ultimate disposition of many contestants.

"There was a period in which a series of middle-aged men followed one another on the program, and we resented this severely because our market for cosmetics was not middle-aged men. So we suggested that there must be some interesting female contestant, or even a child that they could throw into the lineup of contestants. So that a matter of that sort would provoke quite violent discussions."

Merton Koplin, who had become producer of "Bonanza" as well as "Question," confirmed Abrams' comments. He volunteered that "if we had a man with a beard on, the conclusion was that we should get more men with beards. If we had someone with an exotic category, the feeling was expressed we should get more exotic categories. If we had a younger contestant, the cry went up that we should have a young contestant on every show."

The subcommittee eventually came up with an interim report on the affair on February 9, 1960. It proposed a series of amendments to the Federal Communications Act of 1934 and the Federal Trade Commission Act of 1914 and suggested some administrative action by the FCC (Federal Communications Commission). The recommendations dealt with the issuing and renewal of licenses to the companies, any trafficking in licenses, and payments to people promoting products, the well-known "payola" system, a custom not confined to the cosmetics houses, nor by any means to the United States. The rigging of quiz shows was banned, and the committee suggested a series of penalties for any infringements of the regulations.

It was September 1960, before the full subcommittee finally came up with an amended version of a Senate-passed bill. On September 13, 1960, the Communications Act Amendments were enacted. From then on, the rigging of television shows by companies was a federal crime, any payola had to be publicly disclosed by companies, and the FCC was given much broader regulatory powers. Obviously, companies in any field would now have to exercise special care in their sponsorship of television programs.

As for Revlon, its reputation remained remarkably undamaged for all the damning evidence. It kept its lead in lipstick sales, and Revlon stock, which was offered to the public for the first time before the scandal erupted, was trading at $30 a share within three months after the hearings, having been offered originally at only $12.

By the mid-1960s the cosmetics industry in the United States had a tired look. The early entrepreneurs were getting old: Rubinstein died in 1965 aged ninety-three and Elizabeth Arden a year later, at eighty-eight. People were beginning to ask whether the great era of expansion was over, although the industry was basically sound, and sales and profits were still increasing. An atmosphere of uncertainty lay over the industry: people were feeling unsure about their job security, and relations with advertising agencies were poor. As cosmetic companies had gone public, stricter financial control meant that some of the flair and excitement were lost. Although the big mergers and takeovers did not come until the 1970s, the conditions for them were being established during the 1960s.

In this atmosphere, the small companies felt threatened and some of them disappeared into larger groupings. Gradually a small number of very large concerns, like Revlon, Max Factor and Arden, which could afford massive advertising campaigns, began to control most sales outlets. The small companies had made a great contribution to the growth of the industry, facilitating the

mass distribution of cosmetics and the growth of supermarket retailing. Although the small companies had given the industry
much of its flavor and individuality, creating new fashions, styles
and markets, new concepts in cosmetics and much of the excitement of the industry, they either gradually went under or disappeared into the larger concerns. It seemed that the only way that
the industry's leaders could continue to grow was by buying in
ideas from outside rather than through creative activities of their
own.

But from the outside, the industry looked most attractive. To
the financial world, cosmetics companies seemed to have not only
tremendous growth potential but also ample cash resources. In
October 1963, *Beauty Fashion* called what was happening "merger
madness" and said: "Very few of these cosmetic mergers—particularly the ones that make up the daily rumors in the trade—are
mergers of necessity or mergers for clearly defined economic benefits. They are mergers which are the result of an overabundance
of cash and credit pressing on the trade. From an industry of
minor importance in the financial world, cosmetics have acquired
in a bare five years, a fascinating reputation for glamour and
growth."

Beauty Fashion suggested that many companies had been sold
at excessive and unrealistic prices. Big companies, confident in
their mistaken belief that massive advertising was all that was
needed for a marketing success, preferred to buy a "name" rather
than spend time creating a new product for the market.

One entrepreneur who first went public and then sold out later
revealed the painful story. In 1977, Richard Salomon, who had
owned Charles of the Ritz, looked back at what happened to his
company after it went public in 1961. In the September 1977 issue
of the *Harvard Business Review* he concluded: "In retrospect, it
seems to me that for the last ten years of my career the joy of
business had vanished. From the day I went public in 1961 to the
day in 1972 when I retired on my sixtieth birthday, it seemed to
me that I was under constant pressure for performance and not
free to act totally in the interests of the business itself. The inter-

ests of the short-term share owner too often were not parallel to those of the management."

Ten years after going public, Salomon sold his company to the Squibb Corporation. "It seems to me that one act followed another in preordained fashion. The decision to go public led inexorably to our eventually being acquired," he wrote. His experience was typical. He had all the sensible reasons for going public: all his business interests and personal assets were in the one company; he wanted his estate to have an ascertainable value for estate and inheritance tax purposes; he wanted equity to be available as an incentive to executives; he felt that public ownership of his shares would give him personal satisfaction and would mark him as a successful entrepreneur; he wanted more liquid funds; and was advised that he could get all this without relinquishing control of the company.

Unfortunately for him, no one suggested that there might be disadvantages in becoming a public company. First of all, the fifty-five executives eligible for shares in the company began to jockey for position in their attempts to get as many as possible of the 30,000 shares being made available to them. This may sound a trivial problem, but it came to bedevil the operation of the day-to-day running of the business, particularly as the offering price of the stock became an issue. There were external pressures too. Once a company goes public, the analysts, investors and competitors are entitled to a much closer look at it. Salomon felt that a private company could make a quota of mistakes without embarrassment. When there were outside shareholders, such mistakes were public knowledge, and the upshot was that the company took fewer chances than it had when it had been private. New ventures were not undertaken if they had any real chance of early losses, because these would disturb the steady growth in profits and adversely affect the share price. As Salomon put it: "While a privately owned competitor might consider launching a risky product like Clinique or Aramis, this is a luxury not permitted a relatively small public company whose earnings had to increase not only annually but even quarterly."

Eventually Charles of the Ritz began to look for growth that it could guarantee. So it did what other companies were doing: it bought that growth. In 1963 the company merged with Lanvin, a company that, because of the great success of its Arpège perfume, which is still a popular fragrance more than fifty years after its launch, was larger than Charles of the Ritz. Lanvin had just acquired the Jean Naté line of bath products, which was becoming very successful. Salomon became the controlling stockholder and chief executive of the merged group. From this time, the company was able to grow more steadily. It was now able to afford major advertising and promotion expenditures. By the end of 1970, when Salomon was approaching sixty, he realized that no one in his family would follow him into the business and decided to sell out. The Squibb Corporation seemed to him to be the best partner, and the merger took place in 1971. Then, for a brief period, Salomon became an employee of a company, a new experience for him. A year later he retired from active business, although he stayed on as a director of Squibb. Looking back, Salomon had simple advice for others in his position: "Sell out and get out."

What happened to Charles of the Ritz is just one typical example of the method of operation of the industry in the late 1950s and 1960s. It led to the big takeovers of the 1970s by the large diversified industrial conglomerates of the smaller dynamic entrepreneurial cosmetic firms.

Europe did not escape the merger mania: the trend was as strong there as in the United States. Coty was taken over by Pfizer, the American chemical giant, in 1963. Eve of Roma (Eve herself died prematurely in 1969) disappeared into American Gillette in 1968. The following year Cyclax, one of the oldest companies in the cosmetics trade, formed in 1896, was saved by money from American investors. Later, in 1974, it became part of BAT Industries, which already had Yardley, Germaine Monteil, Lentheric and Morny in its stable. BAT has been highly successful in developing its cosmetics side. Eric Morgan, managing director of the BAT cosmetics division, credits the responsibility for this to Sir Richard Dobson, who was chairman of the whole group during this formative period. "Richard," says Morgan, "understood exactly how the cosmetics industry worked. We were able to move and develop as if we were a separate entity, and he was not always breathing down our necks for regular and steady profit growth. So we could take chances."

Goya, a well-known British company, formed in 1937 by Douglas Collins, was bought by Reckitt and Colman, of mustard fame, in 1969. Eight years later Reckitt had realized that the venture was not a success and was looking for a buyer. Christopher Collins, son of Goya's founder, managed to raise enough capital to buy a 25 percent interest in the company, Sutton Seeds taking the other 75 percent. Later on, Christopher was to buy more shares from Sutton to give himself a controlling interest. In 1969, too, the old-established small Harriet Hubbard Ayer company became part of Unilever.

In the 1950s and 1960s the industry became increasingly international in character. As companies began to feel that their home markets were being exhausted, they turned elsewhere, and companies that had suffered from American competition began to hit back. Max Factor, with its West Coast base, had long been doing well in Japan, where it lay second only to Shiseido, the long-established Tokyo-based group. Suddenly, Factor found itself facing strong competition from Revlon, which entered the market offering its regular American lines. At that time, a Western look was very much in vogue in Japan, and the Revlon line immediately captured a large slice of the Japanese business at very little cost by the simple method of using its American advertising with American models offering American lines. Only the copy was in Japanese. The other cosmetics companies, following suit, began to use Western models in their advertising. In this way, Factor was able to recoup its position somewhat: it claims today that it is still second in the market to Shiseido, which has some 30 percent of Japanese cosmetics sales. Avon, too, has gone into Japan, and today it has 100,000 sales representatives there, but it is finding it very difficult to overcome to any great extent the entrenched position of Shiseido.

Until the 1960s, France still had the perfume industry its own way, at least the prestige end of it, although the market was increasing sufficiently in size to allow British and American fragrances in at the medium-priced levels. This situation still obtains today, and some companies have solved the problem by buying out French houses, paying royalties to couturiers for the use of their names in perfumes (Balmain at Revlon is a case in point), or simply by using French-style names for perfumes, as Estée Lauder did for Azurée and Alliage, and Elizabeth Arden with Memoire Chérie and Cabriole.

Avon entered the British market in 1959, when it opened a small manufacturing plant in Northampton, and was an immediate success. Within ten years, Avon had become the biggest seller in the United Kingdom, beating such well-established rivals as Max Factor, Rubinstein, Arden and Yardley with a 17 percent share of the market. By 1979 the share had jumped to as much as 37 percent in facemasks and packs, 26 percent in lipsticks and 25 percent in nail varnish. In no women's cosmetics was its share less than 10 percent of the market. Since 1966 the company has had a large distribution facility at Corby, twenty-five miles from Northampton, which remains Avon's manufacturing and administrative center.

Revlon, doing very well at home, was one of the last American companies to take to the international trail. It began in the late 1950s but made up for lost time, and today it operates in more than 100 countries and is expanding all the time. Michel Bergerac hopes that eventually the group will be allowed to move into the countries of Eastern Europe, where the potential market is very large. Cosmetics production does not have a high priority in these countries, and there is very little manufacturing of cosmetics. As a result Russian women, for example, are prepared to pay very high prices indeed for makeup. Tourists in Russia are besieged with offers to buy their lipsticks, and as living standards rise, the market for cosmetics must grow. Meantime, Russian and other

Eastern European women make do with poor creams and sport an amazing amount of blue eye shadow.

British companies were not standing still either. Weary of the American inroads into its own market, Yardley, after many years of little growth, suddenly began to develop and attacked the U.S. market. This firm, now a subsidiary of BAT Industries, is one of the oldest cosmetics and toiletry businesses. It was formed first in 1670, when a young man named Yardley paid King Charles I a large sum of money for a soap concession in London. Yardley exhibited at the Great Exhibition in Hyde Park in 1851 and again one hundred years later at the 1951 exhibition on the South Bank of the Thames. By the 1930s, Yardley was Britain's leader in an industry upon which women were spending 8.75 cents a week: 1.5 cents on face powder; 1.5 cents on manicures; 1.25 cents on vanishing cream; one cent on soap, night creams, cotton wool and lipstick; and 0.25 cent on white vaseline for the eyelids. The rest of the money went on a fortnightly hairdo. The company had been trading in Canada since 1900 and had to set up in the United States in 1923, when it started to bottle its lavender water—a world-famous traditional product—there. In 1928, a small factory was opened in New Jersey for other products.

For many years Yardley seemed a traditional stick-in-the-mud company, and American groups had no problem competing against it in the United Kingdom. Then suddenly, in the mid-1960s, the British look was in. London was the center of the "Swinging Sixties." Yardley cashed in on the London look—a pale unmade-up look on the face and lips with all the focus on the eyes —and took it to America. The whole campaign was conducted using only one model—Jean Shrimpton, the extravagantly pretty doe-eyed girl who seemed to symbolize the 1960s. On the basis of this one campaign, Yardley was able to establish a toehold in the American market which it has never lost.

In 1966, Mary Quant burst on the British cosmetics scene with a brand-new approach to packaging. Already established in the fashion world, where she was a leading proponent of the miniskirt, Miss Quant and her husband, Alexander Plunkett-Green, backed with money from Gala Cosmetics, brought out a new range that completely broke with the tradition of packaging cosmetics in soft pastels to give them "feminine appeal." She chose instead the hard colors of black and silver. She moved away, too, from a romantic approach in her product names and advertising copy. Everything was synonymous with the new, liberated, independent mood of miniskirted women. Her cleaner was Come Clean, her eye-shadows Jeepers Peepers. The trade thought they would not sell; how wrong it was. The first range went extremely well, and Mary Quant continued her hard message. In 1970, out came the baldly stated Make-up to Make Love In. The range was one of the marketing successes of the year and established the Quant line as a serious producer in the British market. There was no skin treatment product in the range, just four decorative cosmetics for lips, cheeks, lashes and eyes, with a breath freshener.

The company had been working on the idea for eighteen months. It wanted to produce a cosmetics range that could genuinely be said to be long-lasting. Sue Steward, creative adviser at Mary Quant, told Rosemary Simon for her book *The Price of Beauty:* "We thought girls ought to be able to be unaware of wearing make-up. They should be able to put it on and then forget about it, instead of having to worry whether their mascara is smudged or their nose is shiny. Most women want to be able to leave home in the morning looking well made-up and stay that way all day. From there, we began thinking of all the times when girls want to look their best and one of the most obvious occasions is when they are with their boy friend. We wanted to produce a range in which a girl could kiss and cuddle without looking smudged and frightful. Normally if a girl goes to bed in her make-up, she gets up looking a hideous mess."

Mary Quant was breaking one of the fundamental rules of cosmetics by suggesting that women could go to bed without removing all their makeup and putting on night skin cream instead. It was therefore necessary to find a product that would not harm the skin, and the company decided to use gels that do not use powder and are therefore much less likely to clog the skin pores than those that do. Tests did not show any sign of skin irritation at all. Then the colors were chosen and the copy written. Quant had no interest either in the research so dear to the giant companies. Sue Steward: "We all had the feeling that bright colours would be the thing in 1970. No, of course there was no research. It was just a feeling that this was right. I can't explain it. You sense a mood. It's something in the air. It is pointless doing research into either colours or ideas. There is not really time and, in any case, if you ask people whether they would like X or Y in three months, they would say 'no.' People can't forecast their wants." This was yet another heresy in an industry in which it is customary to watch fashion trends closely and conduct a huge amount of market research to ensure that the products are right. But it worked. It also helped the Quant company to increase its distribution outlets. Only one distributor showed the company the door when it went selling—on the ground that he did not want to be associated with disgusting products.

The hard copy line in the advertisements was easy to understand. Women, it was alleged, wore makeup in order to be attractive to men. It did not then need a genius to connect men and love. The pitch was in the magazines for younger women and in *Vogue*. From the beginning, the Quant range had sold to younger women between the ages of eighteen and thirty, and that was the target for Make-up to Make Love In. With its hint of emancipation and its titillating undercurrents, the campaign was highly successful; "fantastic," the company described it. The range ran for several years and established Mary Quant in the British cosmetics industry. A modest export success has meant that the Mary Quant name is registered in the international mind, but basically the company's market has remained the British one. Its experience does show how, even today, in an era of giant companies, there is always room for the really creative entrepreneur.

In the same year as the Love launch, Mary Quant was taken over by the Smith and Nephew group, along with other companies in the Myram Picker Group—Gala, Outdoor Girl and Miners. Smith and Nephew's recent experience with its cosmetics division shows that the problems of the cosmetics industry were not confined to America. After spending ten years trying to get Quant and the other companies established, it was badly hit by a general sales recession in the United Kingdom in 1979. By 1980 the cosmetics division was running at a loss. The company decided it no longer fitted in with the other interests in the group, and the division was sold to Max Factor, a surprising bidder. No figure for the sale was given, but the price was reckoned to be in the region of $20 million. Max Factor released this statement: "We are extremely pleased to add these brands to our list of quality cosmetics, fragrances and treatment products. Their international reputation will augment Max Factor's position as one of the world's leading cosmetic and fragrance companies and we are committed to support these brands with significant marketing, promotional and distribution activities internationally."

The Quant influence remains, however, and in her latest line, which carries the straightforward no-nonsense name Skin Care Programme, Mary Quant, now over forty, uses her own face in advertisements to push the range. Gone are the heady days when "feeling" was behind the product. Now the copy reads:

I WISH I'D INVENTED THIS 20 YEARS AGO

Believe me, I've put some junk on my face the last twenty years. I've tried cucumber, eggs, hormone creams, cold creams, even salad creams.

I fell for all the promises.

Obviously, the sensible thing to do was to come up with my own preparations. A complete, balanced Skin Care Programme, specially formulated for individual skin types.

Simple, I thought.

Only it wasn't that simple. It's taken my skin specialists nearly five years to develop ten different formulations. (A complete list is at the bottom of the page.)

A system of skin care that's bang up to date with all the most effective scientific ingredients built in.

The most magical of these is collagen. It cuts down the amount of moisture that evaporates naturally through your skin by up to 80%.

This is important, because it's the moisture lying under your skin that keeps it soft, supple and less liable to wrinkle. No, it's not the Fountain of Youth and I'm not promising any miracles. But I do promise that if you use my skin care routine every day your skin will become softer and more supple. You'll look younger than you would without it.

Like us all, Mary Quant has grown up.

In 1965, Helena Rubinstein died, aged ninety-three; a year later Elizabeth Arden was dead too, at an age variously estimated between eighty-one and eighty-eight (the latter was correct). It very quickly became clear that, although both ladies had left large personal fortunes, they had also left their companies in a mess. In Helena Rubinstein's will, the only bequests were money and her vast collection of art, furniture, antiques and jewelry was sold. The money which was left after taxes and bequests went to the Helena Rubinstein Foundation, which she decreed would be a family-oriented charity giving money to women and children in need. Her Park Avenue apartment and her Paris one, too, were both bought by Charles Revson who spent over two years and a great deal of money to modernize and renovate them. Elizabeth Arden had never set up a foundation, so the position of her company was even worse. After her death the estate had to find $37 million in taxes. There were said to be sixty inquiries from people wanting to buy the business immediately after she died, but the company decided to stay independent for the time being.

Charles Revson, later on in the 1970s, did not repeat their mistake, with the result that his company has remained independent ever since. It was not long, however, before the giant conglomerates with their interests in toiletries and cosmetics came shopping, their eyes firmly fixed on Arden and Rubinstein. Ever on the lookout for companies to boost their earnings, they felt that the high profit margins of the cosmetic businesses would fit well into their existing interests and be very useful in raising the average profitability of their group. They were right—in theory.

THREE

MERGER MANIA?

*The smell of profit is clean
And clean, whatever the source*
—Juvenal

By 1970, it was becoming clear that a new structure was emerging in the cosmetics industry in the United States. The conglomerates were sniffing around for companies they thought might fit in comfortably with their interests, and their eyes were on four organizations in particular—Elizabeth Arden, Helena Rubinstein, Max Factor and Revlon. Estée Lauder held just as much appeal, but, as everyone knew, her organization was wholly and firmly controlled by Mrs. Lauder and her family. Of the four original prewar entrepreneurs, only Charles Revson was still alive, and of the four companies, his is the only one that has survived until today as an independent. In 1970 the others were all in varying states of disarray.

Nevertheless, these companies, along with Avon, which was already too large and independent to figure in the bid rumors, were to dominate the industry in the United States, and strength there meant dominance in the whole of the Western world at least. Only a few non-American cosmetics manufacturers compared in size: Shiseido in Japan and the Far East; L'Oreal of France in Europe and America, but then mainly in hair products; and BAT Industries of the United Kingdom, which was making profitable inroads in foreign markets. Alongside these companies, the smaller concerns, where they did survive, did so because of their appeal to a very specialized market, and even many of them swiftly disappeared into larger groupings.

The company that was most to engage public attention was Helena Rubinstein. When Madame died, her empire, which she decisively and actively ruled until two days before her death, spanned 100 countries. Alas, her heirs were not made of the same metal as Madame, and her death marked the beginning of what, with hindsight, looks like an inevitable decline for the company.

Rubinstein's arch rival, Elizabeth Arden, left her affairs in an even worse mess than Rubinstein when she died in 1966. The survival and growth of Arden since then, while Rubinstein has declined, is, in contrast, one of the success stories of the twentieth-century cosmetics industry.

At Rubinstein it had become very clear by the early 1970s that there was no one in the company, or among her family, who could run her organization as successfully as Madame. Her own elder son, Roy Valentine Titus, who had been vice president of the firm in his mother's lifetime, failed to take on her mantle. Oscar Kolin, her nephew, who succeeded Madame as president, could not continue the momentum she had created.

By 1970 the company was actively looking for an organization to bail it out of growing problems, which had not yet been reflected in falling profits. When Colgate-Palmolive came along with a $143.2-million offer in 1973, it was not just interested in rescuing the group. There was a further factor: it thought the company would boost its overall profits. On the surface, cosmetics companies appeared to be operating highly successfully, their profit margins seemed enormous by average standards, and they looked as though they would fit very comfortably into a conglomerate, particularly one with interests in toiletries. Had Colgate not bought up Rubinstein, another group most surely would have. The subsequent unhappy marriage between Colgate-Palmolive and Rubinstein has been a chastening example to anyone looking for swift profits from the cosmetics industry.

Things began to go wrong almost immediately after the purchase. Colgate was after a swift return on its investment. But decline had already set in, and changes in executives did nothing to halt the setback. Indeed, each new boss accelerated it. In an attempt to get the company on a better footing, the headquarters were eventually moved out of New York to Greenvale, Nassau County, on Long Island. Three and a half years later, putting a brave face on its problems, the company moved back to New York City to the Colgate-Palmolive building at 300 Park Avenue. The experiment had been a disaster, but with some of Madame's old panache, the company arranged to be welcomed back to New York by Mayor Edward Koch and Lewis Rubin, chairman of the Association for a Better New York. At a ribbon-cutting ceremony David Foster, then chairman of Colgate-Palmolive, told the press how happy the company was to be back in New York. Employees, in an action reminiscent of Helena Rubinstein's launch of her Heaven Scent perfume in 1942—when she had floated tiny samples of the fragrance over New York—showered Park Avenue with helium-filled balloons.

"Helena Rubinstein loves New York" ran the legend on the side of the moving van carrying the company back to the city. The truth was more prosaic: Shirley Lord, the company's vice-president of corporate relations and development, told reporters: "We were spending $50,000 in taxi fares for the executive staff to go to have meetings in the city." Peter Engel, then president and chief executive officer of Rubinstein, bluntly admitted that the move out of the city had been a "dismal failure."

There were other mistakes, too. Helena Rubinstein, Inc., was simply not getting its products across to the public in the way Madame had, despite such widely reported promotion as the Shirley Lord Beauty Breakfasts. These were occasions with Miss Lord pushing not merely Helena Rubinstein products, but what she described as "lifetime beauty." She was always accompanied by one or more of "The Friends of Helena Rubinstein," who revealed their beauty secrets to sometimes startled audiences. Shirley and the breakfasts got a great deal of publicity in the press, but whether they did much for Rubinstein sales is questionable. (The very attractive Miss Lord was being groomed to become Madame II, and for some time it seemed that she would indeed slip into Helena Rubinstein's shoes. It was not to be, however.)

The launch of the first skin-treatment line for the over-fifties—the line was called Madame Rubinstein—did not go well. Madame herself, with her grand Semitic features, could perhaps ignore her age, but most women do not like to be seen at the beauty counter buying a product for "old" women, particularly in an age when youth is all.

In contrast, Millenium, a new Elizabeth Arden line for the 1980s, is for older women too, but its message is far more subtle. It is for "mature," not "over-fifty," skins, and promises that "cell renewal" will be speeded up and occur as quickly as in young skins. The model used in advertising is no teenager, but neither is she an old woman: sophisticated and beautiful, she could be any age between twenty-five and forty-five and carries a promise of beauty for all. Companies are becoming aware that as the swingers of the 1960s reach their middle years, they are still wearing makeup, and the market may now be ready for such a range or ranges, if the story is told the right way.

The biggest disaster of all was the Rubinstein "computer," brought out in 1977. Named the Skin Life Instant Beauty Analyzer, it was described as an electronic beauty-scanner that analyzed the individual needs of every customer and recommended the right skin care and makeup products for their personal skin-color type.

The computer was the brainchild of Peter Engel, who had come over from Colgate in 1973. Launching the product, he said: "The Analyzer is the first and only one of its kind in the industry. At Helena Rubinstein, we pride ourselves on our ability to offer not only excellent products, but also very important service to our clients. Over the years, there has been a certain element of uncertainty in a cosmetic purchase. The result of this has often been a drawerful of mistakes, particularly regarding shaded items, and so a dissatisfied customer. Now, for the first time, Helena Rubinstein has developed the means to eliminate the guesswork, the costly mistakes and the dissatisfaction. If the customer uses the Skin Life Instant Beauty Analyzer and follows its recommendations, she cannot go wrong."

That was all very well, but cosmetics, it seemed, were not yet ready for the computer age. The analyzer flopped badly. Women simply did not want to use it, despite careful marketing. They found it either boring or impersonal. It contained a series of questions about skin texture, color, etc., for the customer to answer. If you had pale skin, for example, a range of colors for foundation, lipstick, hairdo, etc., would show up on a big chart. Whatever the analyzer was, the customers preferred to stick to old methods of buying, attracted by packaging and upbeat marketing and personally assisted by the salesperson at the cosmetics counter. Using the Rubinstein computer was obviously regarded as too lacking in the vital ingredient—glamour. Some observers remark that practically on its own the computer was responsible for almost wrecking the company.

Peter Engel himself was not to survive long. Today he writes novels with events and characters from the industry only thinly disguised in his plots.

Shirley Lord stayed on—at least that time. By now the problems of the ailing cosmetics company were common knowledge in the industry. Estimates were made of the kind of losses being made by Rubinstein: the parent did not reveal precise figures. The international side of the business did not falter as soon as the American, but the American was the bigger, and it was clear that eventually it would drag the rest of the conglomerate down, unless a radical attempt at recovery was made.

And the troubles were spreading. In September 1978 it was announced that the United Kingdom companies of Helena Rubinstein and Coty of Pfizer had merged. This appeared at first to be an attempt by Rubinstein to stop the slide from spreading overseas. Coty's Brentford, Essex, factory was to close, and all production was to be concentrated at the Rubinstein East Molesey plant. To begin with, the joint company had a combined turnover of around £16 million, which put it among the top three or four cosmetic firms in Britain. Executives of both parent companies described the merger as the marriage of a "willing bride with an ardent suitor." In fact, as the industry soon realized, the joint company was formed primarily to make the operation look more attractive to another outside bidder, or possibly Rubinstein hoped that Pfizer might eventually bid for the rest of the Rubinstein group. In its first year of operations the joint British company showed a loss—nothing, it seemed, could go right for Rubinstein these days—whereas a profit of $38 million had been forecast.

Guesses were made as to the extent of the entire group's losses; they ranged from $5 million to as much as $15 million. When figures for 1979 appeared, these were all underestimates: the company had lost $20 million and owed its creditors a massive $50 million. It came as no surprise in the industry to learn, in February 1979, that Colgate-Palmolive was negotiating to sell Rubinstein. The suitor had appeared the month before. It was L'Oreal, the French-based company that is reckoned to be the second largest cosmetics group in the world. Although its biggest business is in hair products, it is well regarded, too, for its Lancôme range of cosmetics and the Fidji and J'ai Osé perfumes and colognes under the Guy Laroche trade name. It was common knowledge that L'Oreal was seeking to expand its North American operation and thought that Rubinstein might be a suitable vehicle. The price tag then was said to be around $140 million, which would have left Colgate relatively unhurt by its excursion. But the talks swiftly broke down, and Colgate began to look elsewhere.

Colgate's first approach to a company to buy Rubinstein might have been to British American Tobacco, although no announcement was ever made about talks. BAT Industries, as it is now known, is one of only five companies in the United Kingdom with sales of over $10 billion a year. It has recently been extending its interests, particularly in cosmetics, in anticipation of a decline in cigarette and tobacco sales. In 1979 it already owned Yardley, Lentheric, Morny and Germaine Monteil, and because it was not an American conglomerate—in the United States a takeover might create antitrust problems—BAT might have seemed to Colgate to be a suitable buyer. Rubinstein was reputed to be now carrying a price tag of $170 million, which would have left Colgate with at least a paper profit on its own purchase price. Nothing came of these negotiations, and it is only former employees of Rubinstein in Britain who allege that any ever took place.

Then in April 1979, Colgate announced that it had agreed in principle to sell Rubinstein to the Kao Soap Company, a Japanese group looking, as was L'Oreal, for an American and international base. By this time Colgate-Palmolive had a new chief executive, Keith Crane, who, in deciding to sell Rubinstein, was taking the first steps to rid Colgate of several companies acquired by his predecessor, David Foster, who had retired suddenly because of ill health. The price asked came as a surprise. It had dropped to only $75 million, which meant that the situation was no doubt far worse than even the severest pessimists had estimated. Colgate-Palmolive was clearly prepared to take a loss of close to 50 percent of the price it had paid in 1973 to get the company.

The bid from Kao came as something of a surprise, even though the two companies were already operating a joint venture in Japan —Kao-Colgate Products—and the larger Rubinstein merger talks had come out of this. It was announced that Frederick Purches, then vice president of Helena Rubinstein in the U.S.—who had himself been a temporary executive casualty under Peter Engel —would move across to be chief executive of the company when the deal was completed. Payment, it was announced, would be spread over four years. William Shanahan, Rubinstein's then-chief, would return to Colgate, whence he had come.

The bid was a rational move for Kao and would have given it an established base in the United States. It was embarking on a different approach from Shiseido, another Japanese company, which ranked number three in world terms in cosmetics and had decided to start from its own small base in the U.S. rather than

moving in by means of a takeover. As far as Rubinstein was concerned, the deal was concluded. Suddenly one of the most controversial figures in the industry, Sam Kallish, threw himself into the
situation. He sued Kao for $15 million dollars, claiming that he
had brought Colgate and Kao together and was therefore entitled
to this amount as part of a consultant's arrangement he had with
Kao.

Sam Kallish, now fifty-two, is a sharp and abrasive man who
sees himself as one of the old school of cosmetics executives. He
has little time for the corporate executive (as opposed to the man
with flair). He describes himself as an ardent "disciple" of Charles
Revson. There is no doubt that he was deeply disappointed when
Revson chose Michel Bergerac to succeed him, rather than Kallish, who had had a great deal of experience is cosmetics. After
that, Kallish departed for the West Coast of America to run Max
Factor, which had been taken over by another conglomerate,
Norton Simon.

That move was not a happy one, and very soon Kallish, after
masterminding the disappointing launch of the Maxi line, had left
Max Factor, following a disagreement with David Mahoney, chief
executive of Norton Simon. Maxi was modeled on Revlon's last
personal and very successful range, Charlie. Kallish was soon back
on the East Coast wheeling and dealing and working as a consultant for a number of cosmetics firms. He reappears again and
again in all kinds of situations in the industry, where he is renowned for his trenchant and hard-hitting comments. No one
quite knows what happened to the Colgate-Kao proposals after
the Kallish intervention, or even whether his intervention had any
impact at all, but suddenly, on May 13, 1979, Colgate announced
that the deal was off.

Neither company was prepared to give a reason for the break-
down, but inevitably there was speculation. Some thought that a
detailed study of the Rubinstein books by Kao showed that the
position, bad as it was known to be, was deteriorating even further;
others, that whatever agreement had been made had been terminated merely for technical reasons. There seems little doubt,

however, that the engagement was broken by Kao and not by Colgate. Disappointed and surprised chief-executive-elect Frederick Purches said that until the day of the announcement, as far as he knew, the deal had been completed. Kallish, of course, did not get his $15 million.

So Helena Rubinstein was back on the market. The talk now was that Colgate would not even be able to give the company away. The general view was that the company had been totally mismanaged by Colgate, and there was no doubt that morale in the group was low. All the employees were aware that the company might well collapse altogether. In May 1979, just after the Kao deal had been broken off, Shirley Lord told me that she was "very sorry" that Kao did not get Rubinstein. The question was, Who would? The group was clearly still on the market, but it was equally clear that Rubinstein was highly unlikely to be bought by a publicly quoted company. "The shareholders would lynch them" was one laconic comment.

The only hope, insiders reckoned, was a bid by someone with what they called the "hots" to be in the cosmetics industry, in the same style as the old entrepreneurs'. Or it was possible, but only just, that a company with very extensive interests could swallow up the company. Another alternative was that Rubinstein could be sold off in bits. This, too, many felt, would be a mistake. Rumor had it that of all the company's subsidiary companies, only the one in Germany was making a profit. Then again, some speculated, it might be better if Colgate retained control. Subsidiaries always have problems in getting loans if the parent company is short of cash, but banks will sometimes lend to a faltering part of a group if the overall performance of the group is sound.

By the summer of 1979, the industry knew that the biggest holdup for Colgate in its attempts to off-load the company was its debt structure. Many millions of dollars would be needed to turn Rubinstein around—if it could indeed be turned round. A group with at least $40 million cash behind it was needed to redeem the company's debts. A further $10–$15 million cash flow was necessary for the day-to-day operation of the business. Few companies, and even fewer individuals, would have $55 million readily available, or have access to that amount.

Despite these daunting facts, however, an earlier suitor returned. In mid-September 1979, Colgate announced that it was once again engaged in talks with L'Oreal with a view to selling Rubinstein. No price was mentioned, but, as usual, rumors were rife. The price, it was said, had now dropped to $35 million. Cosmair, Inc., L'Oreal's licensee in the U.S., would be the vehicle used for the takeover. It then appeared that L'Oreal and Kao had not been the only companies Colgate had approached in its efforts to sell off Rubinstein. Revlon and Fabergé, both American, were said to have been solicited. Neither had been interested. (Apparently the suggestion had been made to Revlon that should it want to buy, it could avoid antitrust suits in America by shutting down Rubinstein in the U.S. and operating only abroad. But Revlon, embarking on a diversification program into other industries, designed at least in part to protect it from the vagaries of the cosmetics trade, apparently had turned down the opportunity.)

At this point, Rubinstein was selling close to $200 million worth of products around the world, but in the United States alone, losses were guesstimated at $5 million. Retailers were upset by the heavy selling methods used by Rubinstein and were returning large amounts of unordered goods to the company. In marked contrast to Rubinstein, L'Oreal has been expanding swiftly. Its profits in 1978 jumped by 50 percent to around $50 million, and its profit margins widened considerably as sales rose by only 14 percent. As a private company, Cosmair, Inc., does not report any sales or profit figures, but its leading executives report themselves happy with the progress the company is making in the United States.

This time the engagement between Colgate and L'Oreal was even shorter. Just two weeks after the negotiations were announced, there came what was beginning to appear inevitable where Rubinstein was concerned. A short, sharp statement was issued by Colgate on September 27, 1979, to the effect that negotiations with L'Oreal S.A. of Paris and its U.S. licensee, Cosmair, Inc., had "terminated." All that L'Oreal had to say was that "the acquisition of Rubinstein wouldn't be of strategic interest to the L'Oreal group." Cosmair was similarly bashful. Its president and chief executive, Jean Caste, would go no further than to tell *The Wall Street Journal* that Rubinstein had been rejected "after a careful analysis."

In January 1980 in New York I talked to James Nixon, general manager of the retail division of L'Oreal, by far the biggest section of the U.S. group. He was equally restrained about the negotiations, remarking that it "had been a useful and interesting exercise and a comprehension of it gives a fundamental understanding of the cosmetic industry today." He elaborated a little: "Helena Rubinstein operates worldwide, but its American business is by far the biggest section and it is losing money significantly. Anyone taking it over has to go in thinking that the rot can be stopped and profits rebuilt. This process has to happen quickly so that interest charges on the debt can be cut. No one is fighting to buy, because, quite simply, companies doubt their capacity to achieve a recovery. The possible choices before Colgate are to sell the company, close it down, or come to an arrangement with someone to try to keep it going under a franchise basis. One could also sell it piecemeal, but I wouldn't want to comment on that possibility. The problem is to assess what one can realistically do. It may not be possible to save the company at a price which makes the operation worthwhile. Whoever takes over will need a lot of guts. Companies are not really interested, and individuals simply do not have the money. The American cosmetic industry is big, but competition is intense, and the market share for many companies is bound to decrease in future."

From September 1979 to July 1980, rumors continued. In the United Kingdom there has been talk that Desmond Brand, who ran the British end of Rubinstein until the spring of 1978, might be interested in buying the British and Irish operations of the company. He is said to have made two attempts to purchase them for $14,400,000 cash, raised with the backing of financial

institutions. That figure, if it was offered, exactly equaled the
asset value of the business in Britain. Even the Lauders were
talked of as possible buyers of the business outside the United
States.

Another man who was said to be interested in Rubinstein is the
American businessman Victor Kiam, who, according to the television commercials in which he appears himself, liked Remington
razors so much he paid $25 million to buy the company. Mean-
while, Shirley Lord has returned to her old journalistic career as
director of Special Projects, Beauty and Fitness, at American
Vogue. When I talked to her she commented that Rubinstein and
Arden were the two great ladies of the cosmetics industry, but "I
have the feeling that neither of them wished her company to
survive after her. Compare this with Charles Revson, who went
to great lengths to preserve his company for his heirs." Lord compared the performance of Arden and Rubinstein since their
founders' deaths. "Joseph Ronchetti has done a great job at Arden
and the company is very healthy." (Perhaps it is significant that
Ronchetti has been at Arden for thirteen years, having joined the
company well before the Eli Lilly takeover in 1971. He himself
points to Leonard Lauder, Estée's son, and himself as "the only
two men at the top of cosmetics companies who have worked for
just one cosmetics company."

Then on July 3, 1980, without warning, Colgate made the surprise announcement that it had sold Helena Rubinstein. The
statement came as a surprise because by this time people in the
industry and investment analysts had assumed that there were
simply no takers around. In a way, they were right. The buyer was
not one of the old-established cosmetics groups, but a new firm,
Albi Enterprises, Inc., set up by Alvin Burrack, former president
and chairman of the Lander Company, a privately held cosmetics
company, and William Weiss, a New York lawyer.

The price was a mere $20 million, and even that was not all it
seemed. The arrangements for payment showed very clearly just
how far the Rubinstein organization had slipped under the Colgate management. Only $1.5 million was paid as the deal was

signed. An additional $3.5 million will be paid in two equal install-
ments on December 31, 1981, and January 30, 1983. The $15
million that remains will be paid in annual installments of
$1,125,000. This means that it will be 1996 before Colgate finally
gets the full $20 million. At the same time as offering this generous
payment scheme, Colgate also guaranteed $19 million in domestic
bank loans to Rubinstein until March 1981 and as much as $24
million in foreign subsidiary bank loans in declining amounts until
January 1988. A Colgate spokesman said that the deal was done in
this way so that the new owners would have "appropriate time to
develop the company." To disinterested observers it appeared that
Colgate was prepared to do almost anything to get Rubinstein off
its hands. All Mr. Burrack had to say, according to the Colgate
statement, was that the sale would "permit a return to a more
simplified management structure."

The new owners set about divesting themselves of product lines
that they felt did not fit in with their plans for the company. The
first to go was Rubinstein's much-admired Heaven Scent, along
with Bio-Clear, a skin treatment cream, and Nudit hair remover.
The aim of the company in its new guise appeared to be to get rid
of the more moderately priced lines and go for a narrower range
of prestige products for the mature woman.

While all this was going on at Rubinstein, there were equally
startling changes at Elizabeth Arden. By the middle of 1970, less
than four years after the founder's death, neither those who had
benefited under her will nor the government, which was demand-
ing the estate taxes, had got any money. The situation was looking
grim. Carl Gardiner, who had been running the company as its
president, resigned. Charles Bliss took over. He also happened to
be chairman of the board of the Bank of New York. Once the
financiers were in, the days of Arden as an independent company
were numbered.

On September 30, 1970 it was announced that the American
Cyanamid Company had been approached to buy Elizabeth
Arden. Perhaps it seemed a strange choice—Cyanamid is known
chiefly for chemicals and plastics—but actually it already had toi-

letry interests, including one market leader in hair products, Breck. First inquiries at Cyanamid had actually taken place five months earlier, in April 1970. Cyanamid had been approached by one Sidney J. Weinberg, a partner in the New York banking firm of Goldman, Sachs and Company, who were said to be the authorized agents for the executors of the estate of Elizabeth Arden. Initially, Cyanamid seems not to have been overly interested, but a month later, following a report from Goldman, Sachs about the Arden business, it decided to undertake its own investigation of the company. When the announcement of talks was made, it was stressed that no decision on whether to go ahead with the purchase had been made, but a price had been discussed in August. The Arden executors were anxious to sell to Cyanamid, because they believed that that company had the management expertise to rebuild Arden. The price was reported to be $35 million; $28 million of this would come in cash, $4.5 million in stock, and the remaining $2.5 million in a contingency payment.

Shortly before the public announcement, the executors informed Cyanamid that the whole deal could be completed more easily if they turned over the contingency payment to Patricia Young, Elizabeth Arden's niece, who was her sole residuary legatee. Cyanamid would not agree to this proposal, but it did not appear to put a stop to the negotiations. Immediately after the announcement of talks, however, things began to go wrong. The next day, October 1, there was a meeting between the Cyanamid officers and representatives of the Arden company and executors, including Charles Bliss. The written agreement that had been drawn up was read to the assembled interested parties and agreed on with one minor modification. The following day, the agreement was approved by the Cyanamid executive committee and delivered by hand to the Arden headquarters. On the same day, Cyanamid informed the executors and Goldman, Sachs that a special meeting of the Cyanamid board would be held on October 7 for the formal approval of the agreement.

That meeting never took place. On the same day that the written agreement had been accepted by Arden, Cyanamid and the executors, the vice president of yet another conglomerate, Eli Lilly and Company, had called Arden boss Charles Bliss and told him that it was interested in buying Elizabeth Arden. An investment broking firm had done a report for Eli Lilly, and Lilly now wanted to go further and do its own research on the company. Bliss told the Lilly man that talks with Cyanamid were moving quickly and would be made final within days. Eli Lilly decided to move fast. On October 2, when the executive committee at Cyanamid was approving the agreement, Eli Lilly told Bliss that they would not bother with their own investigations: they would bid immediately. Cyanamid remained ignorant of the interest of Eli Lilly, and when they received the original agreement back from Arden on the same day, there was a covering letter from Bliss welcoming the deal.

Eli Lilly, also on October 2, said that it would like to meet the Arden board to discuss further details on October 8, one day after the special board meeting was due to take place at Cyanamid. Obviously, October 8 would be too late, unless Arden was prepared to call off the Cyanamid deal without having reached an agreement with Eli Lilly. So Goldman, Sachs, the representatives of the executors, were called in on October 5. They appear to have met the Eli Lilly representatives at the Arden offices, where they presumably made it clear that what they were interested in was getting the best deal for the legatees, Miss Young in particular. Eli Lilly had already been told on October 3 that it would have to better the Cyanamid deal and also put down a large deposit as evidence of good intention.

Work on the new deal went on through October 5, and late on that day, Bliss contacted Cyanamid to say that the executors were likely to go back on the agreement with them and sell the company elsewhere. At 3 A.M. the next morning, October 6, the deal between Eli Lilly and the Bank of New York is said to have been signed at a price of $38.5 million, with $20 million to be paid immediately. The extra $3.5 million over the Cyanamid deal went to Patricia Young—but not straightaway.

Mr. Bliss had some explaining to do to American Cyanamid.

Later on the day after the Arden/Lilly signing, he told the Cyanamid representatives that as far as he had been concerned, a deal had been signed with Cyanamid and that at first he had refused to talk with Eli Lilly. After consulting his lawyers, however, he had changed his mind on their advice and decided that it was his responsibility to accept the best offer for the company. The executors, on their part, also felt that they had acted responsibly, because the down payment from Eli Lilly had been made before the final meeting of the Cyanamid board. The Cyanamid people were entitled to feel aggrieved—and did. They had been approached by Arden—not the other way around—and had acted in good faith. They had been given no opportunity to reconsider their own offer in the light of Eli Lilly's interest, and only when it was too late for them to counterbid were they told of the deal. Not surprisingly, they decided to sue for compensation for the loss of their potential profit. This had the effect of tying up the Arden estate even longer, and there was still no money for the legatees. Cyanamid sued the estate for $60 million and Eli Lilly for another $60 million. The following February it added Goldman, Sachs to its list, suing them for $120 million. Clearly, the company had seen Arden as a very high profits earner.

It was not until Christmas Eve 1971 that the case was settled. The sums paid to Cyanamid were never disclosed, as the matter was settled out of court. The Arden legatees finally got their money. Because Eli Lilly was purging the Arden staff, enforcing compulsory retirement, many of them needed it.

After its shaky start, the merger has proved highly successful on both sides. Elizabeth Arden has fitted easily and naturally into the Eli Lilly group, whose main business is the development and manufacture of chemical compounds. Its cosmetic interests are about 10 percent of the total group, which operates in twenty-six countries. Immediately after the merger, the company's aims became clear. Arden was going to be a high-class, well-researched line. Dr. Cornelius Pettinga became the new president of the Arden company. He had previously been a vice president of Eli Lilly and its senior researcher. Dr. Pettinga's interests were in product development and its relevance to consumers' needs. The profitable Arden salons were improved and developed and the less-profitable ones closed. The packaging was brightened up and a new advertising agency taken on. The company was also fortunate in having a high-flying young executive working for it. Joseph Ronchetti had been working with Arden for three years before the takeover. Previously he had been in retailing, and Arden was, and still is, the only cosmetics company he had ever worked for, a distinction among chief executive officers of cosmetics companies which he shares only with Leonard Lauder. Ronchetti is now the chief executive officer of Elizabeth Arden, and it is generally acknowledged throughout the industry that in large measure he has been personally responsible for Arden's success since the merger. But even so, success did not come immediately to Elizabeth Arden when it came under the umbrella of Eli Lilly. There were still considerable problems that had risen following the death of its founder, and during the first four years under the new regime, the company posted losses totaling nearly $7 million.

Ronchetti told me that the "acquisition syndrome of the 1970s is clearly over. The inherent problem in all conglomerates is their pressure for earnings and profit as soon as they take over a company. The real predicament is the need for a continuous rise on monthly earnings and this is simply not always possible. This problem is sometimes not understood by those who do not know the industry but become involved in it because they see it as a big profit earner."

He explains the success of Arden as part of a conglomerate while others like Rubinstein and Factor have failed: "Elizabeth Arden has learned through experience what it can and cannot do in the industry. We know that our major competitors are Revlon and Estée Lauder and that we have great credibility with the customer. We are trying to position ourselves as a prestige product and we put a heavy emphasis on market research. Our worldwide marketing is done from the United States, where we also do all our research and design our packaging."

The situation at Max Factor as the 1970s dawned was quite different from that at Arden. Max Factor had died relatively young in 1938, but he had left behind a strong company involving his sons and sons-in-law. Max Factor, Jr., took on the main creative responsibilities for the company's future. Innovation and inventiveness carried on into the second generation, and the future seemed assured. Among a great number of products developed in the early postwar period were some that are still sold today. They included pan-stick, the extremely successful creme-based makeup in stick form, rather like a fat, stubby lipstick, which was trademarked in 1948; "color-fast" lipstick; creme-puff makeup; Erace, which was the original cover-up for spots and bags under the eyes; Sheer Genius, makeup in a tube; Geminesse, which was a complete line of very high-priced treatment and makeup products; and Tried & True hair care and coloring products.

The company's slogan, "Make-up for the stars—and you," was highly successful during the period in which films had captured a great hold on the public's imagination. It was translated into many languages, and the company had one advantage over its rivals, in that popular film stars—men and women—were often prepared to appear in its advertising.

At this time, the chairman and chief administrative executive of the company was Max Factor Jr.'s older brother, Davis Factor. He was responsible for much of the growth of the company in this period. All the company-owned branches were established under his aegis, and expansion, building and modernization plans brought the number of the company's employees to 10,000 throughout the world. Alfred Firestein and his brother Chester, who were grandsons of Max Factor, were also active in the business. The former eventually became director of United States advertising, and the latter merchandising director of Max Factor, after some years of working their way up through the business. By the 1950s, Sidney Factor, the youngest of Max Factor I's sons, was also working for the company. First employed in the Export Division, he eventually became senior vice president in charge of the International Division.

Nothing, it seemed, could go wrong. The company had by now acquired Parfums Corday, which meant that it was firmly established in the perfume side of the industry as well. In 1961, class A stock of Max Factor was traded on the New York Stock Exchange for the first time. Another generation of the family was coming along, and Barbara Factor (daughter of Davis), Donald Factor (son of Max, Jr.) and Davis Factor, Jr., all went into the business. Suddenly, however, they all went—for quite different reasons— their separate ways. Barbara decided she would be a full-time housewife, Donald departed to become a motion picture producer, and Davis went into business by himself. Sidney, the youngest son of Max Factor I, also decided to leave the company and devote himself full time to his own business interests.

This left only older second-generation Factors and the Firesteins in the company. Davis remained as board chairman, but in January, 1968, gave up the position of chief executive officer, which went to Alfred Firestein, then forty-three, who also became president of the company. His brother, Chester Firestein, became executive vice president and a member of the Executive Committee. Max Factor, Jr., became vice chairman of the board, and Max Firestein, who had held that position, became chairman of the Executive Committee.

This was the management that was to preside over the merger with Norton Simon. Several approaches were made to Max Factor in the late 1960s and early 1970s, and one, American Cyanamid —later to be disappointed again when it tried to take over Elizabeth Arden—almost made it. Agreements in principle were reached and press releases prepared, but the Factor board suddenly called the whole thing off. Then Alfred Firestein met David H. Mahoney, chairman of the board of Norton Simon. The two men immediately built up a personal rapport, and when Mahoney suggested that the two companies discuss a merger his proposal was sympathetically received. The takeover was put to the public shareholders on February 13, 1973. Approval was overwhelming, and the final details were completed the following day.

Under the terms of the merger, Alfred Firestein was to remain with the company. Then, little more than one month later, he died suddenly at the early age of forty-eight. Eight months later, Mahoney appointed Alfred's brother, Chester, as president of the Factor subsidiary. After three years Chester resigned, saying that he wished to devote all his time to his personal interests. During his period as president the company had launched the highly successful Halston designer fragrance. It seems clear that there was not the same rapport between Mahoney and Chester that there had been between Mahoney and Alfred, but whether or not the resignation had been expected, the company remained for six months without a chief executive. Meantime, its profitability had been slipping. It was apparent that all was not well with the company.

After six months Mahoney thought he had found the right man to succeed Chester Firestein. He chose Sam Kallish, then international president of Revlon, who was still feeling restless following the death of Charles Revson in 1975.

When Sam Kallish had been passed over for the succession by Charles Revson, who had preferred the experienced corporate executive Michel Bergerac from ITT to a man who had worked with him for many years and who had long experience in the cosmetics industry, Kallish was deeply disappointed: he admired Revson enormously ("he was my mentor and I was his student"). When Charles Revson died, there seems no doubt that he thought of himself as the natural heir. So when, in May 1976, David Mahoney, president of Norton Simon, parent company of Max Factor, suggested that he take over the cosmetics company, he did not hesitate. Here was his chance to continue in the Revson mold, but this time he would be the boss.

Sam Kallish had sound experience in the industry. He had started as creative director of the American end of Yardley, the British-based company. Later he became general manager of the DuBarry/Richard Hudnut division of the Warner Lambert Pharmaceutical Corporation, where he was responsible for all marketing. He joined Revlon in 1965 as Charles Revson's personal assistant. "I learned from Charles how to set standards and never compromise them," he told *Women's Wear Daily* on August 27,

1976, after he had joined Max Factor. "Stay with them no matter how small. Revson was able to bring out far and above what people thought they had in them. I hope to apply the good things I have learned."

He was going to prove himself by bringing out a fragrance that would succeed as well as Charlie, the last launch that Charles Revson himself had masterminded. Kallish wanted to show the industry that what his mentor could do, he could do better. But first of all, there was the company to sort out. Max Factor had sales of over $350 million, with a little less than half its business in the United States. The company was nervous. It had been leaderless for seven months, following the sudden resignation of Chester Firestein. Kallish had a reputation as a tough and hard man, and a management purge was expected. It soon arrived.

Orlane, the Paris-based company which was part of the group, soon had two new bosses. Leonce Pacheny, formerly of Rubinstein, became director general, and Leslie Grunberg, ex-Revlon, moved in as international marketing director. They have remained there since. Some executives did not wait to be fired. Within a month Irwin Alfrin, president of the American operation, had resigned. He had known Kallish of old—they had both been senior executives at Revlon at the same time.

By November 1976, with other executives fired from Max Factor and some "high fliers" brought in, *Forbes* magazine reported that things at the company were "grim." Factor cosmetics were still selling well, but profit margins were narrowing, and earnings in the three years that Norton Simon had owned the company before Sam Kallish arrived had dropped by one-third to $20 million. The parent company wanted this trend reversed. What had happened was that Max Factor was still doing well in its basic ranges, which were relatively low-priced. They were not, however, doing as well as Lauder and Revlon in the higher-priced treatment lines, except in the Halston line, which was going very well in the U.S. It had been a relatively late entrant, too, into the fragrance field. There was a great deal for Kallish to do to set the company on a path of increasing profitability. Expansion of overseas markets, particularly in Japan and the United Kingdom, was to be a priority, and from his many years in the international field at Revlon, Sam Kallish knew these markets well.

But he was impatient. He wanted to introduce his rival to Charlie. But the Just-Call-Me-Maxi fragrance launch was a disaster and was to mean that, when Sam Kallish's two-year contract expired in mid-1978, he was to leave the company. David Mahoney had told *Forbes*, in only November 1976: "We looked for the very best cosmetics executive we could find. Sam is a driving individual, a street fighter. I expect we will have differences of opinion, and when we do I will defer to his expertise. Frankly, I see him as an extension of Norton Simon, Inc." He changed his mind quickly and the honeymoon was a short one. Sam Kallish wanted his own way too much, and he and Mahoney were soon quarreling. And this time there was no doubt that Kallish had got it wrong. He could not repeat the Charlie success at Revlon with Maxi at Max Factor. Profits, which had recovered during his first year, fell again to new lows. The market had changed. Charlie was a sporty perfume for the liberated lady; so was Maxi, but by the time it had arrived, women were in another mood and wanted a more feminine perfume, which Revlon again provided with Jontue. Maxi was too similar in sales pitch to Charlie and to other perfumes as well, and the final blow was that women in America just did not seem to like the scent. The adventure had been a costly one: about $10 million was spent in promotion in the United States and only about the same amount was sold to the stores, and eventually about half was returned to Max Factor as unsalable. Investment analysts on Wall Street reckoned that the whole enterprise had cost as much as $8 million in profit. The cosmetic line accompanying Maxi, in contrast, did quite well and continues to sell today. But the launch meant the end for Kallish at Max Factor. He had concentrated too much management attention on Maxi, with the result that other lines like Geminesse, Ultralucent and the Max Factor line itself, which had been doing so well, began to falter. Kallish departed and returned to the East Coast, and Mahoney began to look around for a chief executive more to his taste. Meanwhile, for the second time in less than three years, the company ran for a period without a chief executive.

The whole sad affair was confirmed in Norton Simon's 1978 annual report. No figures were given, but the report stated: ". . . the disappointing initial performance in the U.S. of the new 'Just Call Me Maxi' fragrance had a substantial adverse effect on profits." Fortunately for Norton Simon, the rest of its cosmetic interests were doing well. Sales of the Halston fragrances had now almost doubled. Early in 1978 the first two Halston cosmetic products had been previewed and had done very well, so the rest of the line was marketed. Orlane, too, was booming, and twenty new salons had been opened in 1978 alone, bringing the total to forty in the U.S. In the international markets of Japan, the United Kingdom and Latin America, "profits outpaced sales," meaning that profit margins had widened over the year. Oddly, Maxi perfume, such a disappointment at home, did well in Canada, Mexico, Central America, the United Kingdom, Brazil and Japan.

In November 1978, Mahoney appointed Dale Ratcliff president and chief executive of Max Factor. He had previously been vice president of sales for domestic cosmetics and fragrances at Revlon. Ratcliff set about strengthening his team. He asked George Evanoff, who had been on interim assignment from his post at Norton Simon, to stay on as president of the International Division and chairman of the Executive Committee of Max Factor. And he made thirty-three-year-old Linda Wachner president of the U.S. Division. This was an unusual and a surprise appointment. After the demise of Arden and Rubinstein, women had virtually disappeared from senior positions in the cosmetics industry. Despite her youth, Ms. Wachner had already made a name for herself in the retailing, apparel and textile fields. It seemed for a while that, after a troubled time, Max Factor was to make its rightful contribution to the Norton Simon group. Then, in April 1979, Ratcliff died suddenly, aged only forty-seven. A week later, another Norton Simon executive was brought in to head the Factor company. Robert J. Kamerschen was named as the new president and chief executive officer. Before joining Norton Simon,

Kamerschen had been president of Chanel, Inc., the American end of the French business founded by Coco Chanel, and also of Christian Dior Perfumes. He had also worked at Revlon.

So Max Factor entered the 1980s with a need to pull back from the problems of the past five years. Little wonder that the talk in the trade is whether Max Factor will go the way of Helena Rubinstein, and rumors are that Norton Simon is at this very moment seeking, like Colgate-Palmolive, someone to take the problem off its shoulders.

It has not been failure all the way for American Cyanamid, which lost out to Eli Lilly at Arden and to Norton Simon at Max Factor. The company, which already included John H. Breck, now includes Shulton as well.

Through its takeover of Shulton, best known for Old Spice, Cyanamid has carved a niche for itself in the high-class perfumery trade. Shulton built up the Jacqueline Cochran company, which owned the Nina Ricci and Carven names in the United States. Shulton also brought in Breck hair products to Cyanamid, and the first new line which the company introduced under its new owners was a highly successful Pierre Cardin line for men.

That Revlon did not go profitably the way of Arden into Eli Lilly, haltingly as Max Factor did into Norton Simon, or disastrously as Helena Rubinstein did into Colgate-Palmolive, is a tribute to two men, Charles Revson and the man he chose to succeed him, Michel Bergerac. Revlon today differs from its rivals, who concentrate either on the top end of the market, or go for mass distribution through drugstores and the lower end of the retail market, in that it sells perfumes, cosmetics and toiletries in every price range. By the mid-1970s, Charles Revson had in front of him the experience of the companies of his great rivals after their deaths: he did not want the same thing to happen to his company, and he knew that the critical time for a company often came after its founder died. It also seems likely that, during 1974, Charles Revson was told that he had terminal cancer. He knew then that he was not going to survive to the great ages of his competitors, who, possibly simply by living so long, had weakened their companies.

Looking back, it seems that there might have been problems at Revlon when Bergerac arrived which were not present on the surface. After the sharp growth of its middle-priced cosmetic lines during the 1950s and 60s, sales were slowing down. Revlon was not winning the battle with Estée Lauder in the higher-priced area, and there were problems among the low-priced lines, which were facing increasing competition from such trade names as Cover Girl and Maybelline. Charles Revson had a genius for knowing what women wanted even before they did, but his business was growing to a size where it simply could not afford to take the kind of risks it had taken in the past. When it came to his product, Charles Revson did not mind how much he spent; if it was a matter of getting absolutely the shade he wanted of a color, he would order whole batches of lipsticks, eye shadows or creams to be thrown away if they were not exactly right. Once Revlon had become a public company, its activities were under much greater public scrutiny. Had Revson not had the foresight to employ a man from a conglomerate to take over a cosmetics company that was effectively becoming a conglomerate, the success story that Revlon has been able to report the past five years might not have become a reality.

Whatever the truth about the state of the company, Revlon had grown too large to be run by one man, even a man like Charles Revson. If he had shown genius in developing his company, he showed equal genius when he chose quite a different person to take over the large corporation he would leave behind. In his last full year as head of Revlon, when Revson was sixty-eight, the company was grossing over $600 million in sales each year with $65 million spent on advertising. He was determined that after he had gone the upward progress of his company would not falter. He chose to succeed him, not one of his long-term trusted executives, nor a member of his family, but a man experienced in corporate life. Michel Bergerac came to Revlon from ITT, one of

America's biggest industrial conglomerates. Charles Revson had decided to buy in the industrial experience available in a conglomerate, rather than waiting for one of them to come along and buy up his company.

He was prepared to pay for the forty-two-year-old, and he did. Bergerac, born a Basque, brother of Jacques, a onetime film star who was running the French end of Revlon, was doing well at ITT, and he was offered one of the best deals in American corporate history to move. Simply for signing up with Revlon, he was paid $1.5 million, His guaranteed salary was a minimum of $325,-000 with some incentive and bonus payments linked to the growth in sales and profits; they have now more than doubled the basic figure. He was also given options on 70,000 shares in the company, which brought him a paper profit of $2 million within a year of his joining the company. By 1979, Mr. Bergerac was earning $500,000 in salary and fees, $399,000 in bonuses and incentives, while "securities, insurance and personal benefits" brought him a further $1,442,520. Most of this came through the exercise of his options to buy 28,000 shares of stock for $1,137,500, which by then had a market value of $2,576,000. At the beginning of 1980, Bergerac still had options left to buy a further 100,000 Revlon shares. Revson had been right in his selection of a successor; and Bergerac had known precisely what he was doing when he took on the job, even if it is true, as a rare critic commented, that "he can't tell a lipstick from a suppository."

Michel Bergerac's background is very different from that of Revson. Other men of his kind with broad corporate experience have been brought into cosmetic companies by the conglomerates after their takeovers. Revson simply acquired the expertise by buying the man, rather than by allowing his company to be bought. Bergerac, during his period at ITT (he had studied at the Sorbonne in Paris, at Cambridge University in England and at UCLA), had helped the company to negotiate the acquisition of over 100 companies. In 1971, when he was still aged only thirty-nine, he was made European head of all the ITT operations, running them from a headquarters in Brussels. At ITT many were convinced that he was in the running for the top job there, held for many years by the autocratic Richard Geneen.

Bergerac and Charles Revson worked together until the latter's death, with Bergerac responsible for most of the marketing of Charlie. With just this one perfume, Revlon, previously a small producer of perfumes, had advanced to the front line, a progress it was able to continue later with Jontue. Bergerac soon proved that he was worth the price paid for him. Revlon joined the select band of companies with annual sales over one billion dollars in 1977, when its worldwide sales rose by close to 20 percent to $1,143,324,000, making Revlon the first cosmetic company ever to do this via the retail stores. In the same period, profits had moved up from $54 million in Revson's last full year to $98 million. Bergerac has continued the company's expansion and is trying for a deal in the Soviet Union where there is a black market in cosmetics. Charles Revson had begun to diversify into the health-care market, and Michel Bergerac has continued the process mainly —typically of a conglomerate man—by buying up companies. Today about one-third of the group's profits come from these activities, and by the time the current series of planned acquisitions is completed, health-care products will be 45 percent of Revlon's total business. These moves on the part of Bergerac have resulted in speculation that Revlon will eventually move out of the cosmetics field, or certainly drop its high-priced lines. The company vehemently denies this: "nothing could be further from the truth." This talk first arose after Revlon had been test-selling some of its lines in supermarkets in Dallas, Phoenix, Denver and Seattle. The company replied that supermarkets are the natural place for the low-priced Natural Wonder line. It is absolutely certain that the trend into retailing through supermarkets will grow.

The annual advertising budget at Revlon is now approaching the $200 million mark and is rising steeply. Bergerac believes in the power of advertising, but he also believes in financial control. He has not been prepared to take the risks that were an everyday occurrence for the early entrepreneurs. Strict inventory control has meant that far less merchandise is returned than was common in the days when companies were smaller and great were risks taken, and the rise in stocks has been kept to half the level of the rise in shares. Even so, Revlon believes that it still takes the risks necessary for a business to remain creative. It has, for instance, introduced Polished Ambers, a relatively high-priced line for black women under the Revlon name. This is unusual for two reasons: first, the prestige companies have steered clear of what they see mainly as a lower-middle-class market; and secondly, there is some reluctance to use a highly valued company name in untried areas. Attitudes like these at Revlon have meant that the company has been able to hold its own against other groups with the financial backing of conglomerates behind them.

Michel Bergerac has also got Revlon's customers to pay their bills more quickly. Between 1973 and 1977, he reduced receivables from eighty-two to fifty-three days. Bergerac said at the time that this had saved the business some $25 million in interest charges, because it would have cost $300 million more to finance the growth of the business to 1977.

During his first years heading the business, Bergerac reduced the staff by five hundred, saving $7.5 million, but he took care to keep on those executives he regarded as central to the company's profitability. Those who left at first, like Sam Kallish, who went to Max Factor, and Stan Kohnlenberg, who departed for Calvin Klein, said they were leaving for new challenges. But within about three years of Revson's death, Charles Revson, Jr., had left the company, and his brother John was considering doing the same. Victor Barnett, one of the executors of the Revson estate and a member of the board of the Revson Foundation, had also left the company.

To encourage the people he has wanted to stay, Bergerac has continued to use the same techniques at Revson; he pays well: many senior executives at Revlon earn salaries of $100,000 a year. To keep them happy, Bergerac, with the approval of Charles Revson before he died, introduced the Performance Incentive Profit Sharing Plan (PIP). Under this plan, each top executive receives PIP points, which are worth a considerable sum, each depending on how the company's profits rise. Under the first plan, the profits period was from 1974 to 1976, and each point could be worth $1,875. There was a hitch: anyone who left the company before 1980 lost some of the money earned in the 1974–76 period. This provided a great incentive for some people to stay with the company, particularly as the PIP points money came on top of regular bonuses.

There has been considerable speculation that the PIP plan kept at least one senior member of the staff with the company, the much-respected Paul Woolard, who is president of Revlon's Domestic Division and head of International Marketing. Woolard, like Sam Kallish, was certainly thought to be in the running to succeed Charles Revson, and there seems no doubt that initially, at least, he must have been disappointed when Bergerac was appointed. Since then, however, Woolard and Bergerac appear to have built up a considerable rapport, but then again, Woolard has good reason to stay with the company. In the first year that Mr. Bergerac was running the company, Woolard was earning over $200,000 a year plus bonuses. He also stood to gain 500 PIP points, worth $940,000 for the period 1974–76, if Revlon reached its projected profits growth, which it did. This additional money, however, could not be collected in full until the end of 1980, and Woolard is still with Revlon. It remains to be seen whether having collected his PIP points, Woolard soon says goodbye to Revlon.

After four years as head of Revlon, Bergerac was attracting excessive praise from an industry that views outsiders with suspicion. In June 1978, *Beauty Fashion* wrote: "Bergerac has singularly destroyed the myth which might have been part of the financial analysts' lexicon—'an entrepreneurial business dies with the entrepreneur.' Michel Bergerac did not save the day—he literally created a new era for Revlon."

Growth has not slackened. In 1979, total sales at Revlon rose by over 18 percent to $1,718,000,000, with $387,200,000 coming from sales outside the United States. These figures prove Bergerac's worth to the company: in the five years since he took over as chairman and chief executive, sales have more than doubled.

Among the other major American companies, only Avon and Estée Lauder were completely safe from the hunters. Because Avon, the biggest cosmetics company in the world, is unique in its marketing policy and approach to customers, it is highly unlikely that it would appeal to a conglomerate; and because with its annual sales and profits running at $2,377,506,000 and $480,154,000 respectively, it would be a costly purchase indeed for even the biggest industrial companies. Avon's progress through the 1970s, however, was not without hiccups, and it may find in the future that its old techniques do not work even in buoyant economic conditions. Discount stores, with their very low prices, may well eventually take business away from the Avon lady, unless the company is prepared to increase its "specials" considerably, and this it may not be able to afford to do. In addition, the retail cosmetics business is expanding all the time and moving more and more into those areas where Avon is traditionally strong. Finally, the profit of an Avon sales representative may simply not be good enough for many people in days of high inflation. The profit the Avon lady makes is being devalued as the value of money falls, and the company may find recruitment, at least in industrialized countries, rather more difficult in future than it has done in the past. At the same time, new job opportunities are arising for women which give them a wider choice of activity than previously, and acting as an Avon representative may look less attractive compared with other possibilities.

At present the Avon lady sells door-to-door. The company could easily change its selling policy, so that selling would be done on the party plan, a method—as I will show—that Mary Kay has exploited so successfully. This would increase the possible profits for the representative. Not only would there be several potential customers at a meeting, but a demonstration of makeup techniques could stimulate more sales. Such a move would involve the company in training schemes, but it has the resources to make the change. What it cannot do is sell its existing products in retail stores in the U.S., because regulations of the Federal Trade Commission preclude a company from selling simultaneously through door-to-door channels and in retail stores those products that existed when the regulations went into effect.

One curiosity is why Avon has no black line. It has a commanding lead in fragrance sales to blacks; a survey in 1973 suggested that it had 40 percent of the market. The company is expanding in Africa, too, where the market for black cosmetics is bound to grow. Interestingly, the company some time ago took a decision not to trade with South Africa, because of that company's apartheid laws.

The bottom fell out of Avon's U.S. market during the 1973–74 recession. The growing strength of its overseas interests were not enough to cushion the company, and profits fell. The management was aware that when recovery got underway it would be facing fiercer competition than ever before in the retail trade. In an attempt to keep its customers in their homes and away from the competition of the mass markets of the drug and department stores, the company extended its merchandise into low-priced clothing and cheap jewelry. In 1976, David W. Mitchell, an employee of Avon since leaving school in 1947, became chairman and chief executive officer of the company. He came into a situation where, because people had less money to spend on nonessentials, many of the Avon ladies had vanished. There was no business for them to get. It has been a long haul back, and meanwhile Revlon has been closing the gap between itself and Avon in terms of profits and sales.

The average Avon lady in 1979 did not earn much money. She sells a little under $5,000 worth of goods a year and takes home barely $2,000. Out of this she must pay for her samples, sales books, travel expenses and telephone calls, as well as paying her taxes. The company puts its representative turnover at 100 percent a year—not bad, they claim, for a company with one million representatives worldwide. Some investment analysts specializing in the cosmetics industry, however, suggest that the figure is nearer 150 percent.

In 1978, Avon did something totally unexpected: it bought Tiffany's, the prestige Fifth Avenue jewelry store (situated just a few blocks from the company's New York headquarters). Tiffany's class products are in a league quite apart from the cheap jewelry Avon has introduced, and competitors and investment analysts on Wall Street have been speculating ever since about the purpose of the acquisition. Avon Products stated quite categorically that the two companies would be run quite separately—a wise move, considering the disparate nature of their products. Too close and obvious a link would almost certainly damage Tiffany, and it is doubtful whether the acquisition will be much use in prestige terms to the Avon range. The most likely explanation of the move is that Avon is planning to use its vast research resources to produce an exclusive line of cosmetics, most likely starting with a fragrance, using the Tiffany name for sale in high-class specialized stores. Marketing would probably begin in the United States, where the name is highly esteemed, and then move into overseas markets. Such a move would bring Avon for the first time into direct competition in the retail stores with the other companies, a battle that onlookers would relish, though the firms themselves might not.

Several companies have tried to take on Avon in its own area of door-to-door cosmetics sales. They have all failed. Dart Industries was perhaps the most formidable contender, with its Vanda Products, Beauty Counselors and House of Romney, all of which it had bought as going concerns. But the company was too disparate and tried too many lines, and it has barely dented the hold that Avon has on door-to-door cosmetics selling. Dart had on the surface all the ingredients for successful selling in this way. It owns the Tupperware company, which was, and still is, the biggest earner in the group. The idea was to apply the Tupperware technique to cosmetics, but with three different houses operating; the effort was disappointing. The company's aim had been to get all three companies together by 1969; Vanda had been bought in 1966 and the other two in 1968, but the amalgamation was not achieved until early 1971 in America and late 1971 in Europe. Unlike Avon, which has its own distribution centers and district managers, Dart used independent warehouse distributors as it did with Tupperware, because the company believed that independents would push the merchandise more quickly if they felt they had a stake in the business. All very well, but it is the company-operated distribution pattern at Avon which has made a great contribution to that company's success.

While all these changes were going on in its competitors, the privately held Estée Lauder company was continuing its upward progress and becoming the market leader in the lines in which it specialized. It has eschewed any but the most expensive lines. Mrs. Lauder and her family are credited with flair, expertise and excitement by all their major rivals. No one knows exactly how profitable the company is, and it is not telling. Company president Leonard Lauder professes himself uninterested in what share of the market the company has. He told me: "I just don't know what it is. Our aim quite simply is to sell more products this year than last year—and that is the company's only aim. It is very necessary to bring out two [lines] to keep the market buoyant and only by keeping it buoyant can we fulfill our aim." There will be no room in the foreseeable future for outside investors in Estée Lauder. "We are a very family-orientated business. First of all, there was my mother and father with their two sons. Now we are married and have wives who are involved in the business. Eventually our children will join us. We prefer to stay as we are."

By all accounts Estée Lauder is an extraordinary woman. "She is the company, the company is she," her son Leonard has said. There is no doubt that she believes in the efficiency of her products and expects her employees to do so as well. She has been known to abandon potential moneymaking cosmetics lest consumer belief in her company's message—quality first, sales later —be undermined. It is a message that has worked. In the early days of the company in the 1950s, she built up brand loyalty by careful quality control and careful planning before her products reached the market. She made frequent personal appearances in stores, where she advised women not only on their makeup but on fashions generally. As she traveled widely around the world and in particular to Europe, people in America believed that she knew just what was going on. There is also no doubt she scored in the 1950s because she was that much younger than either Elizabeth Arden or Helena Rubinstein. Those two, even in their youths, could never have been described as beauties; Estée Lauder, in contrast, was and still is much prettier and happens to have very good skin—which, no doubt, many of her customers attribute to her products (although nature probably had more to do with it). She stands as the very essence of the elegance she is selling. Charles Revson, who was also extremely successful, made it clear that he thought that he, as a man, knew better than a woman how women should look to attract men. Lauder, in marked contrast, played upon the fact that she was an attractive woman telling women how to look equally attractive.

Estée Lauder has become as international as her company. She has two homes in France—one on the Riviera and the other in Paris—one in London and two in the United States—one in New York and the other in Florida.

I asked Prudence Glynn, former fashion editor of *The Times* of London, who knows Mrs. Lauder well, what she thought of the company: "The major problem which confronts the Lauder business is that without the living presence of Estée Lauder its existence seems impossible." Many observers would not agree completely with Miss Glynn, though without exception they recognize Mrs. Lauder's unique qualities. They feel that the business now has a life of its own, above and beyond her capabilities. Plaudits come to the company from people throughout the industry. Joe Mann, longtime employee of Helena Rubinstein, was only one who remarked to me that "Estée Lauder was fortunate in having two very able sons who have carried the business forward."

But today Mrs. Lauder is still very much a presence in her company. Miss Glynn: "In this most personal of all morale boosters, conviction is the answer. Mrs. Lauder, gowned and hatted by Givenchy, is absolutely sure that by wearing *her* products any woman can be more youthful, more alluring, more secure in her own appearance than ever. And she herself is there to prove it, goading her salespeople and well-rewarded aides to the Concorde end of the cosmetics market in this time of polarization of all forms of selling. Immaculate and pretty as a hawk, it is said that Mrs. Lauder was once visiting a store when she overheard a salesgirl assuring a nervous purchaser that the Estée Lauder lipstick would never come off. 'Lady,' said Mrs. Lauder, 'if it never came off I'd be out of business.' "

Leonard Lauder obviously has great respect and admiration for his mother. "She is still very active in the business," he told me, and he feels that she has made four specific and unique contributions to the cosmetic industry. "She was the first to discover and develop the idea of women buying their own fragrances. At one time, as much as 90 percent of perfumes sold were bought by men, or were bought as gifts, not by individuals for themselves. Once you can persuade women to buy their own perfumes, it is possible to build much bigger sales and develop stronger marketing. Then my mother built up her business by personal sampling. If she sold a product, it meant that she, as a woman, was satisfied with it herself. She was the first to introduce cosmetic-gift-with-cosmetic-purchase, which was very good for consumer loyalty." Finally, Leonard Lauder said, she made sure that the appeal of every product was strong enough to induce repeat purchases. This last point is very important, bearing in mind the fickleness of the average buyer of cosmetics. The urge is always to try something new.

The Lauder company, through Leonard Lauder, freely admits that it is not the biggest company: what it is interested in is being the best. It certainly has had world-beaters with Aramis and Clinique, both of which have manufacturing facilities separate from the Estée Lauder line of products.

On the company's twenty-fifth anniversary in 1971, Leonard Lauder commented that the company has "spent the first eleven years getting the first million, the remainder getting the balance." No one knew what the balance was, but estimates range from $70 million to (probably extravagantly) $100 million.

Leonard Lauder also made it clear at the same time that Mrs. Lauder might have a reputation for femininity and prettiness but that the company has always been run efficiently. "Women," he said, "may have their illusions about cosmetics, but the concept of selling moonbeams is hardly applicable in an age when we can walk on the moon."

So strong have these American companies become that they have been able to cut themselves a profitable slice of cosmetic sales wherever they set up business. It is also extremely difficult to beat them in their own market. The experience of Shiseido, the giant Japanese-based cosmetics company, in America, shows just how tough entry into that market can be for smaller companies, for big though it is overall, Shiseido has only a tiny share of the business in the United States.

For centuries, European and then American people and companies thought they dominated the cosmetics industry, but there was a much earlier thriving industry serving the vast market of the Middle and Far East, with a much older pedigree. The main industrial thrust came from Japan, where there are over 1,000 cosmetics producers, although there have been hundreds of thousands of small producers throughout the Orient from time immemorial serving local markets.

There is a general tendency to think of American cosmetics companies as holding a considerable edge on the world's trade, but surprisingly, Shiseido of Japan is the third largest cosmetics business in the world. It was established in 1872 as the "Shiseido Pharmacy" and started its move into cosmetics at the turn of the century. In 1957, it began to market its products outside Japan, particularly in Southeast Asia. It was not until 1967 that Shiseido Cosmetics (America) was set up, and the move into the international market was carefully monitored.

Initially, the company did well in the United States, though of course in terms of total sales it remained very small indeed. By the end of 1970, the company was marketing about 275 products in America, all of which were bottled in America, apart from fragrances, which were manufactured and bottled in Japan. Altogether Shiseido has over 600 products in its line. Although it is as large or larger than most U.S. companies, Shiseido in no other way resembles an American or European company. Its whole character is Japanese. Its products are very expensive, but even so, it has managed to create a loyal market of over 10 million women in Japan, gathered together into what it calls the Camellia Fan Club. Members receive a glossy magazine each month called *Hanatsubaki* (camellia), giving beauty tips and pushing Shiseido products. This ties women more closely to the product, and this loyalty is enhanced by "home parties." Altogether the setup combines the approach of both Lauder and Revlon with that of Avon Cosmetics, a combination that would be extremely unlikely and unprofitable in America or Europe. For a time, the Fan Club also had a somewhat less savory aspect, too: it supported political candidates, until the practice was made illegal.

Shiseido has over 30 percent of the Japanese cosmetics market and is thought to have around half of all cosmetics sales in Asia excluding China. But it does not have the market all its own way. Its biggest competitor in Japan is Osaka-based Kanebo, a vigorous, thrusting industrial conglomerate, also more than 100 years old, which now claims a 15 percent share of the cosmetics market in Japan. It bought its way into the industry in 1960 with the purchase of the cosmetics division of Kanegafuchi Chemical Industries. Kanebo, too, has been moving into international markets. In 1979 its cosmetics were introduced into Harrods, London's most prestigious store. The cosmetics line is traded under the name Joset, at higher-than-average prices. Kanebo may be less well known in international markets than Shiseido, but it is the fifth largest cosmetics manufacturer in the world, with sales in Japan alone now totaling over $72 million.

But trying to penetrate the American market where so many home-based firms are strongly entrenched is an expensive business. Despite national advertising and a successful publicity campaign and a feeling among American women that Japanese women keep their looks longer than Western women, Shiseido failed to make a profit in many of its outlets in the U.S. By 1975, its sales were $8 million, less than one percent of the market. In January 1976, it decided to cut its losses: it would no longer be represented in those outlets where it did not make a profit. During that year, it cut back to 170 outlets with only 17 accounts, primarily in the Northeastern states and on the West Coast.

In mid-1977, Andrew Philip, who had spent three years with Chesebrough-Pond's and also worked at Rubinstein, joined Shiseido as executive vice-president. His job was to organize the reconstruction of the business in the United States. "Our early approach to the market was too promotional and we ignored the whole area of quality training of our representatives," he told me. "Our prices then were high, but now we are underpriced. We have still [early 1980] not raised prices above the 1976 level." This time Shiseido is proceeding with great caution in the market. "We opened only one new account in 1977, and by the beginning of 1980 there were still only five new ones. Our aim is to maintain quality and exclusivity, and we are very particular about which stores we go in. Even so, we managed to achieve a 35 percent increase in sales in 1979. We have a long-term commitment to the American market, but we are still very small. In Canada, however, we have reached third place in the market for our type of product, after Lauder and Clinique."

Shiseido has vast resources behind it. It can call on all the research facilities the company has in Japan, where $15 million is spent each year on research and quality control. The Japanese are ultracautious before bringing out a new item and laser-test their products for purity and safety. They also take the training of their sales force very seriously. Each year in Japan, 15,000 beauty consultants are trained. The course is rigorous. It takes place in a multimillion-dollar resort complex where the trainees live in, and classes go on for sixteen hours a day for forty-five days. Trainees learn about regular cosmetic treatments, makeup techniques, hair and nails. When the training is completed they work in stores for three months, after which they are retested and return to the training school if necessary to correct any weaknesses.

In America, Andrew Philip faces all the problems of running a company whose parent is far away. "But I work very closely with them, and the cooperation between us is superb. Imported goods are relatively costly, and we must remember all the time that we are selling a new beauty concept. American women see that Japanese women keep their looks; what they do not always realize is that they also spend more on cosmetics than anyone else in the world."

Shiseido has not yet attempted to break into any other Western markets. It is very probable that it will eventually do so, but in view of its American experience, its policy is likely to be one of extreme caution.

Another company that initially found the going tough in America but, through its associated American company, Cosmair, Inc., is now doing well, is L'Oreal, the second largest cosmetics company in the world after Avon Products. The group is based in France, and although it is a publicly quoted company, many of its shares are held by the Choudon family, descendants of the French chemist who founded the group after he developed a chemical process to change the color of hair. The other major shareholder is the Nestlé Company of Switzerland, and this group, with the Choudons, controls the group. Today L'Oreal leads in hair products worldwide, but it is still not yet the biggest seller in the United States and Canada. That accolade goes to Clairol, owned by Bristol-Myers. Clairol's lines cover every possible hair product, from shampoos, colorings and conditioners, to setting lotions. Its hair colorings include Nice N' Easy, Miss Clairol, Loving Care and, the latest, Clairesse, introduced in 1977 under the slogan "The first major development in 17 years in hair coloring." Well, maybe. Though Clairol beats L'Oreal in North America, it does not present an effective challenge worldwide.

L'Oreal has a long history of international business, and its products were first used in the United States by the Ogilvie sisters, who worked with Elizabeth Arden before the First World War. In some countries L'Oreal runs subsidiary companies; in others, it has set up a separate company, which has the same shareholders as the main group, but which is not a direct subsidiary of L'Oreal. One such is Cosmair of New York. Apart from its hair products, Cosmair is very small in terms of the total retail market for cosmetics in North America. The group has four divisions. By far the largest of these is the retail division, which sells hair products to the mass marketers like J. C. Penney, Sears and I. Magnin. Next comes the L'Oreal professional division, which sells to hairdressing salons only, where it competes with Clairol, Redken and Helene Curtis. The third division, Lancôme, is best known in the cosmetics trade for its extensive high-class line of skin treatment cosmetics. Lancôme has only recently moved into color cosmetics, and it is this part of Cosmair which has been growing fastest in the past five years. Finally comes the fledgling fragrance division, which is just now trying to penetrate this very competitive field.

Cosmair uses all the L'Oreal formulas, and its relationship with L'Oreal is naturally very close. L'Oreal makes its profits from the royalties it receives from Cosmair for the use of its trade marks, and Cosmair with its sales according to its agreement with L'Oreal. The arrangement suits both companies, and there seems no doubt that Cosmair will continue to forge ahead in North America.

But North America is not the only market for cosmetics, nor do companies based in North America automatically beat out all opposition there. Not only have Shiseido and L'Oreal made determined inroads into the market, but in August 1979 the Beecham Company of the United Kingdom made a surprising counterattack in the United States, whose companies had so long been poaching business in Britain from businesses based there. Beecham, a $2 billion sales company, is well known in the United Kingdom for its toiletries and pharmaceuticals, but less so for cosmetics. Its Lancaster line sells only in Harrods in the U.K., but together with Margaret Astor, which does not sell in the home market at all, Lancaster is sold in fifty countries. In the U.K., it has recently launched a new medium-priced treatment line, Evidence, which has started well. In the U.S., however, it has been known mainly for its sales of Vitabath, called Badedas in Europe (made originally in the Black Forest in Germany), where it holds a creditable reputation at a relatively high price.

In August 1979, Beecham announced that it had agreed with the controlling shareholders to buy Jovan, Chicago-based and one of the fastest-growing fragrance companies in the world. The price was $85 million cash. Since it was formed in 1968, the sales of Jovan, Inc., had risen in ten years to $78 million, giving the company an 8 percent share of the fragrance market, compared with the 14 percent of Revlon. Approximately 90 percent of Jovan's sales were in the United States in 1978, but the company was thinking internationally and had nine overseas subsidiaries and sales distribution networks in sixty-one countries. The company had been founded by its current president, Bernard Mitchell, a man of considerable enterprise and initiative, and he, together with the rest of the Jovan management, has stayed on with the company since the takeover.

The bid should not have come as too much of a surprise: Beecham had already had links with Jovan in the form of manufacturing and distribution rights in Mexico and Canada. Beecham made it quite clear that Jovan would be the vehicle through which it could expand in the medium-priced fragrance market in the U.S. In April 1980, Jovan assumed responsibility in the U.S. for Vitabath. One sour competitor remarked to me that the price was far too high and Bernard Mitchell had got "the bargain of the age." There has been talk in the industry that for Beecham, which until its bid had a reputation for dullness in cosmetics, Jovan had been a second choice, after talks with Norton Simon over a possible purchase of Max Factor had broken down. Be that as it may, Jovan has shown impressive and sustained growth since its inception.

Jovan's products were first marketed in the autumn of 1968. It had an immediate success with its Mink & Pearls bath oil. This was mink oil in pearl-shaped capsules with a pearly sheen, which were simply thrown into the bath, where they melted. It was a new and most attractive gimmick. But the company is basically a fragrance house, and Mink & Pearls is only one of its products. Bernard Mitchell was not originally a cosmetics man. He had previously been in the electrical and electronic industries, inventing among other products the room air-conditioner. He also heads an investment business. Mitchell was joined at Jovan by Barry Shipp, a sales expert who had worked at Revlon for a time after leaving the army and before he formed his own sales agency. The two men made an excellent team.

The capsule had been developed on the basis of the glamour behind the idea of a woman dressed in Mink & Pearls. It was not then especially easy to put mink oil, a biotic oil, into a capsule, if it was not to break until used but then melt almost immediately. Previously, only mineral oils had been packaged to behave in this way. Getting a fragrance into the oil was another problem, as mink oil does not take easily to perfume. The final topping was the packaging, a luxurious-looking crystal type of box, which completed the glamorous image. The product took off, and within a year Mink & Pearls was being marketed in twelve other countries, apart from the USA.

Jovan built steadily on this first success. By the time it introduced its Ginseng line—it was way ahead of Yves Saint-Laurent with Opium, and Estée Lauder with Cinnabar, in the trend toward Oriental and Eastern perfumes—profits were running around $20 million. Talking to *Beauty Fashion* in April 1975, Bernard Mitchell discussed his formula for the successful marketing of a product. It ran:

"CR + IP + SO + CO-OP + NATAD + PR = SUCCESS."

CR is the creative research needed to develop a new line with a good chance of success in the market. That produced Ginseng. Next comes IP, innovative packaging, which will draw the customer's eye to something new. SO, the sales organization, follows, and at Jovan the policy is to give the retailer a high-profit margin, backed up by selling assistance, push monies for the salesgirls and national advertising. Then CO-OP comes in. The CO-OP advertising program is part of the merchandising package. No excess product promotions are permitted, and products that have been rejected by the customers are pushed back on the retailer. Banner displays and testers are included when the product is delivered to the retailer. Then follows Mr. Mitchell's NATAD, his National Advertising theme. The aim is to make advertisements for Jovan products different from other advertisements for cosmetics; the primary difference, he said, is fun.

Overall, Beecham's philosophy has spelled success to Jovan. It might well have paid a high price for the company, but in return it is getting one of the most aggressive and successful selling operations of the 1970s in the world of cosmetics.

FOUR

MILESTONES AND MILLSTONES

In all labour there is profit: but the talk of the lips tendeth only to penury.
—Proverbs 14:23

While there is no doubt that the course of the cosmetics industry will be determined by the giant companies in the future, that is not to say that smaller companies cannot survive. They can and will, as many of them have, beginning with the rapid growth of the industry which started with the end of World War II. This chapter shows just how a few of them have done it. The secret of their survival has been to recognize a part of the market in which the giant companies have had no interest—so far—and to appropriate a profitable section of it. When they have done this with considerable success, they have often either reaped the rewards or paid the price of a successful takeover bid, depending on the view one takes. Size is always relative, and some companies—although much smaller than the giant cosmetic concerns—have nevertheless built up annual sales of many millions of dollars. There are, too, always exceptions where companies are family-controlled and where the family has no intention of giving up its company, whatever the blandishments. They remember the experience and agree with the views Richard Salomon expressed after his Charles of the Ritz was taken over.

However disappointed Richard Salomon might have been at the fate of his company, the Squibb Corporation has been satisfied with its purchase. Squibb has been able to provide its new subsidiary with research facilities that had not been available to it before, because it was too small. Further, the very extensive international sales organization at Squibb also meant that Lanvin, Charles of the Ritz and Jean Naté products had access to new markets. These benefits were available at the same time, as the subsidiary operated independently; it is firm policy at Squibb not to interfere with the operation of subsidiary companies, unless something is going seriously wrong.

It is impossible to mention the many hundreds of cosmetics companies that survive profitably today; failure to do so does not in any way suggest that they are unprofitable or unviable. Nevertheless, it is true that some have caught the public eye and imagination more than others, and information about them is more readily available. Take Mary Kay, for example; a company that has been quietly operating for many years in Dallas, Texas, and was started by a woman who had already retired after twenty-five years in direct selling, and who still heads the firm today.

The company, which confounds all the rules about size, was formed on Friday, September 13, 1963, by Mary Kay Ash. Mrs. Kay had been in direct selling for twenty-five years, making $25,000 a year and working a sixty-hour week. She intended to spend her retirement writing a book on direct selling, but it did not work out that way. After a miserable month or so, she decided that anyone could write about the techniques she had learned; she preferred selling itself, and what she needed was a product to prove that her plan for selling cosmetics could work. She wanted something that would appeal immediately to women. Eventually, using $5,000 of her savings, she persuaded the makers of a private-label skin cream to sell the formulas to her and, with her husband, set up business. Her husband died very shortly after, and she continued alone, though she subsequently remarried. Seventeen years later she has over 40,000 salespeople working for her—some of whom earn over $100,000 a year—in the United States, Canada and Australia. Her sales have reached $100 million.

Her method was direct selling, but not in the Avon way. She used house-party techniques to put on a beauty show. The beauty-care treatment lasted for two hours and included a makeup lesson for everyone there. She limited the number to six people. The hope was that at the end of the session those at the demonstration would buy Mary Kay products. The technique worked and remains exactly the same today. Of course, her representatives are not just salespeople: they are trained in the arts of makeup and the use of treatment products. They carry enough supplies to fill any orders on the spot and pay for those supplies in advance at discounts on retail prices ranging up from 50 percent. Top salespeople are rewarded with diamond-studded bumblebee pins—the company's symbol.

This is a no-loss situation for Mary Kay. There are no creditors, nor has the company great liabilities. Everything is cash on the nail. Even in the first three months of business, Mary Kay made a profit from its $34,000 sales, and by the end of the first year, sales, by 318 salespeople, had reached nearly $200,000. A year later, sales had quadrupled to $800,000, and in 1967 the company went public with a net worth of $10 million.

Mary Kay salespeople work in units, and one salesperson may have several consultants working for her—a few have hundreds. No matter how large a unit gets, the company does not sell franchises, nor does it move those who head units from one area to another. A computer keeps track of all the consultants.

The Mary Kay company makes all its own cosmetics apart from eyebrow pencils. This seemingly irrational omission is explained by the contention that the machinery to make pencils is so expensive it would not be cost-effective at the current level of sales volume for the company to make them itself.

How has Mary Kay succeeded in the competitive cosmetics industry today? Its costs are very low; because its products are sold to its units and paid for before reaching the customer, and has had little need for credit. Its advertising budget is very small; it has sponsored some TV shows and advertised in magazines, but basically it depends upon its customers to tell other people and bring them to a session. Mary Kay has said she prefers to use the money that would go to advertising to encourage her top salespeople. For instance, the company has awarded the use of pink Cadillacs to some of its producers whose units bring in more than $120,000 in sales a year. This performance must be repeated each year to keep the Cadillac. Each year, too, in August, the company sponsors a sales conference in Dallas, only it calls it the Seminar. It is the usual three days of meetings with prizes and "Academy Awards" every night. There is also a "workshop" on "how to be a helpful Mary Kay spouse."

The Mary Kay success is quite astonishing and so simple. It is of course still a very small company when compared with the giant Avon door-to-door selling operation, which sells $2,377,506,000 a year. And its territories are much more confined. As women become more aware and more selective about how they spend their money, however, they may well demand demonstrations of products to see their worth, and where better than in reasonable privacy? The Mary Kay formula may become increasingly successful. For some of her representatives, the rewards are high, particularly those, like Ruell Cone of Atlanta, Georgia, who now has sales of $500,000 in her unit every year.

Mary Kay remains independent, but another high-flier, Erno Laszlo, is now part of Chesebrough-Pond's. Dr. Laszlo, now dead, built up an exclusive and profitable business by persuading women to keep their faces clean with soap and water. In his native Hungary, Dr. Laszlo had spent many years on skin research and had opened his own "institute" in Budapest in 1927. He was a doctor of medicine, and his purpose was to treat skin complaints, while at the same time making the skin appear more beautiful. "Patients," as they were originally called, not customers, attended the institute, and eventually, perhaps inevitably, these began to include a number of rich Americans. Twelve years after opening his Budapest institute, he was "persuaded" to set up the Erno Laszlo Institute on Fifth Avenue in New York. The company has been extremely successful, but say "Erno Laszlo" to the average woman and she will never have heard of him. The key to success has been exclusivity and customer loyalty in a very fickle market.

Erno Laszlo operates in very few stores—in Britain, for instance, it sells only in Harrods—and the institute now has "members" rather than customers or patients. A member of the institute who uses Laszlo products will use only those recommended and no others, apart from color cosmetics, which are not in the Laszlo range. In fact, the company will not sell any of its products to anyone who is not a member, or indeed any product to a member which it regards as unsuitable for a particular skin. The basic product is used by every member, and it is a black soap, which is used twice a day. The skin is rinsed many times after the application of the soap. As with all cosmetic products, there is no evidence that the Laszlo technique stops aging, but the women who use it swear by its efficiency in keeping the skin in a good condition. The Laszlo client is treated as if she had come in for a medical consultation. First of all, skin problems, if any, are diagnosed, suitable preparations are supplied and the instructions are explained. The new member is given a membership card, which costs nothing—though the products themselves are expensive—and this card entitles the member to buy replacement products. The client goes away, returning later for the results to be checked.

The gimmick, as always, is in the marketing. It is expensive to use Erno Laszlo products, and there is the exclusivity of membership. No one without a membership card can buy the soap, or this or that cream. Only after the initial analysis and the purchase of *all* the recommended products is the card given. After that, the member can buy as much as she—and increasingly he—wants.

To begin with, the Laszlo products were sold only from the institute on Fifth Avenue. Then, in the 1950s, they began to be sold in specialized stores. In this way, Erno Laszlo has remained a small but highly profitable company. Even after its takeover in 1966 by Chesebrough-Pond's, which distributes most of its products through mass outlets, it has kept to its policy of limited outlets. Moves into international markets have taken place only slowly, and the line remains one of the most exclusive and expensive in the world. The company is not particularly interested in going into the traditional department store and would never consider a drugstore. Its advertising budget is not large, and it goes into only the most prestigious journals. It has no sales gimmicks and does very little promotion. Laszlo products might well be sold in exclusive boutiques or specialty stores that do not carry any other cosmetic line. The packaging is very simple: the various products look like pharmaceutical preparations. Everything is low-key. In the United States it costs about $250 to be a member, in Europe a little less. In total, there are probably only about 30,000 members using the products, but the profit margins are high, and any major increase in members could reduce the company's profitability.

The difficulties facing small companies if they try to remain independent are illustrated by Parfums Christian Dior of Paris. The company was formed in 1947 by Serge Heftler, a childhood friend of the couturier, and its first perfume, Miss Dior, came out with the first postwar fashion collection of Christian Dior. This was the famed "New Look," which gave women their first real fashion following the austerity of the war years, and the fragrance was designed to harmonize with the look. Diorama followed in 1949, then Eau Fraiche in 1953. With the perfumes well established, the company then moved into cosmetics in 1955, when it produced its first lipsticks. Another perfume, Diorissimo, arrived in 1956. Christian Dior himself died in 1957, but the cosmetics company has never ceased to use his name, trading upon the couturier house that has survived its founder. A year after Dior's death, his friend sold out and the company was bought by the Moet-Hennessy group, already famed for Moet et Chandon, Mercier and Ruinard champagnes and Hennessy cognac. The *haute couture* company is now owned by the late Marcel Boussac's textile company.

The upward progress of the company continued after the takeover, and in 1961, nail products were added to the range. The year 1963 saw the introduction of the Diorling perfume, followed three years later by Eau Sauvage, still one of the most successful ranges for men. In 1969, a full range of makeup products was marketed, and the company celebrated its silver jubilee with the Diorella perfume. In 1973, Hydra-Dior, a high-priced, prestigious line of products was added to the regular range. Such a level of activity would have been impossible had the company remained in private hands without the backing of the larger group.

The company has remained very French in character, but this has not meant that it has neglected the requirements of customers for cosmetic products today. It employs chemists, biologists, dermatologists and doctors in its six research laboratories. Every product, after it has passed all the regular tests, is then tried out on at least 300 women before finally being put on the market.

To survive in the 1980s a company marketing a full range of cosmetics need not itself be very large, but it does need money behind it. One that has proved that small (small as compared with Avon or Revlon, that is) can be good is the Noxell Corporation, whose low-priced Cover Girl line has done very well against all opposition. In particular, it has done much better than its most serious competitor, Maybelline, a subsidiary of the giant Schering Plough group. Noxell is one of the smaller conglomerates and sells household cleaners as well as toiletries and cosmetics. It faces heavy competition throughout its range of products; yet Cover Girl is one of the most-used cosmetics in the United States, Noxzema skin cream has a good and steady market, and its stablemate, Noxzema shaving cream, is the second-best-seller in America after Gillette. Rain Tree moisturizer, first introduced in 1977, quickly caught 5 percent of the market.

Although Noxell is a midget among the conglomerates with similar interests and seems to have achieved its success by operating as if it were a small company, it is in fact quite large. The business is still basically family-owned, and although its shares are quoted on the stock market, more than 80 percent of them remain in the hands of descendants of the founder, Dr. George A. Bunting. The key to its success has been its ability to develop new products. Not all of them have been successful, but the company has shown that it is prepared to take the risk of failing. With so much stock in family hands, the company can afford a little independence from its shareholders: it does not matter particularly if profits dip for a time. Indeed, this happened in 1973 and 1974, but recovery since has been very strong.

But, in one way, Noxell is as big as its competitors: it is prepared to spend a great deal of money on advertising its cosmetics lines. It has actually spent more advertising Cover Girl than the much larger Schering Plough has spent on Maybelline. Almost 20 percent of its sales revenue goes to advertising its small range of products—again a decision that can much more easily be taken when the company is virtually family-owned. In a group where the stock is more widely held, shareholders might have something to say about such expenditure. Many companies would like to buy Noxell: for the moment, however, the family, like the Lauders, are sitting tight.

There is still room in the cosmetics industry for new but old-style entrepreneurs, although they are unlikely to find the path to riches as easy as it was for the Rubinstein, Arden or Factor generation. The method of going about it, however, has changed little. The salon route is still the best; getting a line of products into the stores against the competition of the giant concerns is well-nigh impossible today. The new entrepreneur needs a brand-new idea, not always easy today, and absolute determination to stick with it. As with those who first started the cosmetics industry, complete self-confidence is essential, an eccentric personality helps and, of course, a finely tuned sense of what women—and also today men—are looking for in the cosmetics. What is less important in the salon route is a vast sum of money to set up this kind of business.

Sam Kallish points the way to the future: "More and more women will be using salons, places where they can have facials, massages, do exercises and buy their makeup. All that stuff about staying in a beauty parlor for five hours to be beautiful is hogwash. Women are part of the economy now. They have more money, more independence and one way and another will find the time —but not a lot of it—to look good. They are disillusioned with what's being sold and how it's being sold. What makes a visit to a cosmetic center easier is that you don't have to dress up to go to one. No one else does and all the women are there for the same purpose—to look good. It's all part of women's liberation. Stores are still making money, of course, but a trip to a store is much more a big deal. No one likes to stand at a beauty counter looking a mess, and you never know who you will see there, so cosmetic buying means dressing up. Then again, no one wants to be served by some old biddy who has just been moved in from the millinery department and knows nothing about cosmetics, when at a salon you can get expert advice."

Sam Kallish has not been the only one to take the view that this is the way the industry is going. When she was in her teens, just over twenty years ago, Adrien Arpel opened up a small salon in Englewood, New Jersey, where she sold cosmetics and advised women about their skins and the kinds of makeup that would suit them. She gradually developed her own line of cosmetics, but also sold other brands. She at first did not try to take on the big brand names in the prestige stores and country-wide shop chains. She also initially stuck to her home territory. Before she was eighteen she was represented all over New Jersey with seventy-six salons. That was 1959, and the whole operation so far had been financed from an initial $400 provided by Adrien Arpel's father.

Marriage was but a small hiccup in growth, and she began train- ing other wives and mothers who were able to do part-time work in the many beauty salons in New York. Arpel realized that women simply did not have much time to spend in salons, partic- ularly when so many women were out at work. Yet they still wanted facials, massages, manicures and the many other services salons can provide. She hit on what was then a novel idea: she negotiated for space on the main floor of department stores where she set up rooms and counters that could be described as mini-salons, where customer turnaround was swift and no time was wasted. Today, the Arpel salons sell not only her own brand makeup, but skin treatment products, and the business is said to be grossing over $10 million a year. It has now moved beyond America, and Adrien Arpel facials are offered in prestige stores in Europe.

In the early 1970s, the business was growing fast and caught the eye of Seligman and Latz, a big chain of conventional beauty salons. Adrien Arpel decided to consolidate the gains she had made, and became a wholly-owned subsidiary of the larger group. This meant that there was no way that Adrien Arpel could build up an empire in the way an Arden or Revson had in the past. But she recognized a fact of modern cosmetic life—that those heady days are over and anyone obstinately attempting to repeat the 1920s and thirties today could well end up bankrupt.

As in all industries, it is the successes, not the failures, that are remembered. Adrien Arpel, still only just forty, is a very visible character in the cosmetics world and in the company she once owned, offering advice to women and increasingly to men; 10 percent of her customers today are male. In addition, she has, like so many before her, moved into the lucrative beauty-book market. Her book teaching women how to make up their faces was launched in America a couple of years ago.

The salon route has been used not only by cosmeticians but also by hairdressers as well—and with rather more success in stay-ing independent when the founders have wanted to. When Vidal Sassoon, a working-class boy from the East End of London, set up his first salon in the West End of that city in the 1950s, he probably little realized that by 1980 he would be heading an inter-national business with a total turnover of $100 million. At the age of fifty, in 1977, Mr. Sassoon told the press that he was aiming to climb into the Revlon/Lauder league. His turnover then was a mere $30 million. There is still a long way to go to meet his ambitions, but the growth potential is clear to see.

Vidal Sassoon caught the public imagination in Britain with an amazing skill in hair cutting. He also turned out to have a flair for publicity. Before long, many smart women regarded having a cut at Sassoon's as being as important and as normal as a couture dress—and it was, relatively speaking, just as expensive. But the company could not have grown to its present size merely by cutting hair in the United Kingdom. The big market was America, so Vidal Sassoon came here. He immediately hit a problem: the hairdressers association of America tried to prevent him from opening a salon, on the ground that he had not taken their professional examinations. Mr. Sassoon was not to be put off, and by skillful publicity he soon built up as loyal a clientele on this side of the Atlantic.

Since then the major growth of Vidal Sassoon, Inc., has been in America; there are Sassoon salons on the fashionable streets of Los Angeles, San Francisco, Chicago and New York. The salon business—his "flagships," as Sassoon calls them—is now only a very small part of the Sassoon operation, contributing less than $12 million to the total turnover. The company's most famous salon, in Bond Street, London, has now closed. Initial gossip that this meant that the group was in trouble soon ceased: Mr. Sassoon explained that he was not prepared to pay an increase in rent for the premises from $28,000 to $120,000 in one jump. Some provincial salons are also being closed, and the concentration in the future will be on the hair preparations marketed under the magic Sassoon name and on a few prestige American salons. The hair preparations will soon be joined by a range of skin-care products, and thus Sassoon will have become a full cosmetics business.

For a time in the seventies it looked as though the company would dissipate its energies. Sassoon went in for a series of licensing arrangements by which others used his name on clothing, cosmetics and other consumer goods—he got a fee, but the licensees made the major profits from the sales. But real growth for the company began in 1973 when Joseph Solomon, a former hair-dresser, found a biochemist with some new ideas on hair products which fitted in with Sassoon's sometimes rather odd ideas on healthy living. Sassoon has now handed over the posts of president and chief executive in the company to Solomon, who in 1980 was still only thirty-four, but the founder remains very visible, pushing his views on a healthy and active life and constantly pointing out how his products fit in with those views. He has become something of a cult figure in the United States and now has his own television production company, which sells chat shows starring Sassoon himself. As his fame has grown in the U.S., Sassoon has become less well known in the United Kingdom to the new generation of young women. He plans to change all that with a $3.6 million promotion of his products. He has also decided to move into charity and has not forgotten his East End beginnings. In June 1980, when he announced he was planning to sponsor scholarships for minorities and a jazz center at the University of Los Angeles, he told reporters that he knew what it was like to be underprivileged: "I am very much into this minority thing, because I remember being one. Having money enables you to live out these sort of fantasies, like giving scholarships. That is one of the things I like most." Success has its price: Sassoon now has an ex-wife, Beverley, who did much to help him in the growth of his business and who is now embarking on her own advice-to-the-beauty-trade. She won a divorce settlement of a million dollars, and the couple sold their $3 million Los Angeles home after the split.

So far, the major companies in America, apart from Revlon with Polished Amber, have chosen to ignore what to the outsider may appear to be a highly lucrative market: that of cosmetics for black people, and this has left the way open to the smaller companies. A significant percentage of the urban population of America is black, and further, the market is a relatively young one: only around 40 percent of the black population is over twenty-five years of age. In Europe the proportion of blacks in the population is much smaller than in the United States and blacks have usually had to be satisfied with adapting white cosmetics where they can. Biba, offshoot of the now defunct trendy clothing company, has run a limited line for some years, mainly in the United Kingdom, where blacks amount to only 2 percent of the population. A new range, the low-priced Shades of Black, has just been introduced, again mainly in Britain. The problem is that the numbers are probably too small to provide a highly profitable volume of sales.

For a long time black women used either no foundation at all or the darker shades available to whites. The market was confined to some skin creams and moisturizers, and eye shadows, blushers and lipsticks. Nevertheless, the value of cosmetics sales to blacks in the United States is thought to have risen from some $80 million in 1970 to $400 million in 1978.

The decision of most of the leading cosmetics houses in America not to offer a black range so far does, however, make sound commercial sense. Many of these houses are marketing products in the medium to high-price ranges, and they are anxious to maintain their image of exclusivity in the customers' eyes. A mass market could destroy this image. At the same time, there is not yet, despite their large numbers, a substantial enough middle-class among blacks to justify producing many cosmetic ranges for them at relatively high prices. There is, too, the mood of black people to consider. Today many of them do not like to be controlled in their buying patterns by whites. The number of blacks in Europe is infinitesimal in terms of the total market for cosmetics, so there is little prospect in the near future of big sales there. The African states are an increasing market, but they are highly volatile politically and consequently a substantial risk area. Meantime, the major companies argue that their treatment products suit black skins as well as white, and that their color cosmetics anyway have enough variety to suit most black skins. These factors together have meant that it has been left to blacks themselves to develop their own ranges.

An early entrant into the American cosmetics industry for blacks was George Johnson, who came in with all the right ideas about the growing market, but went the wrong way about making the best possible levels of profits out of it. He formed Johnson Products in 1954, after a period of working for Fuller Products of Chicago, another black cosmetics company. His first product was a hair straightener, quite right for the market, and sold directly to the hairdressing trade at a time when many black women wanted to have straighter hair like white women. The company later extended its range to include other hair dressings, conditioners and shampoos, and a cosmetics range, which is a relatively small part of the business. The sales pitch is firmly to the black customer, although there is nothing special in most of the products which demands that they should be used only by blacks. The foundation-cream colors have a wide spectrum to cater to most skins from light golden to black.

Today Johnson Products is the largest publicly owned cosmetics company, which is mainly managed by blacks and sold to a totally black market. But cosmetics analyst Hazel Bishop at stockbrokers Evans and Evans told me: "They went about their whole operation in the wrong way. They tried to sell products in the drugstores and to mass distributors at the same prices as the Max Factor and Revlon ranges. There is just not enough affluence among blacks at the present time to make a success at that level. The black customer who is looking for products in the same class as Estée Lauder is not going to buy lines which are widely available in the mass market." That Johnson sells very much to the mass market is shown by its main customers—Woolworth, Kresge, Walgren and the United States Government, which takes 5 percent of the company's output for army sales.

In the mass market, Johnson was facing competition from, it is true, many much smaller companies, like Posner, Blendique and Nancy Wilson, which are exclusively black ranges, and also from other low-priced brands that are available nationally and have extended their colors to cover shades for black women. There was no chance for Johnson Products in the high-class stores. These are very choosey about the brands they carry, and they could never be persuaded to carry a line that also went into the mass market through drugstores. In the medium-priced stores, cosmetics lines that are not heavily marketed with manufacturer involvement in terms of sales staff and promotion tend not to be well displayed. Again there is competition from other black lines and the ethnic shades produced by the ordinary companies. Johnson also faced competition from hundreds of small regional companies catering for the black community in each area. On top of all this, Avon started selling to blacks in the early 1950s and has always been a formidable competitor, although it does not even now have a specific black line.

What happened was that the Johnson lines did not move fast enough in the shops and were replaced by products that did not sit on the shelves for a long period. Insufficient attention was paid to advertising. Black women, like all women, tend to buy cosmetics on impulse. If they remember a recent advertisement when they go shopping, the chances are that they will buy that product. But this memory is ephemeral and next time around, unless the advertising is kept up, the chances are that another brand will be bought. Johnson Products has now learned the harsh lessons of the early 1970s and is marketing and pricing its products more realistically. That the market is there, there can be no doubt, but that it will remain highly competitive is also true. The black consumer market is growing rapidly as blacks begin to move up to the same salary levels as whites. Yet because of social arrangements, black people often find that there are fewer demands on their money than whites do. They still find it difficult, for instance, to join clubs, and their leisure activities are generally much less costly than those of whites. This should mean that they have relatively much more to spend on their personal appearance, whether on makeup or clothes.

The black cosmetics market is also a loyal one: advertisers can rely on a good response from their audiences. Johnson Products saw this in the early 1970s when it backed "Soul Train," a TV program with an all-black cast. But the running in the black cosmetics market has been made in recent years not by the bigger companies, but by lone entrepreneurs, which may not be particularly large in terms of the total market, but which have built up highly profitable personalized businesses. They have recognized the special problems of blacks, being black themselves. There are problems with foundation cream which at least on the skin's surface do not apply to white women. For instance, all skins regularly shed the top layer. On white skins this does not show: on black it can give a powdery look, which cosmetics must help to avoid. There are often pink tones in even the darkest colors of foundations, and these do not look good on black skins. The upper lip is often darker than the lower lip, so sometimes two shades of lipstick are used to balance out the color.

And black skin is simply not just black, any more than white skin is white. Revlon believes there are thirty-three different shades of black skin, and it has tried to tailor its Polished Amber range accordingly. On the whole, too, black skins tend to be oilier than white (although this is not always true), and special products need to be designed for this, for the use of heavy creams simply exacerbates the condition.

One woman who has achieved a noteworthy success with cosmetics for blacks, although not on a massive scale, is Barbara Walden. Her business was an outgrowth of her own experience when she found that ordinary cosmetics did not suit her and she persuaded a chemist in California to try out her ideas. These ideas have led to a multimillion-dollar business and the sobriquet the "black Estée Lauder." Although in size there is no comparison between the two companies, the aggressive and creative personalities of the two women bear similarities.

Miss Walden, finding that her acting career was not going as well as she had hoped, looked around for a partner to help her develop her ideas for cosmetics. She found Dan Raeburn, who was in advertising, and they each put $350 into the new company. It was not much of a company to begin with, just an office in Watts, a black section of Los Angeles. Miss Walden trained other black women to sell cosmetics door to door. Business went well, and it was not long before there was enough money to open a beauty salon. Miss Walden had the timing just right. The late

1960s and early seventies saw black women getting more, and better, jobs. As they had more money to spend, their interest in looking good increased—and the mood was such that black women wanted other black women to tell them how to achieve this, not the traditional "white" companies.

In 1972, Barbara Walden made her pitch to the department stores. At first she committed the same mistake as George Johnson. Her products went first into I. Magnin, the prestige department store in Los Angeles. The move was a failure. Magnin is a store for white women, and however affluent black women were becoming, they still preferred the medium-priced stores. So Barbara Walden traded down a little and went into the May Company, the Broadway Department Stores and Joseph Magnin on the West Coast. From successful beginnings in these stores, her company has begun to trade nationwide with close to sixty products in its range. The business is still relatively small compared with the giants, and there seems no doubt that it could be expanded rapidly. For the time being, however, Miss Walden has preferred to keep the company very much a personal concern. She appears regularly in the department stores in which her products are marketed, giving advice to customers, and is still much involved in the training of her work force. By this policy she has provided a secure base for her company, and its prospects are bright.

There are signs of more interest from the "white" companies. Some have recently been pitching to black women products originally designed for whites. Clairol, for instance, is taking the matter seriously. It used to offer dark hair shades to blacks, but has recently run advertisements in *Ebony*, a magazine catering to the black woman, suggesting that all its shades are suitable for black women. It has used black models with hair dyed all shades from blond through brunette to black.

There is still room, too, in the hair products market for the smaller companies. Like Barbara Walden, Paula Kent Meehan once entertained hopes of stardom in Hollywood. She failed, but today she is one of the successes from among the cosmetics entre-

preneurs who set up in the 1960s. In the twenty years since 1960,
her new approach to the treatment of hair problems has made her
personally very wealthy. She was cofounder of Redken Laboratories, Inc., a California-based company. Mrs. Meehan, at a time
when most shampoos were for cleaning dry, normal or greasy
hair, decided that the company she was forming would do for hair
what skin treatments did for the skin: hence the "laboratories" of
the name. The company further decided it would not try for a
place in the department stores, supermarkets and drugstores,
where it could not possibly compete on promotion and advertising
terms with the giant producers. Instead it would direct its sales
exclusively toward the 300,000 professional hairdressing salons in
the U.S. Today Redken has some 20 percent of the market for
hair treatment products. Mrs. Meehan has succeeded against
some of the strongest companies in this market, and her business
is still growing.

This slice of the market has been carved out by a simple formula: research and more research to develop products. Redken is
not a marketing-oriented company like some others. Everything
has begun with research, and marketing success has followed.
The company employs more than fifty scientists, rather a large
number for its size. Product development begins and finishes in
the laboratories and does not arise from the demands of the marketing department. From supplying salons in the early days, the
company today has its own retail counters in many hairdressing
salons, just as cosmetic manufacturers have their retail counters
in department stores. Gradually, in this way, Redken has moved
into retail selling, and around 65 percent of its sales are achieved
over the counters in salons. In addition, the company now sells in
selected stores. The emphasis in the company all the time is on
education about hair and its problems. Seminars, which are held
all over the country, are oversubscribed and are sold out well in
advance, so successfully has Mrs. Meehan sold the concept that
her products are designed to produce healthy hair. After twenty
years, Redken's sales have topped $50 million, 10 percent of them
coming from overseas sales. This is small by L'Oreal or Clairol

standards, but experience has shown that this market, in which the products are based on research, rather than on the demand for something new every few months, is a loyal one. Despite its success, Redken at present is represented in about only 7,000 salons in the United States, roughly a mere 2 percent of the total. It seems likely she will be able to withstand the might of Clairol or L'Oreal, which in different circumstances might easily crush her company.

Success in the second line of cosmetics companies is just as varied as in the major groups, and things can go wrong for even well-established companies. One rarely out of the business news in the United States is Fabergé, which in recent years has had a penchant for doing the wrong thing. It is a publicly owned company, but one in which the board is dominated by a single family and, in particular, by one man, George Barrie. His sons Richard and Craig and his sister Caryl are the others. The way in which the board of directors and Mr. Barrie, in particular, behave is reminiscent of the Revlon period, with hirings and firings and general erratic behavior. Describing Mr. Barrie, one observer of the industry told me: "There will always be Queen Bees in the cosmetics industry, and they are not always women. These people will not explain their actions to anyone, nor be accountable to anyone. That attitude was all very well when companies could afford to make mistakes and profits from other sources would make up for them, but in today's competitive world it is more difficult for them to succeed."

At Fabergé, which in the past has used Cary Grant, the film actor, for promotions, shades of the late Charles Revson arose when, in 1978, a line of products featuring "Charlie's Angels" star Farrah Fawcett-Majors flopped badly. George Barrie instituted a general purge of the company of those involved, and one of the victims was his son, Richard. The break between father and son was only temporary, and within nine months Richard had returned to the company as vice president in charge of marketing and sales.

The Fabergé company is known primarily worldwide for Brut, which along with Aramis is the most successful line ever marketed for men. Brut is rather less expensive than Aramis, and there is no doubt that it has persuaded many none-too-affluent men, who previously would not have touched a fragrance, to use one. Its success was, as always, due to very skillful marketing. The whole pitch was to men who are real men. In the United Kingdom, the home-grown boxing hero Henry Cooper was used to advertise the product, not only in newspapers and magazines, but on vast billboards. "Our 'Enery" took an aggressive sweaty pose in the advertisements, and the message clearly was that if *he* used it, there could be no doubt in anyone's mind that it was for *real* men. No one could accuse Henry Cooper of being effeminate, nor the man who has now joined him in the advertisements, Kevin Keegan, Britain's soccer star. This meant that a man could safely buy it for himself, or a woman for him, without a chance of any slur on his masculinity. In the United States, Joe Namath, the virile former football player, renowned for his attractiveness to women and his own attraction to them, was used to similar effect.

Unfortunately for Fabergé, however, Brut has been carrying a great number of less profitable products in recent years. An outstanding failure has been Babe, a fragrance introduced in 1976, which, it was hoped—three years on—would be another Charlie, which has been such an outstanding success for Revlon. This has been a fond but vain hope of many cosmetic houses, and Fabergé was certainly not alone in its failure; it was just that its failure was spectacular. Initially Babe did well, though not nearly so well as Charlie, with million-dollar-model Margaux Hemingway advertising the product. A color cosmetic and treatment line followed in the spring of 1977. This line just did not take off; it made little or no impact on the cosmetics market and was withdrawn in 1978. The fragrance, too, began to falter, as fragrances often do, and sales dropped badly. This was a second failure for Fabergé. Another line, a relaunch of a prewar fragrance Tigress, with supporting model Lola Falana had failed as well. Miss Falana was later replaced by Tamara Dobson, but she, too, was not able to get sales off the ground. In 1980 the Babe fragrance was the subject of yet another worldwide advertising campaign. The signs are that it will fail yet again.

The Fabergé story does not end with Babe and Tigress. Macho, a man's fragrance, was put out by the company in 1976. Initially it did quite well, but then it, too, faded away. Perhaps women in these liberated days, who buy most of the fragrances sold for men for their husbands and men friends, would not take to a product with a name like that. Similarly, the basic Fabergé cosmetic line, which came out in 1977, made little headway against the established Revlon, Factor and Arden ranges. By the end of 1978, all but a couple of the products in the line had been dropped.

The company, faced with these disasters, did what companies often do: it fired its entire sales force and, in the autumn of 1977, hired instead independent sales agents. That did not solve the problem, and within a year the agents, too, were fired and the company was once again engaged in building up its own sales force. Fabergé is very much George Barrie's creation, and he is highly sensitive to any criticism. There is always a good reason why something fails. It is difficult, however, to explain why so many products have sold disastrously after initially promising starts. The company maintains, for instance, that the Farrah Fawcett-Majors line did very well in the circumstances. The company's advertising program had been scheduled in advance— magazines have long closing dates for copy, as the industry knows —but when the ads began to appear, not only had production of the line been delayed, but there was a general lack of coordination between the various sections of the company involved in the launch. This, however, is surely a failure of management. George Barrie frequently, publicly and angrily answers his critics, but as yet there is no sign of another Brut on the horizon. There are, however, two new Fabergé fragrances, Cabale and Partage, and their fate in the market is yet to be seen. But from the evidence so far, Fabergé is just not getting its marketing right; it needs better coordination and efficient functioning in all its departments to succeed.

Another company that has shown how plans can fail when prospects look very bright is Helene Curtis, a firm that was as big as Max Factor twenty years ago. But it never grew properly, and sales today are a mere $130 million compared with $500 million for the admittedly sickly Factor and $1,718 million for Revlon. Profit margins, too, are little more than half the average for the industry. The company appeared to have a good profit potential, an expert research department and a series of excellent products that broke new ground, like its Enden dandruff shampoo. But the benefits of all the development expertise were being dissipated by internal and external problems at the company. In 1964, the federal government seized the company's wrinkle cream on the ground that false claims were being made for its efficacy. This cost the company $6 million and marked the end of dividend payments for shareholders. An attempt to become another Avon, through the purchase of a company called Studio Girl, failed: Avon was not to be shaken, and Studio Girl was sold after several million more dollars had been lost. Two million dollars is still owed to the Internal Revenue Service for taxes not paid on, but deducted from, employees' salaries.

If that were not enough, Helene Curtis (named for the founder's wife, Helene, and his son Curtis) has been badly beaten out in a market it once dominated, the professional salons, by the dynamic growing company Redken, which had actually created the resale market in salons. Helene Curtis, it seems, had never realized that a potential market was there until Redken developed it. Curtis has started fighting back but it will be difficult to shift the advantage that Redken has built up. Like the tribulations of Job, other misfortunes have befallen the company. More wasted advertising was placed and millions of dollars of legal fees were spent when Curtis and Dwight (no relation), makers of Arm and Hammer Baking Soda, brought a case alleging that Helene Curtis had infringed its trademark by selling a deodorant named Arm in Arm (and, incidentally, based on baking powder).

Of course such misfortunes as these are not merely acts of God; they represent missed opportunities and sometimes downright bad management. Helene Curtis was founded over fifty years ago, and it seems to be a story in which the founding father, Geral Gidwitz, who owns one-third of the stock, has hung on too long. The road back to prosperity—if it can be achieved—will be a long one.

One post-1945 development has been highly lucrative for some small companies: health—or as they are more commonly known, "fat"—farms. They originated centuries ago in Europe, but today the health farm, or "spa," differs considerably in Europe and America. Baden-Baden is perhaps the world's most famous. It eschews any hint of cosmetic or beauty treatment. The emphasis is always on health. German citizens are entitled by law to take a "cure," and this can last from twenty-one days to anything up to six weeks. It can be paid for through state national health insurance, and 64 percent of the clients come via that system. Modern health spas are very rarely actually connected with thermal waters —the name just sounds good—but all the old ones—and Baden-Baden is one of the oldest, going back to Roman times—have natural mineral water sources. The waters are the basis of the treatments offered.

The aim of the cure is not to make people slimmer, or more beautiful, but to restore their health and vigor. The treatments, of course, may well help clients become slimmer and more attractive, but that is not the purpose of the spa. The therapeutic facilities are available first and foremost for those people suffering from the strains and stresses of modern life: who isn't, one might ask? No one is offered a facial or beauty massage; treatments are prescribed on strictly medical needs, although it has to be said that not everyone in the medical profession believes that anything more than temporary relief can be achieved through the cure, any more than cosmetic treatments do anything other than keep the surface of the skin in good condition.

Baden-Baden claims, however, to be effective in the treatment of various rheumatic ailments, vascular and women's diseases and respiratory illnesses, and as follow-up treatment for injuries arising from accidents. Most of the health farms are basically a twentieth-century development, superficially copying the old therapeutic spas like Baden-Baden, though they are much less ambitious in their aims and far more expensive. Baden-Baden offers a package deal of $60 for a week's full spa treatment, including attendance by a doctor. Such a figure would barely cover a day at a modern health farm, though those taking the cure at Baden-Baden do not live in the cure house, but in hotels and guest houses in town at additional expense.

It is a far cry from Baden-Baden to the "Spa" at La Costa outside San Diego, in Southern California. There are no thermal springs, and there is nothing spartan about La Costa Hotel Spa, unless it is the ugly togalike toweling garments that women wear in the spa. This is not just a "fat farm"; it accommodates the "spa" facilities within a vast complex of 8,000 acres, which include a golf course, tennis courts and a riding range. When guests wake up in their well-appointed rooms they can choose to eat either an ordinary breakfast, or if they are on the "spa plan," they have the first of three specially planned meals.

The spa begins the day at eight-thirty, with the sexes strictly segregated, except for yoga or dance classes. This is how the daily class schedule looks:

> 8:30—walk
> 9:00—fitness class
> 10:20—water volleyball
> 10:30—aqua-thin-ics
> 11:00—dance (co-ed)
> 11:40—open gym
> 12:20—yoga (co-ed) or open gym

Then comes a break for lunch and the second of the planned meals. And it starts again:

> 2:00—fitness class
> 2:40—water volleyball
> 3:20—aqua-thin-ics (water exercises) or Costa Curves
>   (co-ed exercises to trim the shape)
> 4:00—dance (co-ed)
> 4:40—yoga (co-ed) or specialized men's exercises
> 5:20—open gym

Unbelievable though it may seem, some people actually manage to get through the whole program and toss in a facial and massage as well. Others will do a half-day following a round of golf or a tennis game. In total, 300 people go through these facilities each day, and if any of them spends less than the $150 activities fee while they are doing it, a manicure, a pedicure, makeup lessons or a shampoo and set takes care of the rest of the money.

Altogether La Costa does 100,000 facials a year, and these are just as popular with men as women. Before embarking on a "plan," clients get a limited medical where weight, heart and blood pressure are checked.

The regimen does not halt in the evenings either. There are health lectures, cookery classes, cocktail parties where "diet" cocktails are served along with the usual alcoholic cocktails. Nothing is compulsory: it all depends on will power.

Naturally, La Costa's program is completed by the use of its own cosmetics (specially made in Switzerland), which can be bought only at or through La Costa. That is where Bill Randall comes in. Randall is an old name in the U.S. cosmetics business, never big enough to threaten the major companies, but quite big enough to have built up a highly profitable but limited range, which became very attractive to the giant companies.

A man of many anecdotes about the industry, Bill Randall set up the Sea & Ski suntan products company with $400 that he had left from his severance pay after serving in the United States Air Force during WW II. He took advantage of military medical research, which, during the war, had developed cream for the use of air force personnel forced to bail out over the desert or any hot, sunny area. At first, the cream was a total barrier and excluded all the rays of the sun. This obviously had no cosmetics appeal as the fashion for suntanned skin got underway. Eventually, creams were developed that let some rays through and suntan creams began to be manufactured. The result of this research was made publicly available after the end of the war and Sea & Ski was only one of many companies to set up to cash in on it. Sea & Ski was also one of the most successful ones, and it was not long before Randall had suitors. He told me that Charles Revson was one.

"Mr. Revson spent two hours talking to me and justifying himself and his approach to cosmetics. But I never thought he was a bad guy. I just didn't want to sell to them: I went into the industry to build a Revlon, not to sell to one."

Eventually, Randall was persuaded to sell out to Smith Klein and French in 1967. He kept for a time a sunglasses company that he also owned; he later sold it to Foster Grant.

When Bill Randall joined La Costa, his first product was a massage oil. He quickly realized that customers would want to take it away with them. He opened a shop at the farm and also set up a mail order business. Within five years he was producing a complete line of more than 130 products, which are divided into beauty, bath and shower and sun products. The factory making them is just two miles from La Costa. Bill Randall says he believes that creams do get through the skin and points to a recent ruling by the Food and Drug Administration that some sun products may be labeled "helps to prevent aging due to sun exposure." Equally, of course, this could be an argument for saying that creams cannot get through the skin.

La Costa is typical of many high-class combined health and holiday resorts in America. Other examples are the Greenhouse in Dallas; the Golden Door, which is close to La Costa; Elizabeth Arden's Maine Chance in Arizona (the original in Maine has now closed down); and Palm Aire in Florida. So far the fat farms in Europe have a more spartan air. There will not be a bar, nor will ordinary meals be served, except to those trying to put on weight. The regime is strict and the costs expensive. At La Costa, accommodations alone for three days on the spa plan cost the visitor a minimum of $165. At Champneys, one of the most popular farms in the United Kingdom, a single room costs between $400 and $600 a week, again with additional charges for courses of treatment. Guests must keep to a very strict diet at most of the farms in Britain, and some will "expel" anyone who slips the noose and pops out to the local pub. In Britain it is men rather than women who favor fat farms, and they make up the majority of the clients.

The experience of second-rank companies in the cosmetics industry varies enormously and shows that, despite some great successes, profitability is by no means assured. The demise of some companies and the disappearance of others into conglomerates have not been good for the industry, for these smaller groups provided much of the innovation and genuine creativity of the industry in the past. As the industry enters the 1980s, there are some signs that there will be a resurgence in entrepreneurial activity, but this will not put a dent in the dominance of the major companies in international markets.

FIVE

PAINTS AND OTHER WARS

A desire to be observed, considered, esteemed, praised, beloved, and admired by his fellows is one of the earliest as well as the keenest dispositions discovered in the heart of man.
—John Adams, "Discourses on Devilla"

When people put on makeup, they are trying to project an ideal image of themselves. The woman doing her best to be attractive to men; the young girl trying to appear sophisticated; the African tribesman covering himself with paint to look warlike; or the businessman using dye to disguise his gray hair in an attempt to seem younger—all these, whatever they may think they are doing, are trying to achieve their view of personal attractiveness.

The history of cosmetics is as old as the history of mankind. The impulse to self-decoration has been present in all human societies. From time to time, people have developed prejudices against cosmetics—the Victorian era in England was vociferous on the matter—but these periods have been short compared with the eras when cosmetics played an important and sometimes vital role—as an integral part of religion, myth, medicine and alchemy. Sometimes self-decoration has been confined to one sex, but the twentieth-century view, which prevailed until recently, that only women should use cosmetics, represented a very short period indeed in history, blinking the fact that it has been far more common in many societies for both men and women to decorate themselves. The term "warpaint" to describe makeup for women used to be just that: the early colonists of the United States learned a lot about color cosmetics from the elaborate paint with which the American Indian decorated himself.

The ancient records we first had in the present came from ancient Egypt, where cosmetics and religion were closely linked. Recent archeological work, however, has shown that the Orient and India, and other places with civilizations as old as Egypt, used a variety of emollients and cosmetics on both living and dead bodies: some practices have survived until today in one way or another—in embalming techniques, for example. In ancient times, most products were made at home, but herbs, perfumes and aromatic oils were sold in the shops. Henna, used then, is still a major raw material in hair dyes today; kohl, too, is used now and then for eye makeup. Other materials, like the notorious white lead, which was used to whiten skin but also damaged it, are now banned. In some hands, like those of Catherine de Medici during the Renaissance, white lead was convenient not only as a cosmetic, but also for poisoning one's enemies, although arsenic was Catherine's favorite poison.

The Persians advanced the art of cosmetics and found many more cosmetic products when they conquered India. Cosmetics and medicine became closely linked at this time. In their turn, the Persians were conquered by the Greeks, who made great advances linking medicine and cosmetology. Then Hippocrates of Cos, the "father of medicine," who introduced the oath of professional integrity for doctors which has been used ever since, gathered the available knowledge together, drawing up a code with some semblance of scientific principles. The link between medicine and cosmetics continued for a very long time, through the Roman,

Arabian and Renaissance periods. The Romans, at first rejecting Greek traditions, finally embraced them enthusiastically and went on to refine them. It was the Romans who developed the cult of the baths, rather like a men's club of today, but used enthusiastically by both men and women. The Romans also set up spas wherever possible during their conquering phase, some of which have survived until today: the Roman baths at Bath, Somerset, England, were closed down less than five years ago for lack of money, and there is still talk of reopening them. The Roman baths were the forerunner of the health farms and spas that have become so popular again in the twentieth century.

Galen, who lived from A.D. 130 to 200 and who practiced in Asia Minor and Rome, was considered a very great physician indeed, second only to Hippocrates in that ancient era, and published an enormous number of writings on almost every then-known aspect of medicine. These works were to provide the basic material for the medical profession for as many as 1,500 years. He also created an ointment that was the first version of later cold cream emulsions.

Toward the end of the fifth century A.D., Europe was descending into the so-called Dark Ages, and little initiative seems to have been shown in Europe on the part of the chemists and physicians of this very long period. There were developments in the Arabian countries: from Persia, for example, came the first written reports of rhinoplasty, that is, plastic surgery on the nose, so common today. The growth of Islam brought an increase of interest in beauty culture and pertinent old works of the Greeks were translated into Arabic. Cosmetology fell into disuse and became part of gynecology and surgery. The Arab peoples were interested more in the pursuit of beauty through health, believing that it was part of general bodily well-being, than in the arts of concealing defects or the ravages of time. During the period, the main advances were made in pharmacy and pharmacology.

No one agrees about just how long the Dark Ages lasted, but after about five centuries Europe began to arouse itself. It had gone through what had been described as "a thousand years without a bath," a description not quite true, though bathing was certainly neither a popular nor a frequent pastime and cosmetics appear to have been used only very rarely. Their reintroduction came through medicine, as it had in previous times. Salerno became the first center for surgery. The school there had been used as a hospital for those returning wounded from the first Crusade to the Holy Land. From these beginnings, skills in the use of aromatic materials developed, and the *Antidotarium Nicolai* was published, explaining the preparation of 150 drugs. It was now the turn of the Arabian countries to go into decline.

During the Renaissance, cosmetics became separated from the medical profession, and from time to time, following decrees that the use of self-decoration was against God's will, cosmetics lost their favor. The inclination toward self-decoration was too strong, however, for these periods to last a very long time. The Italians in particular made significant advances. Europe was frequently at war, and one natural effect was an increased interest in the possibilities of plastic surgery. By the beginning of the seventeenth century nose, lip and ear repairs were quite common. The arts of perfume making developed markedly after Europe's many travelers struck out East, returning with many useful raw materials from the Orient.

Then, at the end of the fifteenth century, America was discovered, an amazing source of new source materials, but it was not until the early eighteenth century that the colonialists arrived in North America to exploit these resources. The Spanish by then were already making excellent use of the gums, spices and dyes they had found in South America. But the main center of activity remained in Europe, with France as the leader in fashion and therefore in cosmetics. Marriages between the various royal families of Europe meant that fashions spread quickly from one center to another. In Elizabethan England, for example, cosmetics were used freely, including the notorious white lead.

Hair styles were elaborate and wigs were highly popular, the Queen herself being said to own several hundred. Styles were

Helena Rubinstein

Helena Rubinstein, Polish-born "Madame" of the cosmetics industry, during the interwar years. She referred to her laboratory as her "kitchen."

Rubinstein's great rival, Elizabeth Arden, renowned for both her ladylike manner and her vitriolic tongue.

AN *Extraordinary* CLEAN∫ING CREAM

THAT BRINGS IVORY SMOOTHNESS TO YOUR SKIN

Mme. Helena Rubinstein's famous *Pasteurized Face Cream*, the one truly *scientific* cleanser, has already proved its astonishing powers to women in almost every corner of the world

THE COMPLETE HOME BEAUTY TREATMENT
Pasteurized Face Cream, a penetrative, antiseptic cleanser. $1. Skin Clearing Cream. Stimulates, clarifies, banishes skin "depression." $1. Skin Toning Lotion. A refreshing astringent tonic and powder foundation — to tone combination. $1.25.

If you value youth and beauty you owe it to yourself to give this unique cream a trial. Great European doctors and dermatologists know it as the one truly *scientific* cleanser. No other preparation is remotely like it!

Thirty days is more than ample to prove its powers. And often definite gains can be seen from day to day.

You will notice almost at once that your skin is growing smoother. Softer. More satiny in texture. Then blemishes start to shrink and disappear. And thus slowly but surely your skin regains — and retains — the tone and radiance of youth.

The formula of Pasteurized Cream was discovered in Vienna thirty years ago. Recently, Mme. Rubinstein improved it, adapted it to specific types of skins, and made it available to the women of America at the surprisingly low price of one dollar.

HOW IT ACTS — Pasteurized Cream penetrates through the epidermis to the ducts of the moisture glands. And there it attacks pore dirt by harmless, scientific means. Dissolves it. Brings it to the surface. If blackheads are present they go too. And with each tiny skin duct thus antiseptically cleansed, their return is indefinitely delayed.

Needless to say the formula of this remarkable cream is kept a secret. Briefly it is based on important fruit and vegetable oils. More than sixteen ingredients, from thirteen foreign lands, go into it. These ingredients are mixed and then, carefully

pasteurized. (An antiseptic process discovered by Pasteur, the famous French scientist.) They are actually *heated to more than 350° F . . .* more than twice the heat to which ordinary creams are subjected.

IN TWO CONSISTENCIES — To make this Pasteurized Cream effective for every type of skin, Mme. Rubinstein has prepared it in two consistencies. "Pasteurized Face Cream" for normal skins or for skins that tend towards oiliness. And "Pasteurized Face Cream Special" for skins that tend to be dry.

They are both priced at one dollar. And, being 5 times concentrated, they are extremely economical to use.

A HOME BEAUTY TREATMENT — For a complete skin-clearing treatment, Mme. Rubinstein suggests the daily use of two additional preparations in conjunction with Pasteurized Face Cream.

"Skin Clearing Cream" ($1.00) applied directly after cleansing with your Pasteurized Cream, stimulates the facial blood circulation. Clarifies the skin by natural methods, and banishes skin "depression."

Then "Skin Toning Lotion" ($1.25) should follow. This unique lotion acts as a refreshing astringent and as a perfect foundation for your face powder.

All these preparations are used in the scientific treatments given in her American and European salons. You will find them immediately effective, as well as easy and pleasant to use at home.

HELENA RUBINSTEIN'S Pasteurized Cream
THE ONE SCIENTIFIC SKIN CLEANSER · PRICE ONE DOLLAR

IMPORTANT: Every day thousands upon thousands of women seek specialized beauty treatment at Mme. Rubinstein's Salons in New York, Boston, Chicago, Detroit, Toronto, Paris, London, Rome, Milan, and Cannes.

This continuous personal contact with women of all types has given her an astonishing knowledge of women's skins that could never be obtained by laboratory research alone. It has been one of the most important factors in the development of her scientific skin preparations as well as of her unique ranges, face powders, lipsticks. Her products are sold at all the leading department and drug stores.

Helena Rubinstein

Early claims for the beneficial effects of cosmetics could be quite extraordinary, as this advertisement for Helena Rubinstein's Pasteurized Cream demonstrates.

This portrait of Helena Rubinstein by Graham Sutherland is just one of the many she had painted of herself. Here her grand demeanor belies her small stature: she was four feet ten inches tall.

Helena Rubinstein

Elizabeth Arden did not like people, but she did like racehorses and became one of the leading money winners in the United States. Photographed here with Jewel's Reward, a top two-year-old.

Charles Revson, giving evidence at a 1959 congressional hearing after Revlon was accused of rigging "The $64,000 Question" TV program.

Charles Revson (left) presents a check to Marine Captain Charles McCutchen after the latter hit the jackpot on "The $64,000 Question."

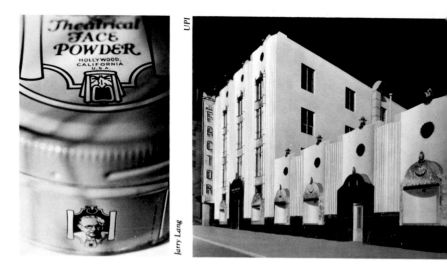

(Left) Max Factor knew the value of the personal touch: his theatrical face powder bore a picture, not of a beautiful woman, but of himself. *(Right)* "The world's greatest cosmetic factory," the $600,000 makeup studio opened with great fanfare by Max Factor in Hollywood on November 26, 1935. There were 3,000 invited guests at the affair and a further 6,000 gate-crashers.

Women wanted to look like their favorite movie stars, many of whom insisted that Max Factor personally do their screen makeup. Here Max Factor and "blonde bombshell" Jean Harlow try out his rouge.

Sam Kallish, a "disciple" of Charles Revson and a controversial figure in the industry. After the death of Revson, Kallish had a short, rather unhappy period as head of Max Factor on the West Coast.

Max Factor, Jr., took on the main creative responsibilities for the family company after his father's death in 1938.

(*Left*) Jean Shrimpton, who symbolized the "swinging sixties." On the basis of her face alone, Yardley of London established a hold in the United States which it has never lost. (*Right*) Mary Quant, the woman who put sex into cosmetics advertising in the United Kingdom in the 1960s.

Opium, the perfume that launched couturier Yves Saint-Laurent as a major cosmetics manufacturer in the United States, and made him the target of attack by the Chinese-American community.

Rebecca Blake/Yves Saint Laurent Parfums Corp.

Serge Lutens/Shiseido

Serge Lutens/Shiseido

SHISEIDO Corporate Image

Practice Shiseido
It gives great pleasure to your skin.

⊕ SHISEIDO

(Left) The lure of the mysterious East comes across in this Shiseido corporate advertisement. *(Right)* This Western model was given an Easternized look in Shiseido of Japan's advertisement for its range of skin creams.

SSC&B Advertising/The Noxell Corp.

The good skin look of Clean Make-up.

The look is pure Cover Girl.
The clean is pure Noxzema.

Cover Girl Clean Make-up

Cheryl Tiegs, currently the world's highest-paid model. Noxell Corporation is paying her agency $1.5 million over five years for the use of her face for cosmetics endorsements. Similarly, her hair is "owned" by Bristol-Myers.

Joseph and Estée Lauder, the aristocrats of the cosmetics world, at the 1981 inauguration of President Ronald Reagan.

Joseph Ronchetti, the man responsible for much of the growth at Elizabeth Arden's since its founder's death.

Michel Bergerac's corporate-executive style has replaced Charles Revson's entrepreneurial flair at Revlon with outstanding success.

severely unnatural; perfumes were widely used and much powder, accompanied by "beauty patches," covered the face. Exaggerated styles in dress, hair and cosmetics were to continue throughout the seventeenth and eighteenth centuries.

During this period, some exotic cosmetics were used. Apart from white lead, there were such products as Aqua Toffana, which contained arsenic. This lotion, like white lead, served two purposes—one to make the skin more beautiful, the other to get rid of one's enemies. Its maker, an Italian woman named Teofania, was eventually hanged in 1633 after a series of poisonings of people using the water, and her activities led to one of the earliest impositions of government regulations. The Italian government decreed that all poisons must be registered and that those buying them must sign for them. Later on, in 1692, a similar law was passed in France, following an equally gruesome episode of poisonings there.

Meanwhile, considerable advances were being made in cosmetics and perfumery, but the industry was of course very small in scale. Cosmetics were made by chemists, and there were a few spice merchants and the like who sold products. One of the names from this era that still exists is 4711 Eau de Cologne, which was produced in the city of Cologne in the early eighteenth century by an Italian family. The trademark of the company has been owned by the French firm of Roger and Gallet since 1862. Other names that have survived from this period are Houbigant, Yardley, Pears, Floris and Geigy. But many cosmetic products were still made in the home, as they had been for years. The housewife bought her materials from the chemist and spice shops, using her own recipes, which were often family secrets handed down from one generation to another.

All this began to change in the nineteenth century with the growth of large-scale industrialization and, in particular, the increasing worldwide economic significance of the United States. The century was one of extraordinary progress; it saw not only the setting up of cosmetics and pharmaceutical companies, but also the development of new kinds of basic materials and the establishment of colleges and other institutions specializing in pharmacology. This in turn led to further developments in cosmetics, notwithstanding the suppression of the Victorian era of many forms of self-adornment.

Many of the giant industrial conglomerates with interests in toiletries and cosmetics had their early beginnings in the nineteenth century. Just a few of the names illustrate the energetic thrust of the entrepreneurs who set up business in those early days. In 1806, William Colgate opened a soap, starch and candles factory in the United States; later, in 1873, his was the first company to make toothpaste; and later still, Colgate-Palmolive was to number the ill-fated Helena Rubinstein among its companies. In 1828 the House of Guerlain was founded; this company remains the property of the founding French family today. In 1835, Eugene Rimmel, who later wrote an enchanting book on perfumes, opened a shop with a backup laboratory in London; later, in 1854, he became the first-ever perfume manufacturer to employ women.

Pfizer entered the American arena in 1849. Although it began as a chemical company, it was later to extend its interests into cosmetics. In 1852, Beecham Limited, now a leading British pharmaceuticals, toiletries and cosmetics company, started making proprietary medicines. It set up a subsidiary in the U.S. in 1895. The year 1854 saw the House of Bourjois products from France on the market for the first time, and four years later E. R. Squibb, now the parent company of Charles of the Ritz, set up a research laboratory and factory in New York. R. A. Chesebrough (later to merge with Pond's) came onto the scene in 1870 with Vaseline, which was to become an important ingredient in many toiletry products. In 1872, Shiseido, the Japanese company that is now the third-biggest cosmetics company in the world, was formed. From Germany in 1882 came Nivea Creme from P. Beiersdorf and Company. Lever Brothers, now renamed Unilever, and the British end of the Anglo-Dutch toiletries and food group, made its first appearance at Port Sunlight, near Liverpool, in England. Eli Lilly, now the parent company of Elizabeth Arden, was formed in 1876.

Perhaps fairly described the "first lady of modern cosmetics," Harriet Hubbard brought out Luxuria cold cream in 1886. She introduced a sales pitch that had not been used before; she asked ladies who were leaders in society to provide testimonials that she could use to impress other customers. Her company, which was bought by Unilever in 1969, is now established in Paris. Johnson and Johnson and Bristol-Myers were both established in 1887, and Richard Hudnut a year later, all in the U.S. The last decade of the century saw the setting up of the Manufacturing Perfumers Association of the United States.

So, by the beginning of the twentieth century, the seeds of the industry were well established. The big names that were to dominate the post-World War II decades had not yet arrived, but, significantly, the conglomerates into which many of them were to be absorbed were already trading. The pace of expansion of the cosmetics industry quickened in the new century, and the developments spread over many continents. In 1905, Coty began to produce perfumes in France, and in America a year later, the Pure Food and Drug Act was passed, the first modern attempt by government to control the industry. In 1905, Charles Nessler, a hairdresser from Germany, developed the first permanent wave, and in 1906 the seven sisters named Ogilvie, three of whom were later to work for a time with Elizabeth Arden, arrived in New York from Canada to specialize in hair and scalp treatments. Over in Europe around this time, Eugene Schueller, a chemist in Paris, was working on a new hair dye that he called L'Oreal Compound Henna, and the Ogilvie sisters decided to use it. Today L'Oreal is the third-biggest cosmetics company in the world, and it is still controlled by Schueller's descendants and the Nestlé group of Switzerland. The pre-World War I period saw Elizabeth Arden and Helena Rubinstein set up in New York, though Madame Rubinstein already by this time had salons in Australia, Paris and London. The scene was set for the tremendous growth that has followed ever since.

This outline shows how in the last century big business has harnessed a fundamental human desire to look good—and made a fortune out of it. While other civilizations have just got on with the business of covering themselves with cosmetics, this has been the century of self-analysis. We are constantly being told why we do whatever we do, and research into the use of cosmetics has told us what we always knew: that cosmetics make us feel good, or as the Cosmetic, Toiletry and Fragrance Association put it in November 1979: "Cosmetic products might touch only the skin, but their beneficial effects on the whole person are profound. Products such as skin and body-care lotions; moisturizers; shampoos; hair conditioners; hair-coloring products; eye, lip, cheek and nail products; cleaners, fragrances, powders and deodorants help people feel at their best *in almost every relationship that life has to offer*" (my italics).

That, in a nutshell, is what cosmetics are all about, our relationships with one another. We are said to feel inadequate without a cosmetic covering. People are judged by how they look—so there is a universal need to look right. A CTFA survey quotes anthropologist Harry Shapiro, who wrote: ". . . so universal is this urge to improve on nature that one is almost tempted to regard it as an instinct. Aside from such fundamental drives as food, love, security and the expression of maternal solicitude, I can think of few forms of human behavior that are more common to mankind as a whole."

One can find all this acceptable, but is it enough to explain the phenomenon of the world's vast cosmetics industry today? It all goes much further than just wanting to help us look good. The trade wants us to look good in quite a different way this year from last year. And next year it will want us to look different again. True, the companies today stress their strong attachment to skin care, but it is in persuading people, and women particularly, that they must change the color of their lipstick, eye shadow and rouge every six months or so if they are to stay in fashion, which has provided the real growth in profits for the industry. As the wise Hazel Bishop remarks: "This is an industry with built-in obsolescence. The trick is to get the new colors out before the old bottles and containers are quite empty. Women can be easily persuaded that these are now out of date and that they must move on to a new color."

This is how it is done.

SIX

LITTLE DABS OF POWDER, LITTLE POTS OF PAINT...

*Darling, at the Beautician's you buy your (a)
hair (b) complexion (c) lips (d) dimples and (e)
teeth. For like amount you could just as well
buy a face.*

—Anonymous

Any illusions one might have that the regular use of creams, tonics and lotions might help to slow down the aging processes vanishes the moment one talks to dermatologists or cosmetics chemists. The best one can hope for is keeping skin in a good condition by cleaning it regularly and polishing it the way shoes are polished. Only plastic surgery offers some hope of *looking* younger, but there is still no way of keeping the skin youthful. Our skin is as old as we are.

"Your skin," a leading dermatologist told me, "is like a mackintosh: creams and water just will not go through it. All you can do by using cosmetics is keep the surface in good condition." National regulations regarding cosmetics confirm this view. According to the American Food and Drug Administration, cosmetics are "articles which are intended to be rubbed, poured, sprinkled or sprayed or introduced into, or otherwise applied to, the human body for cleaning, beautifying, promoting attractiveness or altering the appearance without affecting the body's structure or function." The European Economic Community Directive similarly states that "cosmetic product means any preparation intended to be placed in contact with superficial parts of the body or with teeth and mouth with a view principally for perfuming, cleaning, protecting, keeping in good condition, changing appearance and preventing body odours."

These definitions make it clear that twentieth-century cosmetics are superficial products that are designed to be put onto the surface of the skin and that they do not have any therapeutic effect. If any product penetrates the skin, it moves out of the area of cosmetics and becomes a drug, subject to quite different governmental rules and regulations. It is also clear that cosmetic products are not only the skin creams and decorative colorings that women (and sometimes men) apply to their faces, but also a vast range of toilet preparations for application to various parts of the body, and perfumes as well. Altogether there are close to 300 different products from cold creams, cleansing creams, moisturizing creams, foundation creams, through lipsticks, eye shadows, mascaras, rouges, blushers, to body oils, bath oils, hand creams, toothpastes, shampoos, hair colorings and nail enamels.

Not one of these products can make a fundamental change in the composition of the body; all they can do is clean, soften or decorate its surface. That fact has not stopped manufacturers throughout history from appropriating to their cosmetics products almost mystical powers. It can truthfully be said that never have people been less misled about the properties and possibilities of a cosmetic than they are today. Governments have seen to it that no misleading claims can be made, and the penalties for so doing in most industrialized countries are severe. Not one of the following advertisements from the April 1980 issue of the British magazine *Harpers and Queen* makes a claim that cannot be substantiated:

First, *Millenium*, a new Elizabeth Arden product that offers "a cell renewal strategy" that "not only makes your skin look younger and fresher from the *outside*, it also helps restore its more youthful functioning on the *inside*." It goes on to explain, quite accurately, that skin cells die and are replaced by others and that this process slows down with age as the outer layers of the skin take longer to slough off. The product will help "to emulsify and disperse impurities and to remove stubborn makeup and dulling surface and cells from the outside." Fancy words for keeping the skin clean for the cleanser and tonic in the range. Then, from the inside, the day and night renewal creams will "provide external protection against water loss and environmental hazard, but also act within the skin to replace daily moisture loss, to accelerate the natural skin renewal process and to reawaken the skin's ability to care for itself." Fancy words again, but all they mean is that the creams will stop water from getting out—and this is the chief factor in drying skin—and dirt from getting in. The advertisement does not suggest that using the cosmetics range can keep skin cells alive or create new ones. No cosmetic can do that, and to so claim would put the manufacturer at risk from the Law. The advertisement is subtle, suggesting that the cosmetics range is good for the existing skin, without suggesting any fundamental change in it.

Next, Eterna 27 twenty-four-hour cream from Revlon. "It works fast . . . breaks up moisture instantly. Releases tiny 'moisture molecules' that work within the skin's surface . . . to help supply dry cells with moisture." This cream contains "progenitin," which is said to "plump up cells to fight the dry skin of aging." Again there are no false claims here, and although the cream is said to work from "within," the within is actually the skin's surface, and so no change in the structure of the skin is claimed.

From Helena Rubinstein comes Skin Life Cream with GAM. (We are not told what GAM is except that it is "an extraordinary scientific discovery that closely resembles your skin's own natural fluid".) That means water. It will make your skin "look softer, smoother and supple": it probably will. What it won't do is halt the aging process, which it does not claim to do. All in all, a modest cream.

B23 marks a "new era of Orlane skin preparation." Orlane (a part of Max Factor, not, as one might imagine, a French make) is also after the mature woman. "B23 helps to combat dryness and dehydration (which can look so aging) by actually working to hold the moisture in the skin." In other words, the cream slows down the loss of water just as the other creams do. To enhance the French feeling and lend an air of added sophistication, the advertisement concludes: "Chaque peau a son secret. Orlane l'a découvert."

Lancôme offers Progrès, which is merely a range of "deep treatment creams," which are a "major development." No one could object to the description that they are "gentle and non-greasy, designed to help keep your skin soft and supple." Here Lancôme (a subsidiary of L'Oreal) is relying on its reputation in the cosmetics field and making very few claims indeed. In the same issue of *Harpers*, in a separate advertisement, Lancôme also offers Maquisatin, which is also "gentle": it "smooths on and will not dry your skin." With "Bienfait du Matin," Lancôme completes its offerings. This cream is the "morning skin care cream that protects, stimulates and tones your skin, giving a natural transparent look that lasts the whole day through."

Frances Denney offers a full range of skin products. Again the emphasis is on keeping moisture in the skin. The claim is modest: "Today, Frances Denney offers you a simple truth, backed by years of experience. A routine to protect the natural loveliness of your skin and save it from losses it can't afford." Equalia from Vichy also helps "your skin maintain the water balance essential for beauty." Equalia, it states, "is not a moisturizer in that it does not try to put moisture into your skin." If it did that, it would not be a cosmetic but a drug. "Instead it helps your skin keep the water it already contains."

In that issue of *Harpers* all the other cosmetics advertisements are for decorative cosmetics. It is noticeable that all these advertisements concentrate on the keeping of moisture in the skin. Without moisture, the skin become dry-looking and flaky and certainly will more quickly look old. But just how different are these creams? Is one preferable to another? And perhaps most important of all, are expensive creams, as most of those advertised in *Harpers* are, better and more effective than cheaper ranges?

All the creams advertised today have as their basis the original cold cream formula, said to have been developed by the Greek physician Galen in A.D. 150. This was a mixture of water, beeswax and olive oil with some rose petals added to give the cream a pleasant smell. The most important ingredient was water, as it still is in today's cosmetics, and the mixture was called "cold" cream because the water evaporated on the skin, bringing a cooling feeling.

The twentieth-century cosmetics industry is founded on water. All the modern creams, which have of course changed substantially from the original Galen cream, are still water, oils and wax, plus other ingredients. The proportions used in different creams vary considerably. For cleansing creams, the proportion of water is reduced and oils and waxes, which melt as they touch the skin, are substituted. Cleansing lotions and foams simply contain extra water. Their cleansing effect is no different from that of creams; they merely feel different on the skin. Whatever the formula, it will rarely be as effective in cleansing as soap and water.

Moisture creams, night creams, all-day creams, morning creams, whatever the names—are all also based on the old cold cream. They may look and feel very different, but all are basically similar. They are designed to be left on the skin for some time and therefore have a less-greasy texture than cleansing creams, but once again they are basically oils and water. In modern creams, various other ingredients are added; some contain chemicals to preserve the cream to give it a shelf life of some years, and some have perfumes. A few manufacturers make a virtue out of having no perfume in a product, and then charge more for it; others use fancy oils rather than plain lanolin or petroleum jelly, but there is as yet no evidence that any particular oil is better for the skin than another.

How the creams feels on the skin depends on whether the oil in it has a low or high melting-point. If it is low, it will feel greasy on the skin; if high, it will not. The famous, well-established Pond's vanishing cream has a high melting point and is called vanishing cream because it seems to disappear into the skin. It does not. Putting oil on dry skin will not add moisture to it, as it is the loss of water, not oil, which is the main cause of dry skin, and most of the water evaporates when it is applied to the skin.

This fact inevitably raises the question whether there is any point at all in using cosmetic creams. The answer seems to be yes. Although oil will not add moisture, it can help to slow down the rate at which moisture evaporates from the skin. It also helps the skin to look soft and smooth and thereby improves its appearance. For most customers, the choice of a cream or creams will be a matter of personal preference for a particular texture of cream or lotion or a certain scent or no scent at all, and, primarily perhaps, a matter of cost.

Of the cosmetics dollar, 60 cents goes to the manufacturer and 40 cents to the retailer. Of the manufacturer's 60 cents, only 8 cents are spent on raw materials. The rest is used as follows: 11 cents on packaging, 10 cents on promotion, 19 cents on wages and salaries and administration, 2 cents on interest charges and other small expenses—leaving a 10-cent profit before taxes. Even with such low costs of raw materials, the use of the traditional lanolin and petroleum jelly rather than one of the more exotic oils may mean that the product is cheaper. It is questionable whether these newer and sometimes much-vaunted oils are any more effective than lanolin or petroleum jelly at stopping the skin from losing its moisture. And even it they have properties that can improve the skin, they are unlikely to penetrate it sufficiently to have any markedly different effect.

Throughout history, magical claims have been made for an endless variety of products. At various times, the heralded ingredient has been ambergris, henna, kohl, salts of mercury or white lead. Some of these have been harmless, but others, like the last two, can be downright poisonous.

The twentieth century, too, has not been without its new "breakthroughs" and "discoveries." These have included algae, aloe vera juice, vitamin E, lemon, eggs, collagen, cocoa butter, royal jelly, organic cosmetics, mink oil and turtle oil. The last has a long history of efficacy. There is an old wives' story that a girl would retain her youth (in both senses perhaps) by using turtle oil on her skin on the night of the full moon, provided she was with a young blond man. Apart from the fact that turtles are known to live a long time and therefore might make good advertising copy, there seems to be no scientific reason why their oil should be more effective in cosmetics than any other. The same goes for mink oil. There may be suitable connections that can be exploited for commercial purposes in the public mind between the expensive and beautiful fur of the mink, which may make a woman look elegant, and oil from the animal, which may similarly help the user to be beautiful. Unfortunately, there is no scientific evidence to support such a belief.

Royal jelly, another very expensive product, is extracted from bees. It may be taken internally or used in cosmetics, and it has also been the subject of extravagant claims. Such claims are no longer permitted, but the memory lingers and the jelly has its advocates.

Whenever one looks at such new products, the thought is apt to occur: "There is no scientific evidence . . ." Take algae, for example; claims are sometimes made that it prevents wrinkles from forming and moisturizes skin. Algae is collected from seaweed, and although it does not harm the skin, it is unlikely to offer anything that an ordinary cream does not. The same is true for aloe vera juice. It is more than 99 percent water, the rest being amino acids and fats. Cocoa butter, from cacao beans, also has no special properties and although it is not generally harmful, there is some evidence that certain people are allergic to it. Its main use today is in suntan products.

Eggs turn up from time to time as a cosmetic fad. They are used in facials and in some shampoo products. Once again, there is no scientific evidence that they can offer the user anything special. The same is so for lemon. Lemon juice is acid and if used in shampoos will remove soap from the hair that has been washed in hard water. As most shampoos manufactured today are not soap- but detergent-based, there is no particular point in using lemon, except perhaps for the smell. And that may well be all it is. Most lemon smells in cosmetics, soaps and detergents today are not lemon at all, but an extract with almost no acid in it at all. This may be a good thing, as some people are allergic to lemon juice. There is no scientific evidence to suggest that the use of lemon improves cosmetics. The truth is the people like the lemon smell, and it has a strong advertising appeal.

Organic cosmetics—those made from fruits, vegetables, plants and herbs—are enjoying a vogue at present on the ground that, being "natural," they have more affinity with the skin than other products. That this is so is highly unlikely. It needs to be remembered that all the early cosmetics contained organic materials, and these materials were commonly abandoned when better and more efficient products were developed. There is, in fact, a danger present in organic cosmetics which is not present in others. There is a greater chance of contamination, and such cosmetics may be better kept refrigerated, although today in cosmetics laboratories the organic materials are reduced to dry particles, which diminishes the possibilities of oxidation and therefore contamination.

Vitamin E, the so-called youth vitamin, seems essential to energy, vitality and sexual potency. The problem is an unknown: Just how much of it is needed? The suspicion is that we need very little and that the amount we need is found in any adequate diet.

Nevertheless, in recent years, people have been swallowing Vitamin E pills in attempts to retain their youthful energy, and it was inevitable that the fad would extend itself to cosmetics. There is no evidence whatsoever that the application of Vitamin E cream will keep the skin young. Any improvement that we may think we see is probably psychological. From time to time, other vitamins have been included in cosmetic products; as the extent to which the cream penetrates the skin is infinitesimal, such creams have neither a harmful, nor a beneficial, effect.

Collagen is the latest "miracle" ingredient, and many cosmetics chemists seem convinced by the claims made for it that it penetrates the skin. Once again, however, nothing has been proved, and it is doubtful that collagen does more than any other cosmetic cream that is used frequently and regularly to slow the loss of moisture from the skin. Collagen seems to have something going for it when one looks at the formula. It is a protein substance found in tissues that connect one part of the body with another, in cartilages and bones. It is important because changes in collagen fibers can cause wrinkling and the aging of the skin. The question is whether adding collagen to a cosmetic can also add collagen to the skin, or reverse an aging process that has already taken place. The chances are that it will not, that collagen in cosmetics merely has the same effect as any other cosmetic in slowing down the loss of moisture from the skin. Cosmetics, one should never forget, deal only with the epidermis, the very top layer of the skin. Cosmetics companies often forget this and talk about "deep-pore cleansing" and "penetration." No cosmetics chemist would make this mistake.

Hormone creams are another question altogether. Like vitamins, female hormones can be taken in pill form or injected, and in recent years this form of treatment has become increasingly popular to help women through menopause or to help them retain a youthful appearance beyond it. It also has the strictly medical purpose of hormone-replacement therapy to prevent premature aging in women who have had a hysterectomy very early in their adult life. Even in these uses, there are some doubts about the efficacy of hormones, which, when applied in these ways, may be carcinogenic.

Hormone creams containing female hormones of the estrogen type, however, are now on sale in many countries. Since there is no more evidence that these creams penetrate the skin any more efficiently than other creams, it is questionable that they have more than a surface effect, though the hormone is present in such small quantities it appears to do no harm either. The epidermis in older people is thinner than that in the young, and though claims have been made that the creams thicken the epidermis, there is no evidence that they do. Hormone creams work the same way as other creams in slowing down the evaporation of moisture from the skin.

The claims for hormone creams go further than thickening the epidermis. Some are said to reach the dermis, which is a thicker fibrous layer of the skin which supports the epidermis. This, too, becomes thinner with age and is unable to hold as much water as before. If water retention could be maintained, then the dermis would be able to support the epidermis better, and this, in consequence, would make the skin look less wrinkled with age. There is, however, no evidence that hormone creams reach this second layer. Below the dermis lies a layer of subcutaneous fat. This, too, thins with age, and hormone creams cannot restore fat to this layer. So the implication of the use of hormone creams is the same as with any other skin cream: they cannot restore skin to its youthful appearance, but they may slow down the aging process.

All skin creams have more or less the same constituents, perhaps plus a vitamin here, a hormone there, regardless of which part of the body they are to be used on. Color cosmetics, too, are made in the same way, with the quantities of the constituents depending on the intended use of the product. All lipsticks, for example, contain lanolin, an oil-wax mixture to achieve the right consistency, perfume and color. Their purpose is obvious and the results are visible. Today there is little to make one preferable to another; price differences are the result of packaging and marketing costs and the reputation of the manufacturer.

Skin fresheners, tonics, and astringents are designed to make the skin feel fresh and clean. They often contain alcohol, which is useful for the quick removal of makeup and also makes the skin feel cool, refreshed and tightened. Alcohol, however, does not suit every skin, and some manufacturers virtuously claim that their product "contains no alcohol." It is often said that the use of tonics and astringents can close open skin pores. This is a false claim; pores cannot be shrunk in this way.

Does this all mean that a youthful and attractive appearance cannot be maintained or achieved? Not at all. To begin with, it is only in societies like our own that the pursuit of lasting youth is paramount, that only a youthful appearance is considered attractive. And there are signs even in Western civilization that the youth cult is beginning to diminish, probably as those who were young when this mood reached its pinnacle begin to reach middle and old age themselves and realize the compensations that maturity can bring. An attractive person is attractive at any age, and cosmetics have little to do with it.

Many civilizations have concerned themselves with skin care, but the preoccupation of trying to stop the aging process is a twentieth-century one. In women, obvious skin aging accelerates with the menopause, around fifty, although it actually starts for everyone at the moment of birth. That the effects of the menopause apply to a vast proportion of women is a relatively recent phenomenon because it has not been until our time that so many women live beyond the menopause and therefore experience aging. Previously this was not so. Men age, too, but their aging process commonly starts earlier and is more gradual, because there is not the same fast drying-up of the skin which the fall in hormone levels brings to women's skins.

No cosmetic can stop aging: nothing can, so far. Any claims of miraculous treatment, whether by the application of something to the skin, by diet, by vitamins or by exercise, can be disregarded. But there is one way to maintain and even reachieve an appearance of youth, though this, too, cannot make the skin "young." It is through plastic surgery.

The art and science of plastic surgery has an honorable ances-
try. It is known to have been practiced in ancient times as far back
as the Persians. It originally seems to have been done to change
facial appearance; "nose jobs" (rhinoplasty) have been popular for
centuries. It is in the twentieth century, however, that the range
of operations has widened enormously to take in practically the
whole body, and that face lifts to restore faces to something like
their former glory have become extremely popular with both men
and women.

The first written work on plastic surgery appeared in 1597, *De
Chirugia Curtorum*, by Gaspare Tagliacozzi. In addition to the
text, there were woodcuts showing various kinds of cosmetic operations, including alteratons to ears and noses and repairs to cleft
lips. There was little place for this kind of nonsense in seven-
teenth-century Italy, and after his death Tagliacozzi was declared
a sorcerer. Prohibitions have eased since then, however, and a
major step forward in plastic surgery occurred during the Second
World War, when surgeons developed new techniques to repair
burned and damaged faces with skin grafts and in some cases the
replacement of lost noses and chins.

Today no one knows how many plastic surgery operations are
performed each year, because there is little regulatory control,
but it is thought that in the United Sates alone the number is
approaching 2 million a year and increasing—divided almost
equally between men and women—by around 10 percent a year.
Many of these operations are performed to alter such physical
characteristics as crooked noses and predominating ears, but
today one can rebuild almost the entire body with safety. On the
face, the jaw line can be changed, bags under the eyes removed
and eyebrows lifted. The bosom can be increased in size or reduced; thighs trimmed and abdomens tucked in. The last appeals
to persons who have lost a great deal of weight but have reached
the age when the skin is not so accommodating as it was and does
not shrink back into place where the weight has been shed.
Women tend to go for the full range of operations; men are particularly interested in face lifts. This, too, is an outgrowth of the

youth cult of our modern society; and many working men no doubt feel that if they look middle-aged they will slip behind in the executive race. They could be right.

It is, of course, the face lift that most concerns those who wish to look young, and today it is the most popular of the cosmetic operations. People simply are no longer prepared to put up with an aging appearance—if they can afford to do something about it. Prices vary: a limited face lift can cost a few thousand dollars, depending on where it takes place. As always, surgeons in the fashionable cities can charge two or three times as much as an out-of-town surgeon. The full job can run into several thousands of dollars.

What happens in a face lift is that the skin is loosened, pulled up and back, and cut. This means that sagging skin disappears. Small scars may be created and remain on the hairline, although newer techniques cut the skin behind the hairline, so that there are no visible scars at all. Double and treble chins can also be cut away, and the scars are aligned with the lines that appear naturally on every neck. Droopy eyelids can also be cut away and bags removed by incisions below the eye which allow the fats that have built up there to be removed.

Of course these operations do not alter the look of the skin that remains, and the result can be a taut youthful face with an old-looking skin. Help is at hand for this too, and the face lift can be followed by chemical peeling, which removes the top layer of skin and can restore some of the bloom of youth. This is a long process, however: after the operation the skin stays red and blotchy for several months, and recovery after the operation can be painful. "Dermabrasion" is also tried by some people. This is the smoothing off of the outer layer with wire wheels or sandpaper. It works and will remove small wrinkles and any old small scars resulting from such skin conditions as acne. The price, quite apart from the financial cost, is again a red face for some months.

California has become the world's center of cosmetic surgery today. It is supposed to be the land where dreams come true, and these dreams include being beautiful. Why put up with what nature gave you when art and science can repair her mistakes? And why hesitate when it is—if properly done—safe? Plastic surgery properly done does not harm anyone, unless perhaps psychologically if the new face or shape does not bring the desired change in appearance, in self-confidence or, perhaps the ultimate hope, in life-style.

There are other dangers. It is reckoned now that 20 percent of those persons visiting cosmetics clinics in California are there to have mistakes corrected that were made by another practitioner, who might not have been qualified as a plastic surgeon. At least 30,000 people are said to be working as plastic surgeons in California. The whole of the United States has fewer than 3,000 certified plastic surgeons, so many people clearly are operating without certification, which is not compulsory. Any person who has qualified as an M.D. can act as a plastic surgeon after his or her general training has been completed. And many do. The same is true of doctors in other parts of the world, but there have not yet been abuses anywhere else on the same scale as in California. There is no doubt, however, that the practice could spread.

In an attempt to stop doctors who are in effect charlatans, genuine plastic surgeons have set up the American Society of Plastic and Reconstructive Surgery. The society has well over 2,000 members, or about 80 percent of all certified plastic surgeons. A Patients Protection Committee has also been established. This checks on abuses, and in the three years since it was set up, complaints to the committee have risen sharply. There are five or six major complaints each month and many other small ones.

Operations by charlatans and unqualified doctors could be stopped, but stricter federal and state controls are needed. Clinics, unlike doctors, advertise their services, and their advertising campaigns are often lavish. This could be controlled, and there is no reason why professional qualifications should not be insisted upon.

There has been, however, marked reluctance on the part of the authorities to act to control this very lucrative business, and in the meantime many men and women are spending thousands of dollars to undergo what in effect amounts to mutilation. The situation prevalent today in California could well spread, unless governments and consumer protection groups become more vigilant. There are fewer abuses in Europe, but even so medical authorities there are becoming increasingly concerned about the number of operations which go wrong and the lax conditions under which doctors are allowed to practice cosmetic surgery. A major problem in the United Kingdom is the reluctance of family doctors to refer patients to reputable plastic surgeons, except in cases of gross deformity. Many doctors believe that concern over one's looks is a trivial matter and refuse even to discuss possible referral to a specialist. As a result, those seeking plastic surgery do not always go to reputable clinics. At the beginning of 1981, the British Medical Association urged a code of practice under which plastic surgeons would accept only those patients referred to them by a general practioner. It seems doubtful, however, that without government legislation, which is highly unlikely, the position will improve. The best that can be hoped for is that the attitude of doctors towards plastic surgery changes and that they come to recognize just how very seriously some people take slight physical defects.

Plastic surgery has clear and observable results provided it is done properly, but it often creates as many problems as it solves and does not on its own satisfy those people who not only want to look young, but also to feel young as welll. All too often, after plastic surgery, a tired old body looks in the mirror at a vigorous young face. So people will often adopt diets, exercise programs, vitamin-pill regimes in an attempt to slow down the aging process. The medical profession, too, is studying the problem. One suggested solution is cell therapy. This is not just a twentieth-century phenomenon: skin transplants were mentioned by Hippocrates, and throughout medical history some doctors have maintained that the incorporation of human or animal cells from a young or even unborn body into an old one can have a rejuvenating effect. Greek philosophers like Aristotle and the Elder Pliny mentioned the possibilities—when they themselves got old, of course.

Experiments continued, and in 1771, Dr. John Hunter established in Britain that testes could successfully be implanted into castrated roosters. Later experiments included the transplantation of endocrine glands and the implantation of monkeys' testes into old men. In 1667, Jean Baptiste Denis transfused sheep blood into man. This was the beginning of today's widespread use of blood transfusions in a great variety of medical and surgical situations. The present time has seen the beginnings of similar techniques in bone-marrow transplants, but these are still at a very early stage of experimentation.

Where do cosmetics come into all this? At the beginning they did not, but the past fifty years have seen the development of what Paul Niehans, a Swiss doctor, called "tissular transplantation," which has come to have implications for physical appearance and has now been introduced into cosmetics. In 1927, Niehans first tried out his new technique by injecting eosinophil cells from young calves into the lobe of the pituitary gland of a human dwarf. The dwarf grew about 12.5 inches. Encouraged by this success, Dr. Niehans continued his experiments and in 1931 opened the Clinic La Prairie in Switzerland. In 1949 he used himself as a human guinea pig, injecting ice-cooled cells. At the same time, he began using fetal cells preserved by lyophilization. This process removes all the liquid substances from the cells, leaving them dry and preventing oxidation, which damages and destroys cells. Whether it was the treatment or not, Dr. Niehans lived until he was well over eighty, and it is said that during his career his methods attracted as "patients" such personalities as Sir Winston Churchill, Dr. Konrad Adenauer and Pope Pius XII. True or not, there were and are no shortages of patients at the doctor's clinic.

The treatment is simple and takes between a week and ten days. The patient, who of course does not necessarily suffer from any illness, goes into the clinic and receives a medical checkup. Two or three days later, assuming there are no medical contraindications, the patient receives an injection of the living cells of a special breed of black sheep. In the process, two sheep are killed, the mother and the lamb she is carrying, from which the cells are extracted, and the injection takes place immediately. Then the patient must rest for a few days, as a fever is quite common following the injections. The patient is then sent home and put on a course of placenta extracts and vitamins and told not to drink or smoke for three months. The cost is about $4,000.

The purpose is to make the patient feel well and rejuvenated, not necessarily to make him or her look younger. This kind of therapy is of course in its very early stages of experimentation and not all doctors accept its efficacy. Their doubts arise because of the very commercial nature of the operation, the possibility that disease will be transmitted by the injections or that allergies will develop, the absence of any evidence so far of the long-term effects of the treatment, the problem of controlling the dosage, and the lack of any proof of its efficacy from animal experiments.

Even its protagonists admit that cell therapy is still in its early stages. The problems must be investigated, and more clarification is needed. Even so, the inevitable has happened. Dr. Niehan's successors at the clinic have now produced a range of cosmetics under the name La Prairie.

The project began in 1975 when M. Gerard Fontaine, laboratory director at the clinic, thought that the cell therapy could be extended into the cosmetics field. The products would contain the tissue cells used in the injections and also collagen and elastin, the two new "in" ingredients in cosmetics, as well as various extracts. The clinic approached Dr. Nadja Avalle, a world-renowned cosmetics chemist who operates out of Sion, Switzerland, to formulate the creams. Dr. Avalle spent over two years developing the range, which was then launched in the world's major cosmetic markets. It is of course a cosmetic and cannot be compared with the claims made for the injection therapy. In its cosmetic form, its efficacy remains unproven, and, like all cosmetics, it is doubtful whether its constituents, even if beneficial, will penetrate the skin sufficiently to rejuvenate it or do more than slow down the aging process.

La Prairie has not been the only noncosmetics house to realize the potential profit where a cosmetic has a seemingly medical base. Maurice Messegue, renowned in France for his plant and herbal cures, has recently moved into the market with a range of treatment products based on flowers, plants and herbs. He will not become a major producer, but what he sells will have prestige and a high profit margin.

Even though basic formulas have changed very little in thousands of years, cosmetics companies and individual cosmetics chemists are continuously at work in search of a new scent, a new consistency for a cream, new colorings and new lotions. Every possible new raw material is tested to see if it would be suitable for a cosmetic or a perfume. The aim behind this is of course to make money. If companies do not come out with an endless stream of new products, the customer, who in the matter of cosmetic buying is very fickle, will turn to another brand. Moods change, fashions too, and what people wanted a year ago they do not want now, and what they want now may be passé in three months. This means that all the major companies have teams of chemists, laboratory technicians, creative marketing and product-planning executives, advertising artists and copywriters and salespeople all combining to think up new ideas, test and produce them and bring them profitably to the market.

The process is more or less the same whether it concerns a new perfume or a range of skin treatments or color cosmetics to be developed. First of all, the product-planning department will study the market trends. Their job is to create a product that fills a customer need, or creates one that was not there before. The planners study trends in the market and guess to some extent at changes in life-styles, because it is likely to be more than two years before a product is ready for the market. At a very early stage a decision is taken as to what part of the market the product is aiming for—prestige, medium-priced or low-priced. From this point, the product will have to take on some kind of personality. It will have to be different enough from anything else on the market to find a new niche. While the technical research is going on in the laboratory, the sales promotion staff and art directors and copywriters will be working with the marketing people to produce advertisements and other promotional material that will have an exciting appeal to the customer. During this period, the marketing department will be carrying out consumer research surveys to make as certain as possible that there will be a market for the product when it arrives. At this time, the product most probably will not have a name, at least not the one it will eventually have when it goes out on sale.

Deciding on the product name can be a difficult process. Women found the names of Revlon's Eterna 27 romantic, but Revson had merely taken the number from the number of the floor he worked on. The trend at present is for strong names, like Burberry, Millenium, Evidence. At other periods, romantic names have been chosen; Coco Chanel was actually able to get away without proper names at all and simply numbered her perfumes. It is doubtful if anyone could do that now, although of course when Chanel chose No. 5, there were no numbers 1, 2, 3 and 4. The suggestion—and it appealed to customers—was that she had tried four others and this was the first that she felt was good enough to sell. She went further than this with her next perfume and named it No. 19. Then came 22. What had happened to the rest? A good gimmick, but one that would not work twice. Many, many hours are spent in working out a name which, it is hoped, will find a similar strong and long-term appeal. Bill Randall, now making an exclusive line of cosmetics for the La Costa health farm in California, told me how Sea & Ski, the sun preparations company, came upon its most successful name quite accidentally after hours of discussion. "We wanted something that suggested that our cream was better than anyone else's. We tried Fast Tan, Fantastic Tan, Tan Fast. Nothing worked. Then the secretary said, 'What about Tanfastic?' It was absolutely right. Just one word, which got across everything we wanted to say."

Once a name is chosen and the concept of the range worked out, a marketing profile for the product is built up. This will include the rationale behind the product, the expected cost of the launch, how the product will fit in with existing products, the selling price, the projected level of sales and the target audience.

If these do not all fit together, the project may be abandoned, or the basic research may be begun all over again.

Assuming all is well, the chemists get on with the job of development in the company's laboratory. If a company is not particularly large, it may not have the full resources to do this and may call in outside chemists. I visited one of the chemists, Dr. Nadja Avalle, in Switzerland. Her physical plant is small, laboratory and plant occupying little more than one acre, but in it she produces a full range of cosmetics. She is able to turn out 30 tons of cosmetics in one month and has a turnover of $3.3 million a year. Dr. Avalle divides her time between producing her own cosmetics range and making cosmetics for other companies. Her clients include La Costa and La Prairie. Many of her clients keep their names secret because they want their customers to think they produce their cosmetics themselves.

From a small factory on an industrial trading estate outside Sion, set up twenty-five years ago, Dr. Avalle has developed a worldwide business, with additional factories in France and Milan. The Sion factory concentrates on skin-treatment products using herbs and natural animal products wherever possible, as she believes that these have a natural sympathy for the skin. Her formula for success is simple: she started as a chemist and continues as one, researching all the possible raw materials for their potential in cosmetics. "A cosmetics formula," she says, "is not a formula but a dossier. I must study one idea and test it thoroughly. It must be patch-tested, challenge-tested and then looked at from the point of view of allergies. Then the ingredients must fit in with the various government regulations. These can be a problem as they vary from country to country."

First of all, there is the new idea. Then the idea must be adapted to scientific principles. This may take months and sometimes even years. Dr. Avalle feels that with her small unit with everyone working together, she can sometimes develop a line rather more quickly than the giant companies with their corporate and sometimes bureaucratic structures. The final product must fit in well with the raw material base, so that the product is acceptable to the customer.

Once the basic formula is obtained, it is tested. First of all, it is patch-tested for irritancy. Rabbits are usually used for this purpose, and in an operation as small as Dr. Avalle's, the product goes to a specialized laboratory for these tests. The formula may be tested on a rabbit's skin, or in its eyes, which are far more delicate. All being well and no irritancy occurring, the product is then challenge-tested. This test ensures that the product will stay in good condition for a certain length of time and perform its functions properly through the period. Under various government regulations, a product must have a life of anything up to two years. If the product passes the test, beauticians are approached. They will find out whether the consumer likes the product: is it too greasy, not greasy enough, too heavy, too thick or too light? Most important, even after the animal tests, will it produce irritancy in human beings? If so, the process begins all over again.

The larger companies of course have their own laboratories where creams can be developed and tested. The process is exactly the same as the one used by Dr. Avalle; first the ingredients are tested for purity and safety, then the formulas are developed. Then comes the testing, which upsets some environmental groups, although the companies are at great pains to point out that they treat animals humanely.

If a new product is to be a fragrance, even the larger companies will call in outside experts. They draw up guidelines for the perfume, which are then sent to several perfume companies, who will have one of their perfume artists develop a scent based on these guidelines. The company will then choose the one it prefers about three months later.

Whether the new product is a cream, a color or a fragrance, the design department is meanwhile working on the packaging. Packaging is almost as important as the product itself, and eye-catching bottles, boxes and the use of new colors can do a great deal to achieve a successful launch. The final design is not a matter of chance. Some consumer testing may be done to see what the customer likes, and Andrew Philip at Shiseido told me that in his company in Japan, customers are watched through two-way mirrors to see how they react to different packaging and which they prefer. One way or another, the package ideas become a reality. Different packs on the same theme will be designed for different parts of the range. An engineer, a packaging designer and administrator and someone from the sales force will together iron out any problems concerning coordination of design, so that the look of the whole range becomes a harmonious whole. It is very important at this stage to be sure that the packaging meets the aim of the product. It is no use having a skittish or girlish look to a product designed for mature women: similarly, young women will be put off by ultra-sophisticated packaging. Most desirable of all is an entirely new concept in packaging, which will be so striking that the customer will break her purchasing habit and buy the new product. Mary Quant managed this in the British market when she produced startling black and silver packaging for her first cosmetics range in the 1960s.

By this time, the company will be considering the precise prices it is going to charge. Very early on, it will have decided which market it is going to attack, but the final decision on price may have a profound effect on the sales volume. It is of course very important to assess the realistic levels of consumer demand. A company like Estée Lauder, for instance, has a good idea of its consumer profile. To bring out an unduly cheap product would not produce substantially higher sales and might well damage the company's esteem among its existing and potential customers.

Only after all this is decided does manufacturing begin. Where, the customer may well be asking, does the actual cost of the product figure in this welter of design, marketing, promotion, merchandising, demand and manufacture? It is a reasonable question. Generally speaking, the actual raw materials making up the product are reckoned to cost only about eight cents out of every dollar of the final sales price. This figure may vary a little, but only a *very* little, depending on the raw materials used, but in cosmetics even the most expensive materials go such a long way that the amount in a single jar or bottle of a product has little effect on the product price. An ingredient may sound exotic, but in the amounts in which it exists in a cosmetic, it will not be expensive per item produced. How then does the final price build up? Wages will account for about 10 percent of the cost price of the product, and packaging, along with the raw materials, accounts for another 30 percent. Out of the remaining 60 percent, the company will have a promotion budget that may be very substantial, but if a suitable volume of sales is reached, the overall percentage cost of promotion may be very small. Then there are distribution costs. One way and another, the large producer can expect a minimum percentage gross profit of 20 percent and it may well be more. For smaller producers, profits of between 12 and 15 percent can be enough to keep the business running at a profit. But it was the large profit margins of the larger producers in the 1950s and sixties that made them so attractive to the profit-hungry conglomerates, who saw them as a means of raising overall group profitability.

As we have seen, there is very little basis for choosing one cleansing cream over another, one lipstick over its competitors, one night-cream priced at $25 over one at $5. Indeed, for specialty products, many companies choose the same source for their raw materials although the ultimate final price may be very different. Many cosmetics companies in Britain, Europe and the United States, for example, use the British firm of Smith and Nephew as a source of the basic cream for lipstick. Profit margins at the end of the day may be more or less the same regardless of the selling price. Estée Lauder, Revlon, Lanvin and Charles of the Ritz spend far more in promotion and packaging than is spent on promoting those cosmetics one buys in the drugstores or in cheaper chain stores. The lower the price, the greater the sales volume needed, and the way to profits is to find a proper balance between costs and revenue. The cosmetics companies have not found this task difficult in the twentieth century with the result that the industry dollar-for-dollar has been one of the most profitable for those who have succeeded in it. For many their skill has lain in marketing, which I will come to later.

SEVEN

...BUT IT'S ONLY SKIN DEEP

He was the mightiest of Puritans no less than of philistines who first insisted that beauty is only skin deep.

—Louis Kronenberger

At one time, cosmetics could impair the health of human beings or even kill them. Most notably, white lead ruined skin and made hair fall out, but women were still using it in quite modern times and some died from it. In the middle of the eighteenth century, Lady Coventry, a renowned beauty of the day, died at the age of twenty-seven from lead poisoning, which had been a major component of her makeup. Some cosmetics today can still cause damage to the skin and sometimes even to general health. Fear of cancer has become a major factor in the cosmetics industry, and the companies have developed highly sensitive machines to test a product for carcinogenic materials. It is now possible to isolate one carcinogenic part in every three million, though this process does not in itself indicate how likely cancer is to occur in human beings using a particular product. The attention is drawn to the

well-established correlation between certain biological and carcinogenic substances and to epidemological studies, which suggest
that the elevated instance of certain tumors in hairdressers and in
those engaged in cosmetics manufacture might be due to exposure to chemical carcinogens.

Approximately 1,000 chemicals altogether have been found to
produce cancer in animals: benzene, bergamot oil, tetrachloride
(a chlorinated hydrocarbon solvent), chloroform, cholesterol,
coal tar, DDT, lard, lemon oil, orange oil, phenobarbital and sex
hormones (natural and synthetic) are some of them but of the
total, only about 20 are so far known to cause cancer in man, and
some are known not to do so. The link between ultraviolet exposure and cancer is well known, and this has led the FDA in America to permit some companies to label suntan screen creams as
helping to prevent cancer because they screen the skin from the
ultraviolet rays of the sun.

But cancer is not the only problem: almost any product, not just
cosmetics, can have an adverse effect on someone. This does not
usually happen frequently enough to cause a product to be withdrawn from the market, but enough to warn some people that
they should be careful and stop using a product if they experience
any adverse reaction to it. The most frequent offenders in cosmetics and toiletries are suntan lotions, some skin lotions, bath
oils and soaps. These can contain a variety of products like acetic
acid, ammonia, peroxide, which not all skins care for. They may
cause simple irritation, but in severe cases can burn normal skins.
Some companies, it must be said, do not always issue strong-
enough warnings about the possible dangers of their products.

Allergies are more difficult to cope with than simple irritations.
A preparation that is perfectly satisfactory for most skins can produce nasty rashes on others. Cocoa butter, which appears in many
suntan lotions, is an example. So can vitamin E, formaldehyde,
lanolin and even fragrances.

Cosmetics companies are in business to make money, and one
way they do it is to play on human fear. Women won't get a man
unless they use such and such a perfume; they will age before

their time if they do not buy a certain skin cream and their man will abandon them; no one will love them if their hair is gray. Manufacturers can be quite ruthless in preying on the fears of women, and it is interesting to note that when there is a real danger in a product, women do not always take warning. When the National Cancer Institute issued a report in 1977—it was not the first such report—stating that tests on animals showed that hair dyes could be carcinogenic, very few women gave up using the dyes. Unofficial figures suggested that there was about a 4 percent drop in sales—and some women were actually reported to have said that cancer was preferable to gray hair.

Unscrupulous companies have been known to create artificial fears where no natural human fear exists. One of the real scandals of the 1970s was the ruthless marketing of vaginal deodorants. The market for normal underam deodorants had begun to slow down, but the fear of body odor has now been so well established in Western minds tht it was but a short step to persuade women that they needed vaginal deodorants too.

The advertising campaign was aggressive, and women fell for it. Yet most women canvassed said they had never thought about vaginal odor until they saw the advertisements. The products were worse than useless and actually caused tissue damage and skin irritation. To the credit of the media, there was a strong counterblast. In the United Kingdom, sales of vaginal sprays are now banned, and in the United States they have fallen off dramatically. European companies have carried on selling regardless. What makes deodorant marketing so reprehensible is that even underarm deodorants are unnecessary. Washing regularly and the removal of underarm hair eliminate any unpleasant body odor.

Fear of cancer is a major consideration for most people; yet customers can and do become very irritated when a product they have assumed safe for many years is suddenly said to be carcinogenic, as has happened with some hair coloring products. Improved scientific testing has made possible the isolation of possibly dangerous materials that previously were undetected. But the contribution of science is much wider than that. Today scientists understand such things as the significance of overnutrition and of hormone overdose or deficiency. The advent of computers has meant that available data can be studied to see if there is any unusual pattern emerging from the use of a particular material, not only in cosmetics, of course. And the very interest of consumers in the effects of using certain products has brought a political aspect to consumerism, which in turn has led to greater vigilance on the part of producers.

The whole area is bedeviled by the lack of agreement about what a carcinogenic material is. Scientists disagree quite vociferously on the subject. The problem is that testing a product for carcinogenicity is one thing and measuring just how much of a hazard to health may be involved as a result is another. If a chemist wishes to devise a test that will prove a product danger-free, there is no problem. This means that testing on its own is not enough and that more information is needed.

Hair dyes are an outstanding example of the problems facing manufacturers today. Many hair colorings—whether temporary, semipermanent or permanent—are potentially dangerous. Only hydrogen peroxide bleach and henna, with its herbal base, seem to be safe on the hair itself. Evidence suggests that some materials are carcinogenic, but there are others that cause less serious health risks. Skin irritations and allergies can occur. Permanent-waving solutions are designed to bend the hair in the way it does not want to go. Inevitably, in some cases, hair and skin damage results. Similarly, hair straighteners can damage the hair, burn the skin and even blind people. Cuticle removers and hair removers contain raw materials similar to those in hair straighteners— some of them even contain lye, a material which often appears in products that clear sink drains. The controversy over hair dyes deepened after 1973, when Dr. Bruce Ames in Birmingham, England, saw that a patient with leukemia had used hair dye "more frequently than normal." As a result, cancer tests were carried out on mice in the Department of Cancer Studies at Birmingham University. The first tests showed that there was no significance between the test and control groups. Then when Dr. Ames tested the dyes on cultured human white blood cells, spontaneous chromosome breakage occurred. This breakage was thought to produce cancer, and there was, therefore, a strong argument for stopping the sale of the dyes—at least until further tests had been done.

Two years later, in June 1975, tests showed that 150 out of 169 hair colorants were mutagenic, and this implied that they were carcinogenic. The basis for the belief that carcinogenic in this case equaled mutagenic came from information previously gathered in "Mutagenic Effects of Environmental Contaminants," a paper by Ames, Kanimen and Yamasaki, edited by Sutton and Harris.

There was a further much publicized paper in 1976. Stanley Venitt and David Kirkland of the Institute of Cancer Research, Pollards Wood, England, suggested that "the elevated incidence of certain tumours in hairdressers and in those engaged in cosmetics manufacture might be due to certain chemical carcinogens." They found higher levels of bladder and liver cancer in the British counties where there were chemical industries. Bladder cancer is strongly associated with the manufacture of dyes, pigments and perfumes, pharmaceutical preparations, cosmetic and other toilet preparations. Lung cancer is associated with the manufacture of soaps and detergents. All cancers are more common in counties with chemical industries. The studies also suggest that some hair colorants are carcinogenic in mice.

The companies did not take this attack lying down, and in February 1976 *The Lancet*, the British medical magazine, published a letter from Clyde Burnett, of Clairol Research Laboratories, refuting the Venitt-Kirkland suggestions, which led in return to a reply in March from Venitt stating that they did not suggest that their work was "in any way indicative of a possible long term genetic hazard to the progeny of hair dye users. . . . We did point out, however, that many carcinogens are mutagenic and that many carcinogens cause chromosome damage in vitro. . . ."— meaning in the laboratory rather than in life. They were therefore discounting that their tests had any significance as far as predicting mutagens was concerned, but were still implying that they provided evidence that human cancer might be caused by the use of the dyes.

In March 1976, William F. Benedict of the University of Southern California wrote a letter to *Nature,* another British publication, referring to the possible carcinogenic hazard of hair dyes suggested by the positive results from the use of the Ames test. The evidence that certain hair-dye components could be potential hazards for humans was based on tests with a particular type of laboratory cell culture that had been created from a specific type of damaged cell.

It is clear that most of the evidence that hair dyes may be potentially carcinogenic comes from the assumption that cancer is caused by a mutation. This assumption, however, has by no means been proved. When tested on animals rather than on artificially mutated plants or laboratory cell cultures, several studies have seemed to completely negate a relationship between materials used in hair dyes and cancers.

American hair-coloring manufacturers hit back at the critics through the Cosmetic, Toiletry and Fragrance Association in a December 1977 pamphlet, which claimed that hair dyes were safe. Broadly, it said that the doses used in the tests were too massive to prove anything: that they were the equivalent of twenty-five bottles of hair dye drunk each day for a lifetime by a human being; that no skin tests suggested that hair dyes were not safe; that tests based on human experience conducted by the American Cancer Society and several universities showed no difference in cancer rates between those heavily exposed to hair dyes and those not; that a thirteen-year study by the American Cancer Society showed similar results comparing hairdressers and nonhairdressers; and that total female cancer fell between 1950 and 1975 by 10 percent, when dyes were being used increasingly.

A final decision from the Food and Drug Administration on the matter of hair dyes is being awaited anxiously by the industry. In January 1978 the FDA proposed that cancer warning labels should be put on all coal tar (permanent) hair dyes that contained 2,4—

DAA. Since then the manufacturers have voluntarily removed these dyes from their products while the FDA continued its research. Meantime, there are other substances used in cosmetics which are causing some concern with the American authorities. Among these are nitrosamines, common compounds, which have been found to be carcinogenic when administered orally to animals. In recent years, nitrosamines have been found in some cosmetics, and studies are proceeding to see how these are formed and to what extent. Lead acetates, also found in some hair rinses, are being studied for potential risk. Recently, too, there have been reports of corneal ulcerations following the use of mascara, and regulations about adequate preservatives in mascaras are being considered. This search for protection and absolutely safe products will never end. As substances are discovered, the sophisticated methods of testing them available today means that new dangers will be revealed.

So far, therefore, the case against hair dyes cannot be said to be proven. But how have the cosmetic companies reacted to the growing awareness on the part of the consumer that the products they use can be potentially dangerous? Leonard Lauder was not totally joking when he said to me: "The biggest competitor my company has to face is the United States Government." Companies are well aware that their products must be as pure as scientifically possible if they are to be allowed to remain on the market. Each week the Food and Drug Administration in the United States publishes a list of complaints against manufacturers and retailers, seizure actions filed and products recalled. The sensible cosmetics company does not wait for a product to be recalled. Any hint that a batch might have been produced under contaminated conditions, or that a particular substance causes damage will initiate the recall of the product. An example of this came in 1979 when Revlon initiated the temporary recall of Plus 6 moisturizer because it was discovered that one of its constituents, pseudomonas aeruginosa, could cause blindness or other damage to the eye. The company says that only one batch of 4,000 bottles was affected, but it nevertheless immediately withdrew the product

and informed the FDA, which then put it on its monthly recall
list.

Ironically, too, some suntan lotions that to some extent protect
the skin against cancers by screening out the rays of the sun are
now themselves suspected of causing skin cancers through one of
their ingredients. The suspected substance is 5-methoxypsoralen,
which occurs naturally in the oil of bergamot, a citrus fruit extract
that accelerates tanning. Bergamot, some cosmetics chemists believe, is extremely damaging to the skin. Experiments on furless
mice anointed with 5-methoxypsoralen and exposed to light have
shown that skin cancers occur. There is another chemical closely
related to 5-methoxypsoralen, which is used very successfully in
conjunction with ultraviolet light to cure psoriasis, a distressing
skin disease, and it has been known for some time that the cure
has been effected at some risk of skin cancer.

In the United Kingdom, the government's Department of
Health wrote to all dermatologists in the country in 1978 to warn
them of "the concern expressed by the committee on safety of
medicines" to the safety of 5-methoxypsoralen and related substances. If the substance is used under its own name, it rates as a
drug and could not, under British or European Economic Community rules, be used in a tanning lotion. As oil of bergamot,
however, it is permitted. There seems no doubt that 5-methoxy-
psoralen can damage the genetic material of cells and cause mu-
tations in the same way as the drug 8-methoxypsoralen. Many
doctors are stating quite openly that they feel its widespread use is
ill advised, especially on the skins of fair-haired people. As always
in this kind of situation, there are pros and cons. Some doctors
feel that in order to cure psoriasis the small skin cancer risk is
justified, but not in those cases where people simply want to ac-
quire a tan. The manufacturers of course see it quite differently.
They say that 5-methoxypsolaren works quite differently than the
related chemicals used in the treatment of psoriasis and is quite
safe.

The main brand name using oil of bergamot in Europe is Ber-
gasol, one of the most popular sun creams, which was first mar-

keted in 1969 from a small laboratory in Paris. It was an instant success in Continental Europe and reached Britain in 1975, a year before a very unusual hot and dry summer. It very quickly established itself there and challenged the longtime brand leader, Ambre Solaire, which does not contain oil of bergamot. Sun-by-Sun also has the oil in its list of ingredients, and Biobronze has a "tropical fruit essence" that the makers say is very similar to oil of bergamot and also contains the suspected psoralens. The manufacturers do not as yet intend to remove oil of bergamot from their creams. They argue that they do not regard the skin cancer risk as a significant one and also that exposure of the skin to the sun in any case carries a risk of cancer, so anything that accelerates the tanning process should reduce rather than increase that risk. To anyone not connected with the sale of the oils, such an argument may appear rather specious, especially when creams are available which accelerate tanning and do not include oil of bergamot in their ingredients. Meantime, however, the creams continue to be sold and customers seem happy to ignore the risk. Skin cancers rarely kill, but their treatment can be disfiguring.

All this raises the question of whether the cosmetics industry can ever be reasonably expected to product absolutely safe products. Bruce A. Barron of the Rockefeller University in New York said in 1969: "No clinical trial to evaluate the safety of a cosmetic, however well designed, will provide satisfactory estimates of the incidence of all the important adverse reactions correctly attributable to the substance under test."

The Food and Drug Administration has specific and detailed control over products in the form of statutory instruments of regulation. In 1977, for instance, it imposed strict rules about the labeling of all cosmetics for sale in the United States. Although this may seem like a valuable precaution, making sure that companies do not use toxic materials, it is doubtful whether the labels mean much to the customer purchasing the products. "Mineral oil, isopropyl palmitate, dusopropyl adipate, fragrance, diotyl sodium sulfosuccinate, benzophenone-11, D & C green no. 6, D & C yellow no. 11" described Avon Skin-So-Soft bath oil. Most people would just about make out the mineral oil and the fragrance and guess that the product is turquoise, and it is. In contrast, there is "mineral oil 150, isopropyl palmitate, fragrance, SD alcohol 40-B, nonoxynel 12, propylparaben, benzophenone-11, D & C red no. 17, yellow no. 11." Well, that is just plain pinky-orange Avon bath oil.

Of the other ingredients in the products, isopropyl palmitate and isopropyl adipate are, like mineral oil, emollients; diotyl sodium sulfosuccinate and nonoxynel-12 are detergents (that is, cleaning agents); benzophenone-11 is an ultraviolet absorber, which helps to preserve the product from deterioration in ordinary daylight; and propylparaben is an antimicrobial, a preservative that helps to prevent the growth of bacteria.

Avon's Consumer Guide to Cosmetic Ingredients lists 167 different products used in its cosmetics. It divides them into 21 different categories depending on their function, which is explained simply in the accompanying text. How useful this is to the average customer one cannot be certain, but many cosmetics chemists prefer the American method of labeling ingredients to the more involved regulations of the EEC and its member nations.

Today the companies appear to accept labeling quite happily, but they fought its introduction fiercely, claiming that it would mean that they had to give away commercial secrets. What seems certain is that one or two companies had to do some quick reformulation of certain of their products once it was public knowledge what was in them, though naturally they kept very quiet about this. In some cases, the ingredients advertised as being in the product were not actually there. Whether or not the consumer has been helped is difficult to say: some have been confused by labeling, not always knowing what it means. For instance, if a company puts vitamin A in a product, the label must use the chemical name, retinol, which the consumer may well never have heard of.

Such has been the success of the regulations of the Food and Drug Administration in the United States that a recent survey has shown that there were only 1.8 complaints for every one million units of cosmetics sold. This is far fewer than the number of complaints about food, which is one in every 10,000 units.

The rise of consumer groups, along with increased government regimentation, has tightened the screws on the industry, but the process is slow. With many other countries producing according to American formulas, products are very much the same wherever they are bought. The Europeans, however, have not been prepared simply to go along with American rules, and the European Economic Community Directive, published in 1976 and becoming operative on October 15, 1978, sets out detailed instructions for cosmetics manufacture. It defines and list all those products it regards as cosmetics, and these include toilet and hair preparations as well as the usual cosmetics. It also has a "negative list" of over 400 substances that cannot be used in cosmetics manufacture.

In addition, there is a long list of "restricted" or "provisional" substances, which cannot be used unless a warning is printed on the label. Restrictions on some substances set maximum concentrations of the substances in the finished product. Surprisingly, the "restricted" list includes lanolin, a very common ingredient in cosmetics. The warning must simply say "contains lanolin," and there is no limit on the amount that can be used. Even this limited warning has angered some cosmetics chemists; it has been included because a few—a very few—people are allergic to it. This, chemists feel, is a problem of an individual person, not of a product. If hydrogen peroxide is used, the label must state: "contains X percent hydrogen peroxide. Not to come into contact with eyes. Rinse eyes immediately if product comes into contact with them." Other than warnings like this, the directive does not order any blanket labeling of products.

Even the colors that can be used in cosmetics are subject to rigorous controls. The first law about color in food and other goods was enacted in Germany in 1887. It remained law there as far as cosmetics were concerned until it was superseded by a new German Cosmetics Law ninety years later, on December 16, 1977.

It was not until 1936 that the second ruling came along when the American Pure Food and Drug Act was passed by the United States Congress. What were then called "coal tar" colors were not permitted to be used in cosmetics: today they are known as colorants or synthetic organic dyestuffs. The act recognized that certain elements were unavoidable in cosmetics, so it set maximum levels for their use. In 1952 the German Research Association published a list of approved food colorings and pigments that had proved safety records, stating that these could safely be used in cosmetics. Then came the directive in 1976, but only the German act and the U.K. Cosmetic Products Regulations, 1978, have so far taken account of the directive.

Eric Morgan, of BAT, explained to me how problems can arise over the use of colors, because of different regulations. "Red no. 3 cannot be used in any cosmetic for the Italian market, so we have to use no. 5 instead: in Belgium it is the other way around. And in Germany, where both colors are actually manufactured, neither can be used in sales there."

The problem with EEC directives is that they are binding on all members, but discretion in application is left to the national authorities. Oddly, perhaps, there is a team of EEC analysts who recommend methods of checking restricted substances, but give no suggestions for checking the negative list, which is the one containing substances regarded as definitely damaging to health. This means that companies are merely put on their honor not to include these materials in their products. It is up to governments to take action if they wish. When it comes to the provisional list, the relevant article states that for a period of three years (that is, from October 25, 1978): "Member states shall accept marketing of cosmetic products containing the substances in (the) Annex," when the position will be reviewed.

In addition to safety considerations, the directive also has rules about labeling and advertising, and in particular any special precautions needed in the use of a product must be clearly stated.

In Britain, an EEC member state has no direct legislative or specific statutory control over cosmetic products, but there are many ways in which action can be taken against cosmetics producers. These stem from general consumer laws like the Consumer Protection Act, the Poisons Act, the Medicines Act, the Weights and Measures Act and the Trades Descriptions Act, rather than from rulings specific to cosmetics. Of these acts, it is probably the last one that has most bite for the cosmetics companies today. No manufacturer can make untrue claims about a product. If he does, prosecution can result. This could arise, say, if it was suggested in any way at all that the use of a cold or moisturizing cream could remove wrinkles. There are many people inside and outside the industry who argue that these more general laws can be more effective than the strict regulations of the American government.

The Organization for Economic Cooperation and Development, too, through its Consumer Committee, has also published general guidelines for safety controls over cosmetics. These demand extensive testing of products and their removal from the market if safety is not absolutely assured. Tests for toxicity must be thorough and examine not just a raw material by itself, but also when it is combined with other substances. OECD thinks, too, that manufacturers and importers should be required to submit to a central body, whose job it is to enforce the regulations, full information about all the active ingredients used, and any toxicological data that have been obtained following tests on the final product. This information should then be made public. OECD adds that there should also be provision for a system of information on any adverse physiological reactions that become apparent after the product has been marketed.

So it is that one way or another the cosmetics industry today is surrounded by official bodies determined that the highest standards of safety will apply in the industry. Companies all over the world have heeded the dangers and also the penalties they face if their products cause any damage to consumers. So safety precautions begin at the planning stage of each product. First, the basic raw materials are tested for safety. Then, even if they are cleared, there is always the danger that different materials will react against one another when combined in a product and cause toxicity, even though each alone is safe, so further tests are necessary until the products are absolutely in the clear.

It is impossible to produce a product that one can guarantee as absolutely safe for anyone to use. This is why responsible companies never claim to bring out nonallergic products. The best they can hope for is a hypoallergic range of cosmetics—products that are likely to have an adverse effect on very few people. Occasionally a company has to decide what level of toxicity is acceptable in a new product. As a general rule, this must be as low as or if possible lower than that of any product that the new one is replacing. In all the major companies today, the normal safety precautions include primary tests for irritancy to make sure that the production batch and any subsequent batches of cosmetics have not altered in any way between tests. These are followed by longer-term challenge tests to ensure the safety of the product and also to see that the formula does not change with storage or exposure. These tests cost money, and the cost may be prohibitive for anyone who is not able to recoup the expenditure by a very large sale. This is where the bigger companies gain over small ones, in particular over firms that are trying to break into the field and that may find it difficult to finance the required tests before a product is allowed on the market. There are ways around expensive testing, but those involved in it must be very skilled. Some chemists are prepared to test at the beginning on (voluntary) human guinea pigs. If these tests are satisfactory, they can soon be applied very quickly to larger test groups.

How necessary are all these safety precautions? Many cosmetics chemists and of course companies particularly argue that regulations now go to ridiculous lengths to establish purity. The banning of products is sometimes taken on too lightly as well. In Europe particularly, many chemists are angered by suggestions that lanolin should be banned, particularly as it is used in a highly refined form today. Lanolin, along with petroleum jelly, is a basic ingredient in many cosmetics, but a very small number of people are allergic to it. Chemists feel is is a problem for the individual to solve, rather than requiring a broad sweeping ban on a product that many people find highly satisfactory. "It's like banning penicillin, when it gets the vast majority of people better, just because a very small minority have an adverse reaction to it," one chemist said to me.

Major concern about health hazards in the twentieth century has centered so far mainly around the use of chemicals in cosmetics, but there is a new and growing fear. An age that is thinking about the environment and in which ecology groups are being set up inevitably includes a back-to-nature urge. This has shown itself in the cosmetics world by people making their own cosmetics and by companies providing "natural" cosmetics. The question is whether, without chemicals to preserve them, such cosmetics deteriorate quickly and become dangerous to use. There is no doubt that chemicals added to cosmetics slow down the growth of microorganisms that might be dangerous to health. Those who favor natural cosmetics say that the result of the use of chemicals is far worse than the one resulting from the deterioration of natural products. There are respected scientists on both sides of this argument, which, like any disagreements in the cosmetics business, is likely to go on and become protracted and increasingly acrimonious.

As if coping with and eliminating all the health and safety hazards in producing their products were not enough to contend with, there is another potential threat facing the cosmetics industry in the 1980s and beyond. It is whether the companies can continue to develop their products and ranges using traditional raw materials and manufacturing and testing methods. In particular, they are facing pressure from animal protection groups. These organizations, formed to protect animals and the environment generally from the depredations of man, have already had an impact on the practices of the cosmetics industry. The stronger rulings, too, of the Food and Drug Administration in the U.S. and the European Economic Community concerning what products they will allow to be used, is causing manufacturers to reevaluate their traditional operations. Many of the international companies continue to use animal fats in large quantities—so far they see few alternatives to them—but they and independent cosmetics chemists are turning more and more to the use of plants and herbs as source materials. Dr. Najda Avalle, the leading world cosmetics chemist we met earlier and the 1980 President of the International Federation of Scientists and Cosmetic Chemists, told me that she is now experimenting with the fat by-product that is left when flower petals are crushed to extract the essential oils used in perfumes. Every 1,000 kilograms of petals produces one kilogram of fats, which can be used as a cosmetics base. Though this ratio is very low, the fat is an automatic by-product that was previously thrown away, so the cost is not prohibitive.

Such experiments of course provide only a tiny proportion of cosmetic products, but there is no doubt that companies in several countries are considering the problems raised by the pressure groups, even if in practice they have so far done little about them. In the United Kingdom, an organization called Beauty Without Cruelty was started in 1959 by Lady Dowding, wife of British World War II hero Field Marshal Sir Alan Dowding. Like many groups, it started off as a society to protect animals, particularly those in the wild, which have been hunted, sometimes to near extinction, simply for pelts for fur coats. From its early beginnings in Britain, this charitable organization has become international and is associated today with Compassion in Farming, the International Society for the Protection of Animals and the World Federation for the Protection of Animals. These societies together are a strong world lobby suggesting viable alternatives to unnecessary use of animal products. From their early days of pelt saving, they have turned their attention to the cosmetics industries and have achieved some considerable degree of success in their campaign, at the same time achieving a modest success for their own range of products.

It is the use of raw materials from animals which are unnaturally acquired which is under attack from these groups. One example is spermaceti wax, which is taken from the oil of whales and is used as a lubricant for lipstick, creams and soaps at a time when the very survival of the species is threatened. Animal placentas, amniotic fluids and even crushed snails are used in moisturizers. Mink oil, too, has a wide range of uses in cosmetics.

The manufacture of perfumes often involves the use of animal "fixatives," which help a scent to last. Ambergris—which is either coughed up, or more often extracted from the stomach, of sperm whales—is a popular fixative. So too are musk, most often extracted from a small pod in the abdomen of the male musk deer; civet, scrapings from the sex glands of the civet cat; and castorium, similarly extracted from the Canadian or Siberian beaver. The environmental groups suggest that adequate and efficient alternatives to these traditional products can be produced as by-products of industry, particularly petroleum. They claim that there are more than eighty synthetic fixatives that are just as good as the natural ones. The pressure groups have had some success with the international companies, but cannot rank the French fragrance houses among their converts: these still insist on using animal fixatives for their perfumes to an overwhelming degree. The reason for this attitude is probably historical, going back to the days when environmental protection was nonexistent and France had ready and easy access to essential oils from the East, as well as its own plentiful supply of essential oils from flowers, trees, herbs and spices. The acceptance that synthetic materials could be as effective as the old natural product has come only recently.

In his famous and beautifully produced work of 1864, Eugene Rimmel, in *The Book of Perfumes*, describes the materials used in perfumes. He divides them into twelve groups—the animal, floral, herbal, andropogon, citrine, spicy, ligneous, radical seminal, balmy or resinous, fruity and artificial. He wrote that the animal product resists evaporation longer than any other form. He describes without emotion the hunting of animals for musk, civet and ambergris, though ambergris, he claimed, was found floating on the sea, or was washed ashore, having been thrown up by diseased spermaceti whale: it seems that at that time at least the whale was not slaughtered for ambergris. Rimmel declared then that these animal materials, though by themselves not pleasant, combined with other perfumes to produce fragrances unobtainable in any other way. Had he known of later developments, however, it is unlikely he would have been moved by the thought of cruelty to animals.

There has, however, been some token bowing in the direction of the environmental pressure groups by international cosmetics houses in recent product launchings. Herbs and natural vegetable oils appear more frequently on lists of ingredients than they have in the past. Even so, animals are still used today as a major raw materials source, and also for experiments and testing. In Britain alone, government figures show that 28,000 animals are used in experiments each year. In the United States the figure is much larger; an internal Avon Cosmetics memo, dated November 15, 1977, showed that this company alone used 14,561 animals for experiments in less than a year (165 dogs, 1,037 cats, 6,308 guinea pigs, 2,624 hamsters, 4,303 rabbits, 56 primates, 5 opossums and 63 ferrets).

Beauty Without Cruelty and its worldwide allies claim that Elizabeth Arden, Helena Rubinstein, Revlon, Johnson and Johnson, Gillette, Carter Wallis, Charles of the Ritz and Max Factor among many others all use animals for testing products before marketing. The environmental groups' loudest protests come from the use of animals for testing cosmetics. They cite the practice of Lethal Dosage 50. LD50 means force-feeding 100 animals with cosmetics —either lipsticks, lotions or powders—until 50 of them die. Animal defenders feel that nothing can be gained from such testing: no woman, they claim, would eat twenty pounds of lipstick. Cosmetics companies, in contrast, have argued that such enormous dosages are necessary to ensure that there is no damage or health threat at all to humans through the use of a cosmetic.

Other practices under attack are the Draize Test, under which animals, particularly albino rabbits, have a test shampoo injected into their eyes. Albinos are chosen because they do not have tear ducts, which can wash away the offending liquid. Their eyes are then kept open for long periods. This process, apart from blinding or at best damaging the rabbits' eyes, shows the tester whether any damage at all may ensue to a human's eye from using the product. Major companies are well aware of the distress and anger some people feel about animal testing. On December 23, 1980, Revlon announced that it was setting up a research project with the Rockefeller University of New York to find an alternative to the Draize Test. Revlon is providing up to $750,000 over three years to fund the research which initially will try to determine the feasibility of developing a non-animal test which could replace the Draize. This is the fundamental problem facing the industry— and it is a genuine dilemma—whether testing can be done by machines alone. Testing by machine for product quality by itself may not ensure that there is no adverse reaction on skin, whether for a few specific cases or for a large number of users.

The companies can no longer ignore the protestations of the pressure groups. Their dilemma is increased by the consumer protection against defective products which is legally available in many countries today and which can cost a manufacturer thousands of dollars. Should the producer sell products untested? Or should laboratory-pure products be tested directly on humans? Or does the proper balance of human satisfaction lie, for instance, in the Skin Irritation Test, in which an animal's flank is shaved and the skin subjected to massive doses of a cream or lotion at all levels of skin, for considerable periods in laboratory conditions and under which the animal is unable to move, just to ensure that no skin disturbance results?

Many who would justify the use of animals for medical purposes might flinch at the use of animals purely to enable humans to decorate themselves as they choose, or help them to sustain their youth a little longer. This is a question the leading cosmetics houses know they cannot ignore for long.

Product testing does not stop with animals. Once it is established that there is virtually no chance of irritancy on a normal skin, many companies then move on to see how the product performs on the human skin. Human (voluntary) guinea pigs will spend hours sitting in specially constructed cabins, where all levels of humidity are tested up to 100 percent and in temperatures ranging up to 90 degrees Fahrenheit. Windshield wipers are used, so that researchers on the outside of the cabins can see what is happening inside to the guinea pigs' skin.

In recent years, one safety question has bothered the industry and many outside it. It has nothing to do with the product, but concerns packaging. Manufacturers, governments, regulatory bodies and environmental groups have all been asking the question: Is it safe to use aerosols?

There is no denying that the development of the aerosol was a boon to the industry when it came along. Perfume and toilet water sprays are much more efficient if used in aerosol form. The use of hair sprays and lacquers has been transformed. Various light creams and deodorants can be packaged in this way. And there is some suspicion that when customers use an aerosol they instinctively use more of the product than they would otherwise, so profits are higher. Nevertheless, aerosols may not be used for much longer, as they may be banned. The doubts that have been raised are three: Do they affect health? Are they a fire hazard? And, most tantalizing of all, do they destroy the ozone content of the earth's atmosphere?

It is the way that aerosols work which is behind these questions. All aerosols contain a solvent as well as the liquefied gas propellant, a fluorocarbon that makes the aerosol work. Both elements must be safe. Some solvents, for example, though not dangerous in themselves, are volatile and should only be used in a place that is adequately ventilated to avoid explosions. Some solvents, too, are toxic. The effects of short-term toxicity (poisoning) can be traced quickly, but what is not yet known is the effect of long-term toxicity. One example of long-term damage was found after the use of vinyl chloride monomers as a solvent in car-manufacturing plants. Workers were found to have cancers asscoiated with it, and its use was then banned. Other solvents have been known to cause liver damage.

There are health problems connected with both solvents and fluorocarbons. Fears first began to arise in the mid-1960s, when there was some concern that the use of aerosols in enclosed spaces might cause lung disease. It was found that otherwise normally fit people were having breathing problems and chest contractions after using hair sprays. There is no doubt that the very fine sprays contain particles that are small enough to be inhaled and stay in the respiratory system. Whether or not this matters depends not only on whether the solvents contain poisons, but also on whether they are solvent or not. If they are solvent and poisonous in even the smallest degree, some toxicity will eventually occur in the body as they are carried into the bloodstream. If they are not solvent, they can remain inside the lungs until removed by violent coughing, or they may form sterile abscesses or produce some other type of local reaction in the lungs. Of course not all inhalation is toxic; in the case of medicines, for instance, it can have a local or sometimes continued therapeutic effect.

Fluorocarbons, too, are not always free of toxic elements, but what has most excited public interest about them is the Ozone Depletion Theory. This theory speculates that the release of fluorocarbons into the air lowers the ozone level in the atmosphere. It is this layer that protects the world from the heat of the sun. Fluorocarbons are very persistent climbing gases, and it is argued that they break down the ozone in the upper atmosphere, which filters out excess ultraviolet rays of the sun. The connection between ultraviolet rays and cancer is well documented, and lower ozone layers could lead to increased incidences of skin cancer, a disease already prevalent in sunny climates like that of Southern California and Australia where fair-skinned people in particular take too much sun. Another consequence could be a greenhouse effect, a general warming of the earth's surface, which could have severe worldwide results.

The controversy really developed in 1973. It was at its height in the United States, where mass hysteria seems to be endemic, and where political bandwagoning can bring rapid results through instant legislation and regulation. Many industries, including cosmetics, did not want to see aerosols banned, and research institutes set about disproving the theory. The National Academy of Sciences stated that there was no need for precipitate restrictions. It went on, however, to suggest that labeling should be introduced so that customers could decide for themselves whether they wanted to use fluorocarbons. Various federal agencies saw the illogicality in this: no one can determine his own personal level of ozone. They began programs to phase out the use of fluorocarbons in aerosols.

A big business was at stake. In the U.S. alone, which accounted for over half the world consumption of fluorocarbons, it was an $8 billion industry. Again, the National Academy of Sciences reported, this time on the climatic effects. It suggested that at worst chlorofluorocarbons increase peak ozone (the thickness of the atmosphere) reduction by one percent a year. Assuming that each one percent meant an increase of 2 percent in ultraviolet radiation, it would be like moving 60 miles nearer the Equator. Then, in 1978, the British Aerosol Manufacturers, admittedly an interested party, reported that much more research was needed into how chlorofluorocarbons behave in the atmosphere before any conclusions could be reached about safety. This report had followed a recommendation by the government's Department of the Environment that alternative propellants be sought in case fluorocarbons had to be banned.

The ozone theory has been neither proved nor disproved, and research continues. Meanwhile, however, the United States government ordered that fluorocarbons no longer be used after the end of 1978. The British and the Europeans have not followed suit, and today fluorocarbons are still used in 70 percent of their aerosols. It would be good news for the cosmetics manufacturers if aerosols could be cleared of the charges. The problem is that alternatives are not available or are unsuitable. Halocarbons are expensive and are not immediately available: hydrocarbons are acceptable to consumers, but they have a poor smell, which would have to be masked if they were used; dimethyl needs more testing; and compressed gases produce a much coarser spray, which has only a limited use.

The whole thing may be a storm in a teacup. A contradictory

theory is that the wasteful burning of solid and other fossil fuels, which has been rapidly increasing in this century, has led to an undesirable "thickening" of the atmosphere. Aerosols, some argue, are merely restoring the balance. And ozone layers fluctuate naturally anyway, so the possible maximum rate of depletion may be fairly negligible after all.

EIGHT

OPIUM FOR THE MASSES

*Doing business without advertising is like wink-
ing at girls in the dark. You know what you're
doing, but nobody else does.*
                    —Steuart Henderson Britt

Clever marketing is the key to success in selling cosmetics and
toiletries. As there is very little basis for choosing one brand over
another it is only by successful marketing that one particular
brand triumphs. And what works for one company will not work
for another. Some companies are competing directly, but all of
them like to think the products they have are just right for a
particular market.

It is difficult to get figures for advertising from the industry. It
has been stated that, shortly after he took over, Michel Bergerac
doubled Revlon's advertising budget to $135 million a year. In
1979 the figure had reached $160 million. It seems likely that very
few other companies approach this figure. Avon most certainly
does not; its promotion budget goes elsewhere. At Estée Lauder,
the market the company is aiming at is more narrow, and the
others simply cannot afford budgets of this size: Max Factor re-
fuses to reveal what it spends on advertising, but says that in 1979–

80 it spent $4 million on one product alone under the slogan "Don't you love being a woman?"

Packaging a product usually costs as much as making the product—and often more—and it has a vitally important place in marketing strategy. The difference in cost between one brand and another can partly be put down to packaging, though of course the cost of promotion plays a very considerable part. The producers of low-priced cosmetics using the mass distribution stores are not overconcerned with expensive packaging. As long as the product looks reasonable, the customer will be satisfied. In the higher-priced cosmetics brands, however, the cost of packaging may amount to as much as between 15 and 20 percent of the manufacturers' product cost. Naturally, the companies are not saying just how much. The peak period for cosmetics sales is Christmas, when most of the cosmetics are sold that are not bought by the person who will use them. At this time, extravagance in packaging knows no bounds, the philosophy being that if the recipient of the gift does not like the product itself, there will be something in the packaging that he or she can use. A lipstick, whatever company it comes from, costs only a few cents; yet its price can vary between, say, a dollar in a discount store to even hundreds of dollars. For Christmas 1979 Princess Marchella Borghese (yet another Revlon trade name) put out a lipstick retailing at $200. No matter if the lady did not like the color, it came in a perfume-filled sterling silver purse spray. Also from Revlon, Chaz, their current men's fragrance which is not doing well, could be bought in a wooden case containing a dart board and "executive darts." Estée Lauder was retailing Cinnabar soaps in an oriental collectors' vase and a pressed-powder jar in copies of Estée's own heirlooms.

All cosmetics companies can be divided into one base or another; either they started as marketing companies like Revlon or Avon, or as research treatment product companies like Lauder, Redken or Charles of the Ritz. But however they started, all cosmetics companies today have moved into both areas. Estée Lauder, for example, packaging is designed in house, superintended by Ira Levy, who for over twenty years has been illustrating the Lauder view of life in the market. There is tremendous concentration on the things the Lauders themselves collect. The Christmas powder jar was copied from one left to Mrs. Lauder by her mother. When Private Collection was launched in 1973, the packaging was copied in exact detail from Mrs. Lauder's own stationery. Cosmetic houses today continue old traditions: everything from Elizabeth Arden when she was alive came predominantly in pale pink and blue. Even her racing colors, as we have noted, were the same.

Flamboyance in marketing with the aim of attracting wide publicity has always been a characteristic of the industry. The early entrepreneurs realized that, by catching the public's imagination, vastly improved sales could result. As customers have become more difficult to impress, so the efforts of the companies to ensure a successful launch of a new product have intensified. Helena Rubinstein launched her Heaven Scent perfume in America in 1942 by floating hundreds of samples of the scent on pale blue balloons down Fifth Avenue, carrying the message "A gift for you from Heaven! Helena Rubinstein's 'Heaven Scent.' " Elizabeth Arden first announced Cabriole at the Wembley sports stadium in London. Both the name and the place had horsey associations.

There is no doubt that Revson was the most brilliant marketer of them all. He was also a brute to work with. Executive reward was very high indeed at Revlon; yet the turnover of staff was enormous. Some stayed the course, it is true. Sam Kallish reveled in working with Revson and did not particularly like Paul Woolard, the company's marketing chief, who has now been on the payroll for close to twenty years. For many years too, Kay Daly, the only senior woman on the staff, wrote most of the Revlon advertisements. She survived until she retired, but was often reported as saying how difficult it was to get any praise out of Revson.

If life was tough for Revlon executives, it was worse for the advertising agencies that took on the account. There were many of them, a new one always ready to take on the challenge when yet another one failed to meet Revson's exacting standards. The big advertising budgets first came into being after the end of World War II, and in the following fifteen years Revson went through as many advertising agencies. In the 1970s he finally earned for himself a place on the list of the clients the advertising industry regarded as the ten worst to deal with. Yardley, much smaller than Revlon, was the only other cosmetics company that made the list. Although the Revlon account was a big one and growing all the time, there was often relief in the voice of an advertising boss as yet another of them announced that he had lost the account.

In 1944 the Revlon account was worth only $600,000. By 1979 the company was spending $169 million. In 1944 it went to McCann Erickson; the executive masterminding it there was John McCarthy. He lasted six months, the two men finally falling out because Revson objected to McCarthy's dirty fingernails. Later on, McCarthy described a client meeting to *Time* magazine (September 30, 1957), the pace at which Revson worked and his lack of consideration for others. "It started in the afternoon. Around 7 a waiter from Longchamps came in to serve his dinner. Not a crumb of food was offered to anyone else at the table. The meeting went on through the night." McCann Erickson kept the account for a further three years, and another eighteen failed account executives after McCarthy retired, hurt from the fray. This turned out to be quite a long stint for a company with Revson. In 1948 he moved to the William Weintraub agency, where for a time things went very well. Norman B. Norman, who works for the Weintraub agency, and later bought it out, actually survived for seven years working with Revson. This all ended unhappily, however, when the company sponsored the television program "The $64,000 Question," which, to begin with, Charles Revson did not like.

When Revson left Norman Craig and Kummel in 1956, the value of the account had grown to $6 million. Revson then decided that not all the Revlon advertising money would go to one agency. He split the business, some of it going to three small firms. The bulk went to a major agency, Batten, Barton, Durstine and Osborn. It was a tough agency with plenty of experience with difficult clients, and it was then the fourth biggest agency in the United States. It was not long before the company was agreeing with anything Revson wanted to do, good or bad. Little more than a year later, when BBDO and Revson parted company, one advertising executive said it was like coming out of the trenches after the end of the war. But as BBDO bowed out, others came in to have a go at the very lucrative account, which had grown very quickly to $13 million a year largely as a result of the company's great sales boost following "The $64,000 Question."

Fire and Ice, Snow Pink, Paint the Town Pink, Love That Pink, Powder Pink and Kissing Pink—all Revlon and all names of coordinated lipsticks and nail polishes. At least twice a year Revlon would bring out a new color range; women would sigh perhaps, but dutifully change to the new color. It was irresistible to many women. The advertisements for Love That Pink went "Redheads *revel* in it! Blondes *bloom* in it! Brunettes were *born* for it! *This* is the pink that proves forever . . . pink is for girls! LOVE THAT PINK! Revlon's new pulsating pink." New it might have been, but six months later it would be superseded by yet another set of exclamation marks and a slightly different color. Revlon used the phrase "matching lips and fingertips," poached, it is said, from Coty, which had coined the phrase, but had not managed to get the new product out before Revlon.

Revson's marketing flair was such that by the end of World War II the company had become Number 1 in nail and lip color in the U.S. The advertisements from the end of the war until his death show how clearly Charles Revson understood the changing moods of women and was able to capitalize on them. In 1946, very soon after the war, his advertisements were warm and appealing with feminine, pretty models surrounded by adoring men. At this period, when men had been away at the war, Revson knew that women would be looking for husbands. His advertisements showed women at their most feminine, attracting a bevy of men. The caption ran: "Bachelors but not for long." An obvious message: Wear these colors, get your man. Then came the 1950s when society was once again settled in a peacetime existence and women were ready to behave more aggressively. As they did, they saw Revlon's Fire and Ice, described by many in the advertising industry as the most perfect, well-written cosmetics advertisement ever. The words were by Kay Daly. Charles Revson is reported to have been unimpressed. By now, the lady was not luring men into marriage, but was offering them excitement. She was a "tease and temptress, siren and gamine." All very well, but the temptress went the way of the rest as women became more independent.

During the 1950s, women became more and more alluring and tempting as far as Charles Revson was concerned, and the sexual message in successive advertising campaigns became more and more explicit. Women's attitudes were changing, and Charles Revson knew it. By the early 1970s they were much more emancipated. They were no longer totally absorbed in snaring men: they were becoming free spirits who might well need snaring themselves. For a period the industry was preoccupied with the question of whether women would give up makeup altogether in the "bra-burning" period of the late 1960s 'and early 1970s. This did not worry Charles Revson; his women simply became more sporty and outgoing. In 1972 the Revlon model was on a motorbike—and she was driving. She still, however, looked very pretty. By the time Charlie perfume arrived in 1974, girls were off their motorbikes, casually but smartly dressed; they were twenty-seven, married, liberated, friendly and sexy—altogether the ideal woman in a liberated age. One company executive described her perfectly as "Jane Fonda without the hang-ups."

With the launch of Charlie, it became clear that Charles Revson's marketing genius had never left him. It was the last product that he personally masterminded, and it was one of the outstanding marketing successes of the 1970s. It was also a suitable introduction to the ways of cosmetics for Revson's chosen successor, Michel Bergerac. Bergerac had no experience at all with cosmetics when he joined Revlon, and he and Revson worked together on the project. In its cosmetic ranges, Revlon had always chosen names with a very feminine appeal. With his nose for changing fashions, Revson knew that he could take a chance with his new perfume, and it is perfectly possible that he wanted this new product, which he knew would be the last he would bring out personally, to be a testimonial to his genius in the business. The smell was floral and feminine enough, but the image of the young 1970s woman was a free, independent, liberated one. So he chose the name Charlie, partly after himself, but also to suggest a casual, swinging approach to life. It was a fitting final appearance. Hitherto, Revlon had been rather a second-rate perfume house; only Intimate had anything like a successful sale. Charlie changed all that and pitched Revlon into the front line of fragrance makers and it has never looked back.

The estimates were that Charlie would cop about $3 million in sales in America. Instead it sold well over $15 million in the first year and went successfully into international markets as well. The company capitalized on the success of the fragrance and brought out a full cosmetics range, which has continued to the present time. The perfume was pitched at the young working woman, though 30 percent of those who bought it were not working and 42 percent of them were thirty-five and over. Charlie, a jasmine-dominated scent, has become the best-selling perfume in the world.

The perfume was to be introduced for the Christmas season in 1972. It did not make it: Charles Revson was not satisfied with Charlie and refused to release it. The perfume was developed (the "creation"—the acceptance of the final formula and the marketing—of it was by Revson himself) by François Camail of Florasynth, a company that makes many perfumes for many cosmetics companies. The perfume was reformulated many times until Revson was satisfied. He was ready in February 1973, and out it went, even though the month is not generally regarded as a good one for a cosmetics launch. The promotion work had, of course, been going on all the time Charlie was being developed. Photographs of Shelly Hack, the model chosen to portray the new woman, Charlie, were sent to the women's page editors. The free publicity was almost unheard of, with many of them simply printing the press release as it was written. The department stores played their part. Charlie was first sold at Bloomingdale's, the fashionable New York store. The store was bedecked with over 1,000 Charlie balloons, diners at twenty-six nearby restaurants were invited to "Meet Charlie at Bloomingdale's"; and, as well as being sold at the main cosmetics counter, Charlie was on sale from movable trolleys on three of the store's floors. Other stores had special counters called "Charlie's Place," and the perfume was sold by girls dressed in Charlie clothes—the tailored white trouser suit. Everywhere there were Charlie motifs—buttons, balloons, umbrellas and haircuts, all helping sales along. There were even Charlie horoscopes and a Charlie song.

Others followed the Charlie theme, notably Sam Kallish at Max Factor with his "Call me Maxi." But the formula did not work twice: the mood was changing. "Call Me Maxi" flopped, but at Revlon, with Charles Revson dead, a new scent was ready for the time when Charlie sales began to fall: it was known that they would fall, for however good a cosmetic or perfume may be, people become bored with it and sales drop off. The new scent was ready at Revlon while Charlie sales were still rising. The Charlie girl had been "Sexy-clean . . ."; the new one, using Jontue, was more overtly feminine and gardenia-based. She is "sensuous but not too far from innocence," according to the copy. The market was ready for Jontue, which became the second-best-selling perfume in the world. With these two perfumes Revlon had established itself as a serious perfume maker.

Meanwhile, in 1969, Rubinstein launched the Mykonos line. It was the first really big-style new launch following the death of Madame, who would have surely approved the company's plans. It was the first time a complete range of cosmetics was marketed worldwide at one time. The products had been shipped for sale to all the company's markets around the globe. Advertisements had been prepared for each market in various languages. The whole operation was synchronized; the advertisements appeared in the press, and the products were on the counters immediately following the launch, which took place with 135 journalists present on a boat moored off the island of Mykonos in Greece. The Greek government sent helicopters to the scene, and they dropped carnations on the guests. "All of a sudden," Joseph Mann, a longtime employee of Helena Rubinstein says, "the cosmetics industry became one world." Mykonos started well, but like many cosmetics lines, its appeal soon petered out.

In the 1970s one of the most talked-about launches took place —the Rubinstein bash for its silk-based powders. It took place at the Hotel Villa D'Este, a renowned old hotel on the shores of Lake Como at Cernobbia. The Rubinstein staff of four were dressed each day in a new all-silk wardrobe, no one more glittering than Shirley Lord herself.

The star of the whole performance was the amazing model Veruschka, who at midnight rode into the gala on a white horse. As usual, the whole of the fashion industry and the press cohorts were present. The "powder puff" princess, Shirley Lord, so-described by her erstwhile colleagues of the press, had flown in from New York with a silk wardrobe designed to impress journalists.

But in 1974 Helena Rubinstein showed how it is possible to get a good sales response and still lose money in the cosmetics industry by overestimating that response. In a one-week promotion in Manhattan, New York, the store chosen for the event sold $10,000 worth of goods, taking $4,000 as its gross profit. The company received $6,000 and spent $5,600 for an advertisement in a New York newspaper, $1,200 for two special demonstrators, whom it supplied to the store to deal with the promotion, and a further $3,500 for gifts that went with the product. These were simulated alligator kits filled with Rubinstein products that would have retailed at $15 each. The loss to the company in the one week was $4,300, and this was a rather modest promotion. Had there been any promotional literature, the company would have lost more. It needed at least twice the sales volume to make a profit on the operation.

In 1978 the Opium fragrance descended on the industry. Wherever it was launched it quickly snapped up a profitable share of the market, set a trend toward an "oriental" influence in the fragrance world and sparked off controversy. The perfume had an impeccable pedigree. Brainchild of one of the world's leading couturiers, Yves Saint-Laurent, Opium was first marketed in France by a company rejoicing in the name of Mafia. European women took to the scent immediately. In Australia, however, Opium was banned on the ground that its name did not represent its contents.

In Britain, Yves Saint-Laurent sent the journalists on a boat down the River Thames on the not-so-romantic trip from central London to Greenwich. What was lacking in romance, however, was more than made up for with lashings of champagne and food. The journalists duly produced copy highly satisfactory to the couturier.

Then, in September 1978, came the American launch, the most glittering one of all. America, after all, is the biggest and most affluent market in the world. What's in a name? The name Opium was chosen by Saint-Laurent himself; this was his choice and he was determined to stick to it. It seems that some attempt was made by Charles of the Ritz, a subsidiary of E. R. Squibb and Sons—a group not renowned for commercial adventurousness—to persuade Saint-Laurent to abandon "Opium" for some less controversial name. His name alone backing the perfume, it was suggested, would be enough to provide the American distributor and the French couturier with at least a modest success.

Saint-Laurent was not to be moved. Opium was what he wanted it to be called and Opium it was. In Europe, it was argued, sophisticated customers had enjoyed the joke implicit in the name, and American women would do the same. All opposition was to be overcome by a spectacular launch. It was indeed dazzling. The party cost over $250,000 for a perfume that was to retail at $100 an ounce. One enterprising journalist was to speculate that, at this price, the perfume, at its launch date, was more expensive than opium itself. Heroin, derived from opium, was retailing, he said, at $150 an ounce.

The night chosen was September 20, 1978, and Opium—the

formula is 71 percent ethyl alcohol and water, 10–15 percent clove oil extracts, artificial jasmine and benzoin, and a smattering of vetiver, myrrh, sandalwood, benjamin, pepper, coriander and opopana—hit an expectant public.

To succeed, the perfume had to convey an atmosphere of oriental mystery and romance; the ambiance was just as important as the smell itself. The launch therefore had to suggest all this, just in case writers and journalists failed to get the message conveyed in the name. Saint-Laurent had plotted his product carefully. First of all came the name with its associations and hints of drug peddling and exploitation. Then, to reinforce the aura, he rented a tall ship, the *Peking*, at the South Street Seaport Museum, and transformed it to conform with the idea of the decadent and sumptuous East. There stood the *Peking* in New York's East River with twenty banners in red, gold and purple silk and gold lamé floating from each of its four masts. Aboard sat a 1,000-pound bronze Buddha surrounded by white cattleya orchids from Hawaii, brought in at a cost of $50,000. Each flower was wired into a small water vessel to prevent wilting, and guests helped themselves to them as the evening wore on. There was a disco and six bars.

Finally, there was the reception area. Here there lay a 50-foot sisal rug designed by Saint-Laurent and covered with eight-inch-wide ribbons in oriental colors. Bamboo furniture and fans wired to the masts and were hand-painted in blacks, reds and golds (the guests later helped themselves to the fans before leaving) completed the image. Saint-Laurent stood awaiting his guests, surrounded by six (imported) models dressed in black, white and gold brocade in sumptuous oriental style. Eight hundred invitations had been sent out. They were hand-addressed and had cost $2,000. Delivering them by hand had cost a further $1,500. "Everyone" from the President and Vice President was invited, although many celebrities did not show. However, the fashion industry was there in full force, including Bill Blass, Halston, Oscar de la Renta and Mary McFadden. Zandra Rhodes, the zany British designer, turned up without eyebrows, but with ZZZZZZs drawn in their place. The singer Cher wore a transparent black dress. Writer Truman Capote arrived wearing a deerstalker hat and matching jacket. Unfortunately, no one had remembered to send a written invitation to a party of six from the South Street Seaport Museum who had difficulty in getting in. They owned the *Peking* and they were not pleased.

The evening wore on. Guests reclined on beige down-filled cushions casually strewn around the boat. Rumor had it that real opium smoking was going on below deck. Black-clad waiters served the food, which consisted of 160 pounds of veal and steak tartare, 13,000 oysters, clams and mussels, 20 pounds of red sturgeon and caviar, 50 Peking duck, and strawberries and other fruits. Guests seem to have managed eight drinks apiece. The champagne was French, not American, and 720 bottles were drunk.

The evening ended with fireworks and the well-shoed guests appear to have stripped the boat of everything detachable. Then it was off to fashionable disco Studio 54 to finish off the night. The gamble had paid off. The name was a gift to headline writers, who chose many permutations on opium, mystery, pushing and peddling. The staid *Wall Street Journal* had earlier come up with "Mafia launches a big opium push—at about $100—in Paris." The next morning the media was full of the story; almost every paper in the United States ran something. The party was more than paying for itself in terms of free publicity. The momentum was maintained by an advertising campaign relaying the same message. A beautiful jewel-bedecked woman wearing a black and gold velvet gown designed by Saint-Laurent (cost, $6,000), reclined, looking stoned out of her mind. The message was clear.

It seems that such a hullabaloo was not necessary, for Opium was sold out before its launch. The market was ready for a sophisticated perfume after some years of girlish or flowery scents. What the launch did was to bring Saint-Laurent the sort of fame he already had as a designer, but which he had not previously achieved in the perfume world. That was presumably its purpose, and at $300 a person for almost blanket coverage in the media, it was cheap at the price. And in the first week of sales between $4,000 and $5,000 worth was sold every day. Bloomingdale's alone sold $1,000 worth in the first hour of selling. The flacon containing the perfume was cleverly modeled on the antique box in which opium was originally shipped to China by the British East India Company in the 1800s.

The cosmetics world is like fashions: people tend to get the same ideas around the same time and Estée Lauder was just launching her own new perfume with an Eastern influence—Cinnabar. The subsequent battle between the two companies became known as the Opium Wars, or the War of the Tassels: Opium featured a tasseled necklace upon which the perfume could be dangled, and Cinnabar, too, featured tassels in its packaging. Estée Lauder is no slouch. To begin with, her perfume retailed at half the price, $50 an ounce instead of $100, but those testing the scents said that Cinnabar was "just like," but "better" than, Opium. The Lauders managed to get their Cinnabar promotion into Neiman-Marcus of Dallas just before the push by Opium. Observers in the industry were surprised to see how fast the relatively large Estée Lauder company could move. It was a battle the Lauders could not lose. The outlets for Opium are far fewer than those available to the much larger Lauder company, and after the first initial thrust in 1978, there is no doubt that Cinnabar outsold Opium in 1979. Lauder often claims, and is accorded by many of her competitors, creative leadership in the industry. In this case, however, the pushing of Cinnabar onto the market was seen as simply a "marketing and sales effort of amazing ferocity and energy."

Nevertheless, Saint-Laurent, Charles of the Ritz and E. R. Squibb had good reason to be pleased with the market reception for Opium. What they had not expected, although the earlier American reservations about the name might have warned them, was that the Chinese-American population would be angered by the whole exercise. No sooner was the product on the market than an umbrella group covering sixty Chinese-American organizations was set up. Coalition Against Opium Perfume and Drug

Abuse charged that the product's name and advertising program romanticized narcotics and insulted the Chinese people. It was Jim Tso who led the opposition who told the New York *Post* it was "as bitter and anger-provoking for us as it would be for the Jews if someone called a product Holocaust." He added: "We won't rest until the name is changed and we get an official apology." Lotus —not quite the same aura—would be a nice alternative name, he thought. The battle will be long and hard, although the advertising of the product has been toned down. E. R. Squibb has been a sympathetic listener to the complaints, but Charles of the Ritz knows a good thing when it sees one, and the good thing in this case is a sales figure of $3 million for the first nine months, from a promotion expenditure of $750,000 according to *Advertising Age*.

It is only when a major new line is being marketed that there is an elaborate national or international launch. When it simply is a matter of new colors, cosmetics companies tend to rely on press comment, point-of-sale display and special promotions in stores. Lipstick and nail polish colors, for example, change so often— twice or even sometimes three times a year—that the expenses of a major launch cannot be justified. In these cases, the success of the new look depends upon the skill of the copywriter and the creative designer of the advertisement. They must catch the changing mood of the customer in as new and dramatic a way as possible.

All the early entrepreneurs had great marketing gifts, none more so than Charles Revson when he moved into the lipstick market in 1940 with his "matching lips and fingertips" campaign. Only Revlon lipsticks, of course, exactly matched Revlon nail polishes, and Revson saw and seized the opportunity of effectively doubling his sales figures. When a new color was launched, it was always just that tiny bit different from the color that had gone before, and it was the "in" color. Thousands of women ditched their existing lipsticks and bought the new ones. With a first-class publicity director, Bea Castle, and a brilliant copywriter, Kay

Daly, Charles Revson went from success to success. The names of Revlon colors meant little, if anything: Pink Lightning, Fatal Apple, Plumb Beautiful, Where's the Fire?, Paint the Town Pink, Rosy Future, Pink Vanilla—all nonsensical names, but they all sold. Full color came in with Pink Lightning in 1944.

The one that topped the lot was Fire and Ice, and Kay Daly's advertisement was named the best advertisement of 1952. It was a two-page full color spread with model Dorian Leigh dazzling in a silver sequin dress and scarlet cape, showing off her matching lips and long, long nails. She filled one page: the other was taken up with a long questionnaire headed: "Are *you* made for Fire and Ice? Try this quiz and see." In America at that time, the view was that European women were sexy and exciting and American ones homely and ordinary. What Charles Revson wanted was to break down this belief. He wanted to make American women feel that they had all the homely virtues, but that lurking beneath them was a vibrant sensual woman. If you were made for Fire and Ice, you would answer yes (and there was a box provided for the answers alongside the questions as in any quiz) to at least eight questions, then, ran the implicit message, you were comparable with Dorian Leigh, who no one could deny was glamorous and exciting. The questions were:

Have you ever danced with your shoes off?

Did you ever wish on a new moon?

Do you blush when you find yourself flirting?

When a recipe calls for *one* dash of bitters, do you think it's better with two?

Do you secretly hope the next man you meet will be a psychiatrist?

Do you sometimes feel that other women resent you?

Have you ever wanted to wear an ankle bracelet?

Do sables excite you, even on other women?

Do you love to look *up* at a man?

Do you face crowded parties with panic—then wind up having a wonderful time?

Does gypsy music make you sad?

Do you think any man *really* understands you?

Would you streak your hair with platinum without consulting your husband?

If tourist flights were running, would you take a trip to Mars?
Do you close your eyes when you're kissed?

Millions of American women, it was clear, said yes to the required number of questions in the advertisement. The press and
department stores responded too. Almost every newspaper in the
United States mentioned the promotion in their fashion columns;
radio announcers talked about it; there were Fire and Ice beauty
contests; Fire and Ice appeared in window displays all over the
country. It was all an enormous success, but for Revlon it was just
one—admittedly a startlingly successful one—promotion in a
whole series.

Avon's marketing policy is quite different from that of any other
cosmetics company. While the advertising budgets of Revlon,
Estée Lauder, Max Factor and others run into many millions of
dollars, Avon spends its money on promotional literature for its
sales people. Its corporate advertising is very small, and more
frequently classified advertisements appear in local papers asking
for Avon representatives. The policy is the same whatever the
market, and Avon is now operating in thirty countries, where it
has subsidiary companies, having found that its first efforts abroad
operating directly from an American-based export division did not
work.

Ever since Mrs. P. F. E. Albee, working with David H. Mc-
Connell when he founded the company in 1886, started calling on
her neighbors in Winchester, New Hampshire, to sell them the
perfumes of the California Perfume Company, the marketing policy has been the same: to use housewives and women who want to
work from their homes to do the selling for the company. Today
there are over one million Avon ladies around the world, close to
400,000 of them working in the United States, mainly part time.
Each lady sells into between 100 and 150 homes on average, although some go as high as 300. Avon divides its selling year into
twenty-six separate campaigns, and each fortnight a new brochure
or brochures will go out to the representatives. In 1978, 400 million brochures were distributed, and the figure will be higher now.

Some of the Avon representatives are now men, and, as well as containing cosmetics and fragrances, the range has expanded into jewelry and clothing products. With Avon probably approaching a point in the American market where eventual growth is expected to be no more than 5 percent a year in cosmetics, the move into new lines is a natural one. And Avon cannot lose on the operation. The representatives order only those products they have already sold, so there is no question of returns.

In America and some other markets, like the United Kingdom, the 1,300 or so products in the Avon range go out with only suggested prices on them. Most will sell at these prices, but if the representative can get a higher price, the extra profit goes to her, not the company. The main problem is to get the orders out quickly. It is very important, for a steady flow of business and to keep customers loyal, not to "short" representatives when their orders come in. This means that inventory control at the warehouses is very critical to the success of the business. In the United States, delivery from the company's Springdale, Ohio, center, which is the size of forty football fields, takes about a week. There are similar centers in the main European markets and Japan and South America, but in some smaller markets, where the customers are scattered and isolated, delivery may take longer. In these cases, delivery and ordering may be by mail.

Millions and millions of small orders are dealt with each week, and by expanding its overseas markets, Avon has been able to achieve a 12 percent growth rate in cosmetics sales in recent years. It does not automatically go into every market where cosmetics are sold. For instance, it made a decision several years ago not to enter South Africa, because of that country's apartheid policies: a decision, the management says, made on moral grounds, but also pleasing to the very many black women among its representatives and administrative staff. With a preponderance of women among its representatives, there are rather more women in management at Avon than in the other companies. Over 80 percent of the management staff in the field are women, and 70 percent of all the employees are women.

A local area manager will appoint the representatives who will come to the company either through recommendation from an existing representative, or through classified advertisements which started in 1886, the first year the company was operating. There is some local training in how to make the "step calls," as they are known; sales kits are issued; and the aim throughout, although the company is the biggest in the world, is to make selling a very personal business, so highly motivated people are needed who like working on a one-to-one basis. To encourage representatives to stay with the company, there are biweekly sales meetings, various contests and prizes and awards to those who have the biggest sales turnover.

Products are carried in the brochures for some time, but each year there are eight or nine major promotions to tempt jaded appetites, not only those of the customers, but also of the representatives, who must be kept enthusiastic about the products they are selling. For instance, when Tempo, an Avon perfume, was launched in late 1978, an ocean liner was charted for a four-day cruise around the Bahamas. All representatives were eligible for the cruise, which was something they could rarely afford in the normal run of their lives. A sweepstakes was held with winners guaranteed from every state in the Union. To qualify for the sweepstakes, an initial purchase of Tempo had to be made. Winners in districts got a prize of some merchandise and then moved onto divisional drawings. In the end, 600 representatives and their spouses (Avon management wants to keep its reps happy) went on the trip.

Of course it was not just a holiday. Tempo was everywhere, in gift packs, T-shirts, menu covers, etc. etc., and promotional literature. No one could come away with any impression other than that Tempo was an important product as far as Avon was concerned. It paid off, and Tempo is the most successful perfume Avon has ever had. After Tempo came Tasha and in April 1980, 300 prize-winning customers and 300 representatives from the United States went to Monaco after a sweepstakes. The result of all this is that some representatives stay with the company all their working lives. Those who do not like the work find out quickly and usually leave after not more than six months or so. Turnover of representatives throughout the world is 100 percent a year, which does not mean that everyone leaves, but that if there are, say, 100 employees in any one year, 100 persons will come and go. The company feels that the turnover level is acceptable for a firm dealing with one million representatives in very different environments.

With one notable exception, Avon has not moved from its door-to-door selling policy, and it is doubtful, with its reputation in the middle-priced value-for-money lines, it could profitably adapt to a combination of direct selling and outlets through stores. The exception is Tiffany's, New York's famous high-class jewelry store on Fifth Avenue. The financial community in New York was intrigued by the purchase. Both companies issued statements saying that they could continue to operate independently, but not everyone takes these at their face value. A fragrance under the brand name Tiffany would go down very well with those who only know of the store by repute. This could downgrade Tiffany's image with the monied classes, however. Another course would be to open more Tiffany shops and ally them to Avon's jewelry sales. This, too, could not be good for the Tiffany image. So far the company has made no moves since making the purchase, but many are speculating on what may happen, and some openly state that the marriage of the class name Tiffany with the mass name Avon could be a grave mistake. The only logical move for Avon is seen as the launch of some kind of expensive Tiffany range of cosmetics or fragrance through the store itself, in its mail catalogue and through a few other specialty stores. If so, it would be the beginning of Avon's attempt to break into the retail cosmetics market, perhaps as a competitor to Revlon. It is a daunting task.

Whatever their current policies, new approaches to advertising and marketing by the cosmetics companies may become necessary as women change their views of themselves. Charles Revson knew what he was doing when he invented the Charlie girl, bright, attractive and sexy, but above all, independent: quite different from the clinging romantic creature of earlier years. But there is more to the successful marketing of cosmetics than just finding a new image: no matter how liberated women have become or feel that they are becoming, experience has shown that they will still use makeup, toiletries and fragrances. It is the pitch they respond to that has changed. Even in the United Kingdom, where women are much less aware of their new roles and potential position in society than in the U.S., they have been objecting to the stereotypes of their sex so common in advertising.

When canvassed, women say that they no longer wish to be portrayed—if they ever were—in advertising as completely stupid, overglamorous, or idiotic, and when they are, they are beginning to ignore the sales pitch. If this is so, cosmetics companies will in many instances have to change their approach to women to some extent in their advertising. In early 1980, British women were criticizing the Optrex Eye Dew advertisement as sexist when it suggested that it "makes the most of a quick Flash" and Miss Worth "when he calls across the oceans at 3 a.m." In contrast, other advertisements have been applauded as nonsexist. Cacharel's Anaïs Anaïs lady, for instance, "models herself on no one" and the independent, attractive and sexy Charlie girl is admired. So, too, is Max Factor's Blasé "for the girl who doesn't have to prove a thing." But sex-object advertising like Sure deodorants exhorting "Get out of the jungle" is not praised, and there is doubt about the role reversal in Unilever's Denim Male Toiletries advertising. Advertising that preys on the narcissistic element in everyone's character is viewed with suspicion. Such advertising includes Badedas' "things happen after a Badedas bath," and Fenjal, another bath oil, has a similar slogan. Saint-Laurent's Opium perfume is also felt to be too narcissistic. Female stereotypes are readily recognizable, but there are male stereotypes too. Pour Monsieur, from Pierre Cardin, suffers from this, whereas the Brut deodorant poster showing boxer Henry Cooper, "the deodorant with muscle," does not. Such awareness of the reality behind advertising seems certain to grow rather than diminish. It is a trend that the cosmetic companies ignore, at their peril.

Fragrances and their marketing are almost an industry on their own within the cosmetics business, and the public is almost totally unaware of the names of some of the biggest producers in cosmetics in the world. Italy provides companies all over the world with color cosmetics which eventually go out under the name of well-known companies. Many companies use the same suppliers, but sell at vastly different prices for basically the same products when they reach the market. Nowhere is this more true than in perfumes. Paco Rabanne perfumes, for instance, emanate not from the couturier, but from Puig of Barcelona, Spain. What happens is that cosmetic companies come up with an idea for a perfume, and a specialist company produces it for them. These companies operate from all over the world with names like Norda, Givauddan, Florasynth, Roure DuPont, Naarden, but most of all, International Flavors and Fragrances, an American-based company, which towers above the rest.

Most of the fragrance houses are in private hands, but International Flavors and Fragrances went public in 1961. Like many companies in the cosmetics industry in America, it was founded by a first-generation immigrant, A. L. van Ameringen, a Dutchman, who set up in business in the 1920s: IFF itself was not formed until 1958, although van Ameringen had been making a good living in fragrances for years. It was the explosion in scents not only for cosmetics and toiletries but also for perfumed air fresheners, detergents and the like that brought a boom to IFF. Its growth was spectacular, and the company has become a worldwide operation with laboratories and manufacturing plants in more than twenty countries, including one in Yugoslavia. Within a decade of going public, the value of the shares had risen by an incredible 5,000 percent.

The international strength of the company was clear from its 1978 results. Sales rose by 14 percent, from $274 million to $314 million, and profits did even better, rising by over 22 percent to $85,509,000. In the mature market of North America, sales are rising slowly, by around 7 percent a year, but the company's strength internationally has brought increases in sales in Europe between 15 and 16 percent and even more in Latin America and the Far East, where they improved by between 20 and 25 percent.

Fragrance companies have always been very profitable. They each have their secrets, and no company is able to copy exactly the fragrances of another. It is also a very competitive world: if a fragrance does not work in a product, the customer will go elsewhere next time he is looking for a fragrance. What makes the business so highly profitable is that the fragrance, in soap, for example, will probably be only one percent of the cost of the product once it has been developed and accepted. The fragrance house is then out of the picture, and its risk in terms of the total product is minimal. It has moved on to another project, while the cosmetics or toiletries manufacturer is the one involved in the costs of product development, testing for impurities, test-marketing, advertising and distribution. The only problem for the fragrance house is to pitch the price of its contribution at a profitable level.

A fragrance company will have several perfumers, or "noses," as they are known, working for it. These people have access to up to 4,000 synthetic fragrances, and 300 to 400 natural ones. From these they will work to fulfill the customer's specifications. At IFF there are stores of as many as 23,000 flavors and fragrances. To find a perfume, a "nose" may perform thousands of experiments before he or she is ready to put a selection before the client. Whatever a perfume smells like in the end, it will have basically the same ingredients: nearly three-quarters of it will be ethyl alcohol; there will be some water, of course; some essential oils, which may come from Grasse, France, or from the Soviet Union, which is a big producer; and some other scents of spices to give the perfume its distinctive smell. Altogether, the cost of these ingredients in a one-ounce bottle will be somewhere between five and ten dollars and the final product will cost anything up to ten or even twelve times as much. The rest of the money goes in the same way as the cosmetics dollar: in advertising and promotion, packaging and profit to the maker and the retailer, and the costs are the same whether it is a male or female perfume that is being marketed. Up to 70 percent of wholesale costs may go to promotion. In 1979, Lever Brothers, the Anglo-Dutch conglomerate, spent between $10 and $12 million promoting Denim, its new male line. This is thought to be the highest advertising expenditure ever for this type of product. As more and more money is needed in the development of products, there are those who feel that the traditional European (and particularly French) perfumes have had their day. Only the very large companies can afford the vast sums of money needed to capture the market with a new perfume. Once again, it all comes back to money.

Some cosmetics houses do develop their own perfumes, and here again Estée Lauder comes up trumps. She is considered to be one of the leading judges of fragrances in the business—a natural "nose." The Fabergé company also brought out its very successful Brut by itself, and also the less successful Babe. But these instances are rare. In the overwhelming majority of cases, companies go shopping to a number of fragrance manufacturers when they are searching for a new perfume. Fashions change in fragrances just as they do in cosmetics and the first company to spot a change from, say, flowery to spicy, or light to heavy, fragrances can be on to a winner.

A mere list of all the ranges of cosmetics that have come out in the thirty-five years since the end of World War II would fill a book. Every company brought out, if not a complete new range, at least a new product in the range, or a new set of colors every year, and new companies were springing up constantly. The plethora of choice which descended on the market can be seen by the number of new perfumes from the period—and they were few in comparison with skin-treatment products and color cosmetics. What makes the perfume launches so interesting is that they show just how successfully the French could compete in any international market if they wish to do so. The perfume industry was slow to revive after the war ended. The reason for this was the then concentration of all the best perfume houses in France. But as early as 1945, Weil brought out Antilope, followed two years later by Dior, now part of the Moet-Hennessy group, with Miss Dior and, a year later, in 1948, Nina Ricci's L'Air du Temps. In 1950, Lancôme introduced Magie, followed in 1953 by Estée Lauder's first perfume, Youth Dew. Dior was back again in 1955 with Dior-issimo, sticking to the couturier name (Dior himself did not own the perfume company), as did Givenchy in 1959. In 1956, Chanel made the bold step from women to men, calling the fragrance simply Chanel for Men; no numbers for them. Apart from the Lauder scent, there was no significant perfume line from America and none from Britain during this period.

It all began to change in the 1960s. In the first year came Mémoire Chérie, the last major perfume produced by Elizabeth Arden herself. Lauder brought out Aramis, a line for men, in 1964, quickly followed by arch-competitor Charles Revson with Braggi in 1965. Fabergé had also introduced Brut in 1964, a cheaper but very successful men's range. A year later Fabergé followed Brut with Musk for Men, not nearly so successfully. Dior, with Dior himself dead, had Eau Sauvage in 1967. Women's perfumes were still coming from France in the early 1960s. In 1960, Nina Ricci added Caprice to L'Air du Temps; in 1962 Grès brought out Cabochard. In 1964 came Yves Saint-Laurent's first perfume, Y; Imprevu from Coty in 1965; and during the decade, Jean Patou launched two new perfumes, Caline for women in 1966 and Lacoste for men in 1969. Estée Lauder was there also with two new names for women, Estée in 1968 and Azurée a year later. L'Oreal, through its subsidiary Guy Laroche, introduced the continuingly successful Fidji in 1968, and finally Revlon brought out the not-so-successful Norell a year later. The decade also saw the first perfume from the Italian Florentine couturier Pucci, in 1965, named simply after himself. The 1970s have seen Pucci joined by other Italian designers like Gucci and Valentino, who, like the French couturiers, later moved into cosmetics.

If the designers were establishing a leading place in the 1960s, they were to dominate it during the 1970s. This time the American designers would be involved too; where they could, cosmetics companies were buying up designers' names for perfume lines. In the 1970s, almost as many lines were introduced for men as for women. Givenchy III for women came in 1970, followed in two years by Givenchy Gentleman. Weil added Weil de Weil in 1973; Nina Ricci, Farouche in 1974. Grès pour Hommes made its appearance in 1972, as did Cardin's Cologne for Men.

In the same year Dior was back with Diorella, and Chanel with another number, this time 19, followed in 1977 with Cristale from the same company. Bill Blass, the American designer under the aegis of Revlon, brought out his own-named scent for women in 1970, followed eight years later by Bill Blass for men. Paco Rabanne reversed the process, and his first scent, Calandre, was for men. Three years later in 1973 he brought out Paco for women. Oscar de la Renta, Diane von Furstenberg, Calvin Klein, Pauline Trigère, Charles Jourdan, Geoffrey Beene, Mary McFadden and Lagerfeld all brought out perfumes alongside their clothes, either independently or under the wing of a larger cosmetics group. The big companies were in the market as well, notably Max Factor. Call Me Maxi may have flopped, but the perfumes brought out by the company under the Halston (yet another designer) label, Halston for women and 2-14 and 1-12 for men, did a great deal at Norton Simon to make up for the disappointing showing by Max Factor. The Halston cosmetics have been doing well, too.

Coty introduced Nuance, Masumi, and Smitty (yet another copy of Charlie) with varying degrees of success in successive years. Elizabeth Arden brought out its first perfume after the death of Miss Arden, Cabriole, in 1977. Rubinstein, which had bought up designer Anne Klein, introduced her to the public with the briskly named Blazer perfume. And of course Estée Lauder was there with Alliage in 1972, Private Collection in 1973, and her "new romantics," White Linen, Pavilion and Celadon in 1978. In the same year, Cinnabar was rushed out quickly to compete with the dramatically launched and highly successful Opium from Yves Saint-Laurent, via, in the United States, Charles of the Ritz and its parent organization, the Squibb Corporation. Finally, among the major launches, Revlon brought the decade to a close with the launch first in France and then in America of the world's most expensive perfume, Ivoire, backed by Pierre Balmain, a highly respected name in the world of fashion. In the last three months of 1979 alone, seventeen new fragrances were introduced in France, and of these Ivoire de Balmain had the most favorable reception. Fragrance sales in France account for a quarter of all cosmetics sales there, and as much as 10 percent of the total is to men.

Former model Baroness Fiona Thyssen takes a dim view of some of the couturiers' moves into fragrances: "I do think that many of them launch themselves into the mainstream of the cosmetics industry, relying on their names to sell products and perfumes which are mediocre. One is dealing with an infinitely more selective and informed public nowadays, and a sound proven article should outweigh a heavy publicity campaign."

During the 1970s the women's fragrance market in the United Kingdom took off. With total sales in 1978 of just over $170 million, it is a small market compared to that of the United States which in the same year was close to one billion dollars, but it is growing very fast. In five years it had more than trebled in value, with the great surge coming between 1976 and 1977. As the industry enters the 1980s, there are seventy-five perfume houses operating in the U.K., offering around 250 different fragrances, about the same as in the United States.

The reason the market opened up so suddenly and quickly can be put to one product—Revlon's Charlie, which was just as successful in the U.K. as in the U.S., and, moreover, it increased general customer awareness of and interest in perfumes. The boom in sales following Charlie induced far more companies to enter the market, and in 1977 fifty new perfumes were introduced, compared with a previous average of two in normal years. Stimulating the sales has naturally brought a significant increase in advertising, and this now amounts to around 10 percent of the total revenue from cosmetics sales. This figure is rather more than when sales were much lower. Then the figure was around 7.5 percent. Sales were also helped in 1977 and 1978 by the low pound: international visitors found that they could get the best value for money for expensive perfumes in the U.K. and bought accordingly.

There was not simply a great spontaneous boom in fragrance buying by the British public. In order to succeed, many companies had to try marketing techniques that they had not tried in a big way before—sample sizes, special offers and giveaways. The ten most popular perfumes in the United Kingdom differ quite markedly from those in the U.S. Charlie comes at the top, but out of the top ten, six are British, five from the BAT Industries house: Lentheric with Tweed, IT, Tramp, Just Musk and Panache. The other one, In Love, comes from Norman Hartnell, late dresser to the Queen and other members of the Royal Family. Coty, owned by Pfizer, Inc., has one market leader, L'Aimant; and Prince Matchabelli, from Chesebrough-Pond's, the other, Cachet.

There was a sharp change in the market in the 1970s. At the beginning, there was no doubt that Yardley, also part of BAT Industries, was the leading fragrance house. Today it is nowhere among the best sellers. By 1975 the company had an aged appearance; only older women were using its perfumes. The reason was Charlie, which swept the young market as soon as it was launched in Britain. Yardley reacted by bringing out a series of perfumes pitched at the modern woman, like Laughter (1976), Je Suis (1977) and Intrigue (1979). The company has not yet, however, discovered how to marry this market with its older perfumes like Freesia, Old English Lavender and Bond Street. While these sell alongside one another, it seems unlikely that Yardley can regain its leading position.

In contrast, Lentheric, Yardley's sister company at BAT, is one of the marketing successes of the fragrance trade in Britain. The company succeeded by using a mass-marketing approach. It brought out a whole series of fragrances and marketed them all together on the same stand in Boots and other chains of drugstores. This might have taken the mystique out of the idea of an individual perfume for every woman, but it worked and sold on a self-selection basis. Lentheric became Britain's leading fragrance house in 1977, a position it has maintained since. Altogether with its three house names—Lentheric, Solitaire, a cheaper range, and the older Mornay label—the company had fifteen perfumes on the market in 1979.

The upmarket U.K. perfume buyer has a great liking for French perfumes or at least French-sounding names, and, apart from Charlie, it seems that to get any start in the prestige market at all, French names are essential. For this reason, L'Oreal, with careful advertising, has built up a good reputation for its "French Quarter" line, four different fragrances that link in the one line the names of four couturiers—Courrèges, Laroche, Ted Lapidus and Jacques Fath. Only the Fath name comes from the older couturiers who have a recognized standing in the market, but even so, a sound base has been established and the perfumes are well liked. Of the top twenty perfumes sold in Britain, eight of them are French or have French-sounding names.

NINE

MILLION-DOLLAR FACES

Beauty gets the best of it in this world.
—Don Marquis, *archy and mehitabel*

When it was announced that Margaux Hemingway, an American model, was to be paid one million dollars over five years to promote the Babe perfume brought out by Fabergé in 1977, the amount of money involved caused more comment in the media than the product launch itself. Miss Hemingway's name, though well known in the modeling world, was not known to the general public, which was told that, in addition to being beautiful, she is the granddaughter of the late novelist Ernest Hemingway. Staggering though the figure she was going to be paid might seem, however, it is only one of the many lucrative contracts which go today to those girls fortunate enough to be blessed by nature, not necessarily with a very beautiful face, but certainly with an extremely photogenic one.

Almost alone, along of course with the couture clothing industry, the cosmetics industry has virtually created the photographic side of the modeling industry in the postwar period. Gone are the days when a mannequin—not a model—urged an emaciated body along the catwalk and then went home, to a frugal diet and a

short-lived professional life. Today's model is a breathing, walk-
ing, talking, girl-shaped (though not too shapely) young woman,
who looks more human, healthy and attractive than most of us,
but not extravagantly so.

Never before has a photogenic face been worth more to its
owner—and her agency. In her short professional life, in most
cases generally reckoned to be about six years, though some do
manage to survive much longer, a female model can set herself
up for life if she manages her money properly. So, too, can a male
model and on the whole his effective working life is much longer
than a woman's, for it is a fiction of the fashion and cosmetics
industries that people find middle-aged men acceptable in advertisements but not middle-aged women. This view may of course
change as the major portion of the cosmetics market ages as the
birth rate falls and there are fewer teenagers.

Some outstanding girls do survive for a considerable time. Lauren Hutton, now making a career in films, is still, at the age of
thirty-seven, modeling the Revlon Ultima II line, for which she
has appeared since 1973. Her contract is worth $200,000 a year.
Karen Graham, who models the entire Estée Lauder line, has had
a very long career, too. Her earnings are a closely guarded secret,
and the company would like her life to be equally unknown outside her job. To them she is not Karen Graham but the Estée
Lauder woman, and nothing else about her is of any interest at
all. Since it began national advertising in 1962, the company has
used only three models to advertise the Lauder range; the Clinique line brought out by the company is marketed completely
separately. Miss Graham has now been putting across the Lauder
image for ten years, a long time in the life of a model, especially
as she is now thirty-five and was not young for a model when she
first signed her contract. The image is of a young but not too
young international woman of worldly grace and sophistication,
glamorous but not remote, and versatile and lively, even sporty.
Miss Graham's own background reflects the image she portrays:
she comes from a well-to-do Mississippi family, and her education
included a stint at the Sorbonne in Paris. She is also married to

Delman Coleman, a businessman who specializes in company deals and found himself under investigation by the American Securities and Exchange Commission in 1969. That was before Miss Graham married him, and also before she almost became Mrs. David Frost. The nuptials were canceled at the very last minute, and Miss Graham then immediately married Mr. Coleman. Apart from that brief flare of publicity, however, Miss Graham has led the quiet, well-heeled life as behooves the Lauder woman. She might well be Estée Lauder herself some thirty years ago. The impression she gives of her background and style is the same.

The Revlon woman is blatantly sexy; the Lauder woman is not. She is equally at home in metropolitan town life and in the suburbs, and obvious sexiness is out. The appeal is more to sensuality. Miss Graham's fee may be a secret but will compare well with those broadcast abroad, by companies who seek extra publicity for themselves by broadcasting just how expensive their models are. Miss Graham's days as a model must be drawing to an end now, but during her time with Lauder she will have made enough money to keep herself comfortably for the rest of her life.

The tales of large sums of money hide the realities of a business that is tough and has a high casualty rate. Only one girl in every 1,000 is suitable for any kind of modeling at all; yet it remains an overcrowded profession—and always has been. For every girl who hits the headlines, there are dozens who spend their professional lives in the hard grind of store fashion shows, or doing the least popular jobs, like modeling underwear. Only about one percent of the girls who enter the industry are immediately successful, and that is usually not because they are more beautiful than the others, but for some reason catch the eye of the advertising agency, because they are different or striking in some new way. One out of every two newcomers in the industry drops out within a few months, and for those who remain, earnings may be erratic and low. It may take years to get into the top earning brackets, and only a small percentage ever do.

Those women who make it to the top can easily earn $2,000 a day and up to $200,000 a year. Top male models, who are beginning to be used more and more in cosmetics advertising, do not earn as much as the women, but even they can command fees of $1,250 a day and up to $150,000 a year.

It was possible in the past for a girl to become a photographic model without using an agency. To get some modeling assignments, a girl would take herself around to the advertising agencies and magazines in search of work. As demand grew, it became almost impossible in this way to find the right kinds of girls to fill the needs, and inevitably a new business to provide them sprang up. Once again, it is Americans, or American-based companies, who control the business, mostly from New York, where four large agencies fight bitterly with considerable personal enmity for business, which in 1979 was reckoned to be worth around $50 million a year. The four—Ford Models, Zoli, Elite Model Management and Wilhelmina Models—have between them 60 percent of all the billings in the industry in the world, and they carry on in the style of the old-time cosmetics manufacturers, stealing one another's models and generally indulging in personal vituperation.

The reason for this is that, until four years ago, Ford Models, Inc., run by the husband and wife team Jerry and Eileen Ford, virtually controlled the whole of the modeling industry worldwide. The Fords set up their business in 1946, selling their car to get the $900 they needed to set up the still privately owned company. Two years later they had total billings of $250,000 and 43 female models. By 1978 the figure had risen to close to $12 million from 259 women and 93 men. Out of this, the profit was around $2,500,000. Their "stable" includes many well-known models like Candice Bergen and Lauren Hutton, and America's most popular model of 1979 and 1980—Cheryl Tiegs.

Choosing a good model is rather like having a good "nose" for fragrances, and Mrs. Ford picks the "girls," as they are always referred to, with Mr. Ford selling them to the advertisers. The secret of success for the agency is in the product. Provided a continuing stream of the right girls can be found and then dissuaded from leaving for another agency, marketing them is not particularly difficult. The search for girls goes on worldwide, and the Fords have talent scouts looking out for appropriate candidates all over the United States and particularly in California, where to be beautiful seems to be a law of nature, and in Europe, especially in Germany and Scandinavia, where the best blondes for modeling are found. The agencies look for girls who are tall, at least over five feet seven, and preferably taller than that, long-limbed with good bones and slender frames. At the Ford Agency, the price for the introduction of a suitable girl from a foreign agency is between 3 and 5 percent of the income she makes in the first year. In addition, the Fords consider about 5,000 American girls each year, rejecting the vast majority.

For years the Fords brushed aside all opposition. Even when Wilhelmina Cooper, their top model in 1967, left them to start her own agency with her husband, there was no slowing down in their growth. Wilhelmina, who had modeled for Revlon, ran into nothing but trouble for the first few years and incurred heavy losses. Then she changed her tack and decided to leave the high-fashion and cosmetics models to the Ford agency, which was supreme in that area and could not be budged. She went into those parts of the business which the Fords had ignored. By adding black and brunette models to her stable—the demand from cosmetics companies is heavily biased toward blondes, who, it is believed, can sell anything—and moving into the broad television area, which does not require its models always to be amazingly beautiful, her agency turned the corner, and was soon nudging the Fords in total billings.

Since Wilhelmina and the Fords were operating in different markets, there was no need for extensive piracy between them, but the arrival of John Casablancas in New York in 1977 changed all that. Previously he had run his agency, Elite, from Paris and had exchanged girls with both the Fords and Wilhelmina. He had also, both alleged, promised never to compete with them in New York. Although there were no written contracts between the parties, both Ford and Wilhelmina are now suing Casablancas for multimillion-dollar damages. His arrival on the scene pushed the previous third agency, Zoli, which is especially strong on male models, into fourth place. Casablancas, a man of great energy, came from Paris with enough money behind him to embark on an extensive publicity campaign and also to defend himself in the lawsuits he faced. He also offered a lot more money to his models and immediately won girls over from the Wilhelmina and Ford stables. His girls on average earn nearly twice as much as they do at Ford and 25 percent more than at Wilhelmina. All the agencies charge advertisers 10 percent commission and their girls between 15 and 20 percent on their earnings.

The business the model agencies most covet is the cosmetics business and, most of all, the exclusive contract to represent a cosmetic range—like Lauren Hutton with Ultima II; Shelley Hack for the Charlie fragrance and cosmetics, who, like Farrah Fawcett, did a stint as a Charlie's Angel; Clotilde, a Ford model on a $190,000-a-year contract to model for Shiseido in Japan; and of course Cheryl Tiegs. Miss Tiegs has gone one further than the others and has been portioned out between several manufacturers. Noxell Corporation has her face and will pay her and her agency, Ford, $1.5 million over five years for her face; she models their Cover Girl range of color cosmetics and foundation creams. Her hair, for the time being, is owned by Bristol-Myers, whose Clairol subsidiary is using her for its Clairesse hair color. A rumor that her legs are also available to another purchaser has been denied by Jerry Ford, whose most profitable girl she is. Miss Tiegs has had the ultimate accolade of a *Time* cover story, on March 16, 1978. She has had a long life for a model and is now thirty-two, though she looks about twenty. She is said to charge well over $2,000 for a day's modeling, which is rather more than many other top models, though none will step in front of a camera for less than $1,000 a day, and on some jobs, say in Japan, where the Western look is much admired, they can earn up to $5,000 a day.

Not surprisingly, advertisers—and none more so than the cosmetics companies—complain about the prices they have to pay for models, but pay they do, because there is no other way that they can economically seek out the girls they need, or believe they need, to get their products across. It is impossible to say how much a particular girl adds to sales and profits, if anything, but even at $2,000 an hour a model is a minuscule charge in the total cost of advertising. Some cosmetics and fragrance manufacturers do object to the prices, and some take action. Sears, for example, once refused to use the Ford male models for a two-year period because it thought they were too expensive. Most cosmetics companies pay the girls full fees, though Revlon can often get away with less, claiming that a girl it has used will be able to command a much higher fee afterward.

But are annual earnings of between $100,000 and $200,000 for a top girl excessive? The agencies would argue that they are not. The life of a professional model is short by the standards of any other profession, even for a girl who lasts ten years or more. And it is a fact of modeling that the same girls seem to appeal at the same time to most of the companies in the cosmetics industry, and the chances are that, at any one time, there will be only about thirty of them. Naturally they go out to the highest bidders, and however much they may dislike doing it, the companies are prepared to outbid one another to get the girl who they believe will best help them sell their product.

It is difficult to define what makes a girl a good model. So many fill the requirements of beauty and size and are photogenic as well. A girl who suits one period will not suit another. Jean Shrimpton, the British model who was the darling of the 1960s and did much to establish Yardley as a swinging up-to-date cosmetics company in the U.S., suited the mood of the 1960s. She looked vulnerable with enormous, innocent eyes. Behind them was a worldly-wise look, but she did not have a liberated image. The American models of the same period were similar. Then the mood changed, and in Shelley Hack, Charles Revson with the Charlie range found a new look that had instant appeal—a liberated, healthy woman who was also attractive and sexy.

Cheryl Tiegs is another look altogether. She has the "California Look," which is almost always blond and blue-eyed, is always long-legged and well, though not extravagantly, shaped, and most certainly wholesome. Twenty years ago, the public would hear nothing about the lives of the women they see every day modeling some product or projecting some makeup. Today everyone knows about Miss Tiegs: she—or rather her agent—tells all. She is five feet ten and weighs 120 pounds. She was not always thus. After her marriage in 1970 when she was twenty, she fattened up to 150 pounds and half-retired. The story has been told so that women everywhere can sympathize with her: they have the same problems. She solved it by not eating, and her career took off. She is in demand quite simply because her face—and figure—sell products, any products. She appears to be sexy and therefore attractive to men without apparently seeming threatening to women, who therefore are also sympathetic to anything she is advertising. And it's not just cosmetics: *Harper's* magazine found that when she was on its cover, sales increased by 70 percent.

Miss Tiegs grew up in Alhambra, California, the daughter of an undertaker. Her mother worked in a flower shop, and the family were Quakers. She did well at school and was first noticed by a talent scout when she was sixteen. College as an English major at California State University lasted only one year, because by that time Miss Tiegs had been "discovered." In 1964 she appeared in a swimsuit advertisement for Cole of California in *Seventeen* magazine, and Nina Blanchard, a West Coast talent scout, offered her a contract. Thus armed, she moved to New York in 1966 and in the next three years was photographed for seventy magazine covers. From then on it was a matter of consolidation, and Miss Tiegs's career developed steadily until, by 1978, she was the highest-paid model ever in the industry, earning at least $200,000 a year. But time marches on, especially for models, and Miss Tiegs has begun to work out what will happen in the rest of her life. First of all, she has been clearly determined to get as much out of her modeling life as possible. She proposed herself to Pro Pop Arts, the company that had made at least $1 million from its posters of Farrah Fawcett-Majors, who had flopped so badly promoting a cosmetics line for Fabergé. She hired a public relations company to promote her as a personality and embarked on a very public social life. She signed a contract with Simon and Schuster for $50,000 to collaborate on a book, *The Way to Natural Beauty*, and is reported to have lamented that there was so little money in publishing. Like Suzy Parker, Lauren Hutton, Candice Bergen and many others before her, she is embarking on a film career.

Not bad for an undertaker's daughter with an extremely pretty face who has been described as reticent to the point of being inarticulate. But she is not the most beautiful girl in the world, and her success is due to those qualities—in addition to luck—that all successful models have. Baroness Thyssen, who, as Fiona Campbell-Walter, was one of Britain's most successful models of the 1950s and 1960s, put it well when she told me that she had been "blessed with a good head," but brushed that attribute aside for the disciplines that she possessed and that are vital to every model—"punctuality, totally professional outlook, patience, clothes sense and charm."

The world's most public model face in the 1960s was Jean Shrimpton's, who appeared on around 350 magazine covers after her first appearance in *Vogue* in 1961, when she was eighteen. The photographer was London East-Ender David Bailey, with whom she was professionally and romantically involved for many years. In 1980 she told the *News of the World*, a British Sunday paper: "Famous I might be, rich I wasn't. I'd refused to do advertising or TV commercials, which is where the money is. I preferred working on *Vogue*, which was more fun but very badly paid. I got £10 a day and my lunch." But at some stage in her career the Shrimp, a nickname she was said to hate, was reckoned to be earning $1,000 a week, a sum that, at $50,000 a year, looks meager against the $200,000 that top models command today for contracts that are often not exclusive and leave them free for other work. (Models have always been relatively highly paid, though the sums available today are startling by any standard.)

Fiona Campbell-Walter was reputed to be the highest-paid

model ever in the United Kingdom at the time she was modeling, and recalls: "When I started modeling I seem to remember my fee was £3 an hour and eventually it did go up! If it is true that I was earning £4,000 a year at my peak, I must have been fully employed." She describes herself as "bustier" than was normal and remembers that the Ford Agency in New York wanted to take her on, but also wanted her to take off ten pounds, which she did not want to do.

It was when Jean Shrimpton modeled the Yardley cosmetics line in America in the mid-1960s that she moved into the big-money league. She took the fashion world here by storm. No one had imagined that an English girl could look like that. She was on the cover of *Newsweek* on September 23, 1965, and the magazine commented: "Ersatz Shrimps are already proliferating around the globe. In the U.S. women and childwomen from the Bronx to Beverly Hills lavishly round their eyes, install canopies of false eye-lashes, let their hair fall in carefully combed disarray and imitate the Girl's gangly, coltish stance. The Shrimp, it can be argued, is the embodiment of America's current love affair with people and things British. She symbolizes the emergence of London—once the citadel of gentlemen's fashion—as a new-world tastemaker in pop culture.

"That once stodgy city seems to possess the world's most 'dolly' girls, the most 'gear' combos, and the most 'switched on' singers, artists, designers, models and photographers." With magazines writing editorial copy like that, Yardley and their gorgeous girl just could not fail. The company, alas, found no one to replace her. When the Shrimp was at her peak in 1963, it was forecast that if she survived as a model for ten years she would earn $100,000 over the period. It turned out to be more than that, but even to her Cheryl Tiegs's earnings today would appear to be a fantasy.

Shrimpton followed the usual model path, wrote her autobiography, *My Own Story: The Truth About Modelling*, in 1964, at the advanced age of twenty-two, went to live in New York for a few years and, then, at the age of twenty-seven, bored with her job, retired to Cornwall, in the southwest of England, where she has remained ever since.

What Jean Shrimpton did in the 1960s, Lauren Hutton repeated for the 1970s, and before the amazing Miss Tiegs, she was almost certainly the world's highest-paid model. She personified the Ultima II Revlon line and was personally chosen by Charles Revson to model the whole range to the exclusion of anyone else. Her durability in this industry of short professional lives is legend. She first appeared on the cover of *Vogue* in November 1966, photographed by Richard Avedon, who has photographed so many famous women and made so many others famous. At first she made $50 a week and was turned down by all the agencies she tried. With an obvious gap in her front teeth, she was perhaps not at first an automatic candidate for stardom. But she had not tried the Ford Agency, which was then absolutely dominant; when she did, she was accepted. Even that did not mean instant success, and it was only when Diana Vreeland, then editor of American *Vogue*, saw her and immediately put her into the magazine that her career took off.

When she thought her modeling career had reached its peak, Hutton turned, as so many models have done, to Hollywood, made four forgettable films, and that seemed to be the end of that. Then came the Ultima II job and her future was assured. A tiny false tooth filled the gap in her teeth for the cosmetics advertisements, and her face became immediately familiar to millions of women. Not all models are distinguished by their intelligence, but Miss Hutton proved she knew what she was doing. Her Ultima contract left her free to work for *Vogue* and also to pursue her film career. That, at her second go, has proved much more successful too, and at thirty-seven, when most models' careers are finished, she continues in the commanding heights of the industry—with or without her porcelain filler, as the director or advertiser demands.

Lauren Hutton was said to have been romantically involved with Charles Revson, but this is certainly untrue, although she seems to have been fonder of him than the other models personally selected by him. She did not, however, contrary to rumor, meet him until the day she signed the contract with Revlon in 1973, after months of negotiations. Miss Hutton has lived for many years now in Greenwich, Connecticut with a free-lance stockbroker.

It took advertisers quite a long time after the end of World War II to realize the marketing benefits that could accrue when the public could identify a range of products with a particular model. Until the 1950s, if a model did a cosmetics job—and it was quite rare that she did—it was generally a one shot and some other girl would be used next time. It was Charles Revson who first realized the potential in using a glamorous, very sexy woman to represent a complete range of cosmetics.

Many women have appeared in Revlon advertisements and then moved on to other careers. Candice Bergen, daughter of comedian Edgar Bergen, has had a highly successful film career since she modeled Tawny for Revlon in 1964. Wilhelmina, with her agency now locked in combat with the Fords, helped Revlon's Moon Drops lipstick along its profitable path. But two women in particular became associated with the Revlon image in the 1950s, and it so happened that they were sisters, Dorian Leigh and Suzy Parker. Miss Leigh, the elder of the two, was first used by Revlon for the Fatal Apple promotion in 1945, but her real claim to fame was her modeling for Fire and Ice in 1952. This advertisement is regarded in the trade as one of the best ever in cosmetics and was designed to give the ordinary woman a completely new idea of herself. Miss Leigh was dressed in a silver-sequined, tight-fitting dress under a brilliant scarlet cape. The accompanying copy suggested that women were two people—an ordinary normal woman, with a smoldering siren underneath. It worked and sales rocketed. *Advertising Age* named it the best advertisement of the year, and *Business Week* wrote: "Perhaps more than any previous ad, this one successfully combines dignity, class and glamour [a trade euphemism for sex]."

It was known that Miss Leigh was very friendly with Charles Revson; her sister, Suzy Parker, was not and is reputed to have told people that she did not like him. Miss Parker, now Mrs. Bradford Dillman, was perhaps the most dazzling model of them all. Before she and her sister came along, models had been aloof and elegant. The incoming sisters did not go for the pretty, casual and relaxed look, as typified by Cheryl Tiegs and Shelley Hack today. They were women of almost flawless beauty, although Miss Parker always wore false nails, much, it is said, to the annoyance of Charles Revson. They were, however, extremely elegant, and there was little of a "liberated" image of them in the advertisements in which they appeared: they were obviously approachable —by men. They also happened to be intelligent and articulate, and for the first time real women came out from behind the glamorous façade of the model world. They spoke up for themselves and did not allow anyone to use them in a way in which they did not wish to be used. Miss Parker was featured on the cover of *Life* magazine in 1957, the first time such coverage had been given to a female model.

The relationship between Miss Parker and Charles Revson was a stormy one. He clearly thought that she was the best face in the business, but grew to dislike her, simply, it would seem, because she did not behave like other girls and do as she was told. She made it clear she was working for money, not for love, and that in her view the money was not all that good. She could get fees of well over $100 an hour in the late fifties, but such a figure even then was not so impressive as it sounds. A photographic session lasting, say, four hours could net Miss Parker $500, but she would not be needed again for several months. In those days, there was no question of the exclusive contracts that are so sought after today, and that was what Miss Parker wanted in order to guarantee her income, although BBDO, which was then Revlon's advertising agency, is said to have suggested the arrangement. In the end, Miss Parker refused to model for Revson, and he later, contrariwise, refused to use her, although on one occasion, for the Cleopatra look, Sphinx Pink (could anyone actually say that when trying to buy it?), she was the model and Revson was told that the advertisement actually featured her sister.

There is one famous shot of Charles Revson and his senior aides with Suzy Parker which was taken for publicity purposes in 1960. Miss Parker—with her glamorous long fingernails—is laughing happily, as Mr. Revson, with lipstick shades on the palms of his hands, is admiring her. But the reality is that Miss Parker insisted that this session be treated as a modeling assignment and that Revson pay her a fee.

Following her successful modeling career, Parker moved into films. Her sister ran a modeling agency in Paris for a time and later a restaurant, Chez Dorian, outside Paris, before writing her autobiography, *Girl Who Had Everything.*

Other girls made money from Revlon, but none achieved quite the glamour of the Misses Parker and Leigh. Barbara Britten, however, who worked for Revlon for twelve years as an anchorwoman in television commercials probably made more money out of the company than the rest, possibly put together. In her best year with Revlon she made $130,000, and she did nine commercials a week, three in each of the shows Revlon was sponsoring, "The $64,000 Question," "The $64,000 Challenge" and the "Walter Winchell File." Miss Britten did not appear in the advertisements; she just did the talking at a time when all commercials were live performances. When advertisements began to be taped, her career faltered and finally died.

Today's girls, with their high earnings, will be yesterday's girls in a very short time. The mood changes, and the sporty liberated models of today could be old hat within a month or two. There is no doubt that women have often no idea of how they want to look until the cosmetics manufacturers and the fashion trade tell them. Then they tend to follow like sheep. A new trend in fashion and cosmetics automatically demands a new look and therefore a new girl. Thousands of new girls approach and are approached by the model agencies every year, and even the most established models are under threat. In less than a year's time, Lauren Hutton, Cheryl Tiegs, Shelley Hack and Karen Graham could be just as much names from the past as are Suzy Parker, Dorian Leigh and Jean Shrimpton, who are still relatively young women, and the trade will be talking about and fighting for girls like fifteen-year-old Jodi Foster, who already has a successful film career to her credit.

TEN

AN INDUSTRY IN NEED OF A FACE-LIFT

*Beauty in Distress is much the most affecting
beauty.*

—Edmund Burke,
Sublime and Beautiful

As cosmetics, "this industry of artists, neurotics and queers," as
the chief executive of a very large company described it to me,
enters the 1980s, it is beginning to show its age. Some parts of it
are definitely in need of a face-lift; others, many believe, should
be laid quietly to rest. Compared with many other industries,
cosmetics had a long and healthy childhood followed by an
equally impressive maturity. It was fortunate in its early entrepreneurs, who, although they might have been pretty ghastly people,
had distinct flair and business ability and in some cases maintained their vigor and competitive approach into their old age.
What is happening now is that the old competitiveness has been
maintained, but in a new atmosphere. For the most part, the old
bitter personal rivalries have gone; what is left is straight, hard and
intense competition. No longer do a few individuals square up to

one another, copying each other's ideas. Quite simply, there are
large groups, with a great number of public shareholders who do
not care who brings out what first, or who steals whose formulas,
but who are concerned about the level of monthly earnings in the
companies in which they invest. Not only must these earnings be
maintained, but they must also rise if investors are to see their
dividends increase and the capital value of their stock rise. Any
diminution in growth and they are off into other stocks and share
prices fall. This has already happened in the cosmetics trade, but
without any decline in industry profits. In 1979 and early 1980,
both Avon Products and Revlon were trading at their lowest prices
for some years.

The explanation of this new situation is that an increasing percentage of total sales going to a few very large companies. There
are still many thousands of small cosmetics companies scattered
throughout the major cosmetics markets. There always will be,
but the pattern will be for new companies to be constantly set up,
while their predecessors disappear into larger companies or go
under. It was only in the 1970s that the companies of the first
entrepreneurs were taken over: those of the 1950s and 1960s like
Erno Laszlo, Adrian Arpel and Mary Quant are already part of
larger concerns. The parent companies today are aggressive mass
marketers that know what risks can be taken, and where. Against
these, the smaller companies have very little chance of long-term
survival, although there will always be a few companies that catch
the imagination. These will survive if they limit their attempts to
grow and operate in a confined way with a limited number of
outlets and products.

As soon as the smaller companies move into the mass markets,
they find it very difficult to compete. They cannot afford the vast
advertising campaigns required today—a million dollars is beginning to look like a minimum for a launch—to get a product or a
line off the ground and bring it sufficiently to the attention of the
customer to capture a profitable number of sales from its rivals.
The pattern of distribution has been changing as well in the past
decade. The department stores, traditionally the area where prestige cosmetics have been sold, have been losing their place to the

drugstores, supermarket chains, discount stores and other mass distributors. These changes have not meant that the producers of the higher-priced ranges are giving up the department stores: they are simply fighting harder for a place in them. This, too, is bad for the small manufacturers. These changes have put severe pressure on cosmetics companies to find new ways of marketing if they are to hold their own.

The new ways do not always have the flamboyance and excitement of the past, and many people feel that the industry today has become dull. Others, working in the vast conglomerates with plenty of experience behind them, and the financial cover of other interests in the total group, are optimistic and look forward to the battles of the 1980s. Sam Kallish, as I write, is without a corporate base and is among the most pessimistic.

It is difficult not to like Sam Kallish at first meeting. His toughness and go-getting mentality soon emerge in his conversation. Although he may be difficult to live with in company terms, his approach is invigorating and exciting. Since he returned to New York from the Max Factor debacle, he has been advising companies in the industry. That he will one day attempt to run his own company again, there is no doubt. He attacks the industry vigorously and accuses it of lacking entrepreneurial spirit. "Dull," "boring," "repetitive," "unimaginative" are words he often uses, although he is generous in his praise of those he admires in the industry, such as the Lauders.

He sees the industry as one in which many executives have no loyalty to a particular company, but who move around constantly. The major companies, he charges, are becoming too cumbersome, but he sees changes for the industry in the 1980s as a result of the shifting role of women in society. He does not like the industry as it stands today. "There is very little innovation in the cosmetics industry and very few entrepreneurial people indeed. It is a cliché to suggest, as many people do today, that the entrepreneurial, innovative creative people in the industry were and are financially irresponsible. The industry has been and continues to be its own worst enemy. Look at the executives. They move from company to company, two years here, two years there; there is no

loyalty. I feel very strongly that any company in the fashion business—and cosmetics are fashion—needs strong leadership. All
the wonderful, dynamic crazy people are dead. Now all one ever
hears are words like 'accounts receivable' and 'cash flows,' and all
decisions about products are taken by committees. The cosmetics
company needs to have its decisions taken by one person—one
person with the courage to take risks is what is needed, because in
the end profits are made by one person having the courage to
fail."

Strong words, but are they appropriate to the cosmetics industry
today? Margaret Hayes, chief cosmetics buyer at Saks Fifth Avenue, tends to agree with Sam Kallish. She takes a somber view of
the industry but points out that at Saks she is concerned only with
the top end of the business: "The mass market is flat at present
and there is little sign of creativity. In terms of incremental business, the industry continues to expand, but the same cannot be
said for profits, and margins are narrowing. I believe the market
for fragrances is growing faster in the U.S. than anywhere else
and that there will be further growth, but the industry has not as
yet come to terms with the recession in the economy and inflation." She too points to the Lauders as trend setters in the industry. "No one knows what their profit figures are, but they must be
good. They have the best management and standards and the best
understanding of the long-term prospects for the industry."

But at Cosmair, Inc., associate company of L'Oreal, James
Nixon takes quite a different view. "In my opinion the industry
overall is very healthy. It is growing faster than the growth in the
population, but the major growth areas are concentrated in certain categories. There has, for example, been a tremendous renaissance in color cosmetics with the ending of the natural look
craze. The whole resurgence started with clothes. Everything
today is unnatural and a woman just doesn't look right if she looks
natural. Toiletries, too, have considerable growth potential.
Shampoo sales have been growing astoundingly for many years.
Both men and women are washing their hair frequently now.
Fragrances, too, appear to have plenty of growth left in them."

Eric Morgan, managing director of the cosmetics division of BAT Industries of Britain, would not agree with Mr. Nixon on the question of color cosmetics: "In color cosmetics you are dealing with the most fickle market of all, teenagers. They like to be fashionable and will abandon a product very quickly for something new. Then one has to have such an enormous range—say, twelve different shades of lipsticks, six of blusher and the same of eyeshadows. This means that relatively small amounts are produced of each item. There simply isn't sufficient run to make a profit.

"There are three different levels. First of all, there is a level of production below which people fail. They simply cannot make a profit. Then there is the second threshold where the company is so strong in the particular market and its sales are such that it cannot fail. This is true at the moment of Estée Lauder in America, Lentheric in the United Kingdom in fragrances, Yardley in South America and Shiseido in Japan."

Leonard Lauder, too, takes a cautious view of the future: "The industry is reaching maturity after a period of explosive growth. It will get more and more difficult for new companies to enter the industry, and saner growth will be the pattern of the future. So much depends on the way the economy moves and, in particular, how the price of fuel affects the economy. We have noticed how government changes can affect sales. In the United Kingdom there was a severe jolt for a time when the government raised sales taxes [called "value-added tax"]. It didn't mean that women stopped using cosmetics: it simply meant that they used up their old cosmetics completely before buying new ones. This kind of action can have a marked effect on sales."

Joseph Ronchetti, chief executive of Elizabeth Arden, agrees: "The big companies will get bigger, and it will become increasingly difficult to get into the industry. The problem today for those using the salon route is that their profit margins are too low for growth. A return of 10 percent or so may be fine for a small business, but 15–20 percent is average for the industry, and that is the level which is needed. When new ventures are set up, people ask themselves why they should trust these people and their products when they have no experience of the industry." Government regulation and control of the industry is bound to increase in the next decade as it becomes more and more easy to identify toxins in raw materials.

Former model Fiona Campbell-Walter, today a customer, reflects Ronchetti's views: "I tend towards using the big names, rather like buying a painting or a horse with a good pedigree. One hopes it will be miraculous as they claim and, at worst, it will be good."

At Revlon, Michel Bergerac is more optimistic: "The industry will continue to grow as more and more women enter the market during the next twenty-five years and as life expectancy continues to lengthen. In addition, more women will continue to join the working force as the two-income family becomes the norm and they will have more disposable income." He sees the biggest area of growth in treatment products, followed by fragrances for both men and women. He forecasts, too, that international business will grow at a faster rate than domestic U.S. trade. The biggest growth-potential lies, in his view, in Latin America, the Far East and the Pacific rim. "At Revlon we will continue to develop the cosmetics business both domestically and internationally. The company will continue to develop its health-care products based on ethical pharmaceuticals and on less-regulated pharmacy" (those products that do not face rigorous controls by the U.S. authorities).

From Shiseido, Andrew Philip comments: "The cosmetics market is getting polarized and will become more so as time goes on. Women are becoming more quality-conscious and more aware that there is more to looking good than cosmetics. For this reason, the number of salons will continue to grow where women can go for advice about diet and exercise."

Andrew Philip was also enthusiastic about Boots, the British manufacturers and retail druggists: ". . . quite simply, it is the best merchandising operation in the world," he said, adding that it is difficult for anyone to make a profit on cosmetics sales on any large scale in Britain without the cooperation of Boots. Indeed, the company is variously praised and cursed by the cosmetics industry. It absolutely dominates the market with 34 percent of total retail cosmetics sales. It also produces 12 percent of them with its own brand, No. 7. Moreover, it has 1,112 outlets, and to be able to sell via Boots is obviously desirable for a company. Yet it is very choosey about whom it takes on. One disgruntled European manufacturer who approached Boots told me: "We just couldn't afford to go into Boots. They asked me what advertising budget I was planning and made it very clear that if we were not thinking in terms of at least a million pounds, they were not interested in taking us in. This added to the fact that cosmetics are so incredibly cheap in Britain, even though the value-added tax is high, means that we cannot get into the market."

It is indeed true that the British market is very mature. The growth in sales is slow and even the higher-priced brands like Lauder, according to Leonard Lauder himself, have suffered from the almost doubling of the tax on sales. For a large company, an advertising budget of a million pounds may not seem like much, but for a small or medium-sized company trying to break into the British market for the first time, it is often prohibitive.

Boots not only offends some foreign and domestic British manufacturers who wish to sell in its stores; it is also at the center of a row in Britain for, it has been alleged, trying to force some of its suppliers not to sell to other chains. In March 1979, Sainsbury, a leading grocery chain that has been trying to get into cosmetics retailing, attacked the cosmetic companies for refusing to sell to it. The reason given by Sainsbury was fear of loss of prestige on the part of the companies if their products were sold alongside food, but it also charged that there was pressure from Boots on its suppliers not to sell to the supermarket chains. Boots denied the charge, but did state that it did indeed believe that a cosmetics line might lose some of its status if it was sold in a food store. If Britain follows the U.S. pattern, however—and it usually does—Sainsbury's may not have too long to wait before cosmetics join its food lines.

Commenting on the British market and others outside North

America, Leonard Lauder said: "You have to divide the British cosmetics industry into Oxford Street and Knightsbridge, London, and the rest. The London market is very mature and sales can only develop slowly from now on. The rest of the country is different and growth will be faster. In Europe, the French and Swiss markets are very mature; Germany is slow and Italy very buoyant."

Wherever one looks, except perhaps in the Latin American or African markets, all the signs are that the explosive growth in the cosmetics industry is over. Eric Morgan thinks that growth in the industry has always been closely linked to the growth of a country's gross national product: "Cosmetics sales are always equal to around 0.15 percent of GNP and the rate of increase in the growth in the major industrialized countries, which are the chief market for cosmetics, is slowing down."

Add to this problem the definite signs that young people today are using fewer makeup products and less of those that they do use than teenagers did twenty years ago. They still use them, but much more sparingly, and it could be that in its massive marketing and promotion the companies are defeating their own aims. Not all products can be better than every other product and the new customer in particular is faced with a bewildering array of products and, not to be discounted, an often fearsome sales assistant with a superior manner, aggressively pushing the customer to buy more than she wants.

Not only is it becoming more difficult to persuade young people to use cosmetics indiscriminately, but there is a further very fundamental change coming in the industry in the next decade. There will simply be fewer teenagers around. For the first time since the industry became very large, the number of teenagers will be falling and there will not be the automatic overall rise in sales that there has been in every decade of this century. By the year 2000, it is expected that the teenage market will be down by about 20 percent, a significant decline. There are several implications for cosmetic companies in this, and not all of them will go the same way about improving their position in the new situation.

Women have more money to spend than ever before, but also more calls on their money: they also have more sense and will ask themselves whether in buying a cream for $30 they are in fact getting much better value than one for $5, or whether they are simply paying for the packaging and advertising behind the product. Men have never been quite so credulous as women.

There are other problems to be faced. Tariffs, high taxes, falling living standards and price controls are just some of the problems facing the cosmetics industry today. And there are problems even in the affluent North American market. After centuries of self-decoration people are not suddenly going to give it up. But they are going to become more selective. Some of the sales are already moving away from the drugstores and department stores into the new kind of beauty centers which are growing up. These are not beauty salons as such, but places where a woman can go to exercise, get advice on cosmetics and spend not too much time doing either. The days when many women can or will spend all day in a salon are over, and the friendly, relaxed approach of the expert advising the customer about cosmetics is very welcome, to working women particularly.

One thing is certain: competition will not cease, and it is likely to become increasingly bitter as companies fight for an increasing share of a falling market. Success in that market consists in getting a six-foot space on a cosmetics counter in a department store. In the lines they run, Revlon and Estée Lauder between them take up about 45 percent of such space available in North America. Smaller companies get their share, as there is always a section of the market in search of exclusivity, but their position is always perilous. Newcomers must buy their markets, and this implies high spending on promotion and advertising. The retailer is not interested in whether the supplying company is making or losing money: his interest is confined solely to the cut he gets from sales. Diane von Furstenberg, who started out designing dresses, has still not managed to get her cosmetics and fragrances division into the black after four years. Calvin Klein has failed to make profits, too. Looking back, the designer must regret that he did not take the offer when Revlon tried to buy his company.

Forecasts of the increasing strength of the large companies are certain to be fulfilled. The strong will become stronger, and there will be no room for the weak. Companies will increasingly diversify into related products, following the lead of companies like Revlon, where, after the current phase of acquisitions is ended, cosmetics will be reduced to 55 percent of the total business. With fewer young people the emphasis in cosmetics will turn from the young and companies will change their strategy as the age profile of the cosmetics user increases. Cosmetics users, of course, do not get old; they simply grow up and the companies will grow up with them. Helena Rubinstein brought out its over-fifty range too soon and its pitch was wrong, but today Elizabeth Arden with Millenium and, in the United Kingdom, Mary Quant with her Skin Programme, have the right ideas.

So just where do the big growth prospects lie for the industry in the next decade?

Men's toiletries and cosmetics could be among them. But it is a much more resistant market than the women's market. As Eric Morgan of BAT Industries says: "The men's cosmetics market is always said to be on the verge of an explosion, but it has never really happened." That could change in the 1980s if men can be persuaded that they need cosmetics as much as women do, or think they do. It is certainly a message that the cosmetics companies have been pushing across to the public since the end of World War II. The signs are that they are now succeeding. During many periods of history, men have worn as many cosmetics as women —and color ones at that—but since the Victorian era in England and the growth of the Protestant ethic, it has been regarded as effeminate for men to indulge in self-decoration. Some of the first film stars refused point-blank at first to put makeup on their faces, but quickly changed their minds when they saw themselves looking, not manly, but washed-out on the screen. (Tom Mix, an early cowboy, swore never to use makeup, but was mortified when he saw what he looked like on film and quickly changed his mind.)

But this was not enough to persuade men outside the theatrical profession to use, if not color cosmetics, at least deodorants, after-shave lotion, colognes, talcum powders and, ultimately, skin creams. It has been a hard market to crack, but it is being done, and in the U.S. alone sales are now running at over a billion dollars a year.

Men today appear to be becoming as convinced as women that to have a good-looking skin is an asset, but the market is highly sensitive, and the trend could change sharply and suddenly. The reason for the growth in interest by men is the same as for women —the cult of youth in our society. If one does not actually have youth, it is felt necessary at least to have a youthful appearance. This applies, if anything, more to men than to women in business. The aging executive fears for his job, and the man who once touched out the gray in his hair—no longer is this a sign of distinction, but mere age—now may use the full gamut of creams, and eventually have his face lifted as well. The way the message was got across was by making it clear that it was not only manly, but also sensible to take care of the body and the skin. It was easy enough with talcs and deodorants. First, all a company must do is to persuade women that the natural smell of a man is not pleasant and she will provide the first sales. Then a man has to be persuaded that to be attractive to a woman he must smell pleasant. While the industry had little problem in persuading women to buy for their men, it proved more difficult for many years to get the follow-up sales from men, who, it appears, simply left the products on the shelf and continued in their old ways. But gradually, resistance was broken down, and since the 1960s the overall market has grown steadily.

The men's fragrance market is also expanding, but no one has yet discovered a foolproof method of marketing a product successfully for men. During the past fifteen years the market grew from $67 million in 1963 to $395 million in 1978 and as much as $445 million in 1979 in the U.S. This is an average annual growth rate of just over 12.5 percent, compared with an average annual increase for all toiletries and cosmetics generally in the U.S. of 9.4

percent. Ten companies control 80 percent of the market there, with Avon by far the biggest, with 20 percent. Altogether there are some 250 brands of fragrances alone on the market.

Outside America, the prospects for growth in men's lines is even better. It is reckoned that over 80 percent of American men use deodorants, but the figure for Europe is highest in Sweden, where it approaches 60 percent, and lowest in Italy, where men are very conscious of their masculinity, at about 30 percent. The problem is that although the potential market is there, this does not necessarily mean that one can develop it. Some people do prefer the natural smell of bodies to scent. Living standards in Europe are generally not as high as in America, and there has never been as much idle cash lying around to spend on nonessentials. It is a strange man or woman who is actually going to do without meat to buy high-priced nonessential cosmetics.

But men still like to feel that they are men, even if they smell nice. Revlon's Chaz man was holding a bunch of daisies in his hand, intended by the advertisers to be for his girl friend. The public, however, clearly thought otherwise: a guy with daisies was just too much. The company has not yet given up with Chaz, however, which is now being marketed in thirty-four countries. Another way of getting men to buy fragrances is to push his and her versions of a scent in the hope that a woman will buy for both. Perhaps Jovan had the best gimmick here: the two bottles snuggled suggestively together with curved sides.

The expensive ranges at Chesebrough-Pond's products in contrast have been doing very well indeed. In particular, Prince Matchabelli, which the company bought in 1962, has been outstanding and chalking up sales increases of close to 20 percent. Aziza, Wind Song and Cachet have done well for the conglomerate, too, in the female area.

It was a tough enough job to get men interested in personal freshness and fragrances and yet another one to persuade them into skin care. The market is by no means fully developed, and care must be taken to avoid words like "cosmetic" when referring to products for men. When suntans became a status symbol, men realized that they needed protection from the sun just as much as women if not to prevent wrinkles, then to protect themselves from skin cancers. Men who participate in sports that exposed them to extreme weather conditions have always used skin creams as a matter of course. Members of the Chris Bonington Everest expedition in 1972 took along lip salves and creams to protect their skin at high altitude. Most men, as well as women, use some form of protective cream when they are skiing, or sailing, in hot or cold conditions. By using sportsmen, or other men of proved masculinity, in their advertising and promotion, the companies have gradually worked up a good and growing market for men's skin treatment. Erno Laszlo now has a questionnaire for men, and the regimen is the same as that for women. Clinique has extended its line to skin supplies for men, and the stable companion at Estée Lauder, the Aramis line, which was first introduced in 1954 as a cologne, after-shave and soap, now has over seventy-five items in its range. Aramis now also comes without a smell. It is called Aramis 900, but so far men seem to prefer the fragrance.

It was thirteen years before Estée Lauder introduced a new cedar-smelling men's fragrance, Devin, in 1977, to sell alongside the very successful Aramis, after Chaz, which appeared in 1976. Devin, despite a million-dollar advertising campaign at its launch in the autumn of 1977, has barely touched the dominance of Aramis. Although the men's quality toiletries market is now reaching a value of a billion dollars a year worldwide, men are still reluctant to buy cosmetics and fragrances for themselves, and 65 percent are bought for them by women.

If the resistance can be broken, there is no reason why men's cosmetics should not eventually be as big a market as women's. Once the barriers are broken down, however, another problem will arise. How does a company get a man to buy skin products different from his wife's? After all, fragrances and color cosmetics are readily identifiable, but who knows if a man is using Revlon's Natural Wonder or Arden's Millenium instead of a cream marketed for men? If two people are using a product, the company has garnered the sales anyway, but, in the building up of brand loyalty, it is important to make separate unit sales. And the industry fears that a man might be put off for good should someone accuse him of using a skin cream. Many believe that the industry can forget about men as far as color cosmetics are concerned, but even here, there are signs: from using tan-without-sun lotions, some men are beginning to use colored skin creams, not that they are ever referred to as "foundation creams," of course. The emphasis is on a healthy glow, winter and summer.

Although it would be good business for the cosmetics companies if they were to persuade men to use skin creams as a matter of course, there are genuine problems, because men's skins are quite different from women's. Dermatologists and cosmetics companies are agreed that almost everyone who sunbathes needs a sun screen: even black people can get burned if they expose themselves suddenly to the sun after a long period of being covered up. A few men, too, whose skin is dry, are advised not to use soap and water, but most men have oilier skins than women. Too much cream can irritate their skin because their sebaceous glands and hair follicles are much larger than those of women. Creams can clog the pores as a result and cause acne.

Men are taking to face masks and facial treatments as well. Every health farm in the United States will have a quota of men taking full skin treatments appropriate to their skin type. As an average, men comprise about 10 percent of health farm customers, but in some cases, the figure rises to 20 and even 30 percent, generally on the beauty-conscious West and East coasts of America.

Meantime, while it puzzles over the future, the industry has plenty of other things to think about. Those in it spend a lot of time trying to work out what difference there is between cosmetics and toiletries—if any. And if there is, whether it matters. David Mahoney of Norton Simon has confessed himself unable to tell the difference—perhaps that is why Max Factor does not sit comfortably in his group—and two years after taking over Charles of the Ritz, Richard Furland, president of the parent company, the Squibb Corporation, said that he was still waiting to be told where cosmetics ended and toiletries began. To the outsider, such differences may not seem to matter, but they are important, as the two products require quite different marketing strategies. The definition of the difference is easy enough. Toiletries are utilitarian products, mass distributed at relatively low prices and used by most people, men or women. So defined, a toothpaste, soap, shaving cream, shampoos and deodorants are all toiletries. Cosmetics, on the other hand, are designed to make people look what they are not; they are meant to create as good a look as possible for a person and they are clearly not utilitarian. As a result, they are more personally valuable to the customer who uses them, though they will not be used by everyone and will inevitably be less widely distributed than toiletries and more expensive.

But the lines are blurred. Some inexpensive after-shaves, for instance, are quite simply regarded as toiletries and will be found on supermarket shelves. Others, with an expensive perfume (and a perfume is almost essential to cosmetics apart from some hypoallergenic lines), are certainly regarded as a cosmetic. On the other hand, there is some temptation to say that anything for a man is a toiletry, in an attempt to keep any suggestion of effeminacy away from the product, but a glance at the display in any department store will show that this is not so.

Hair coloring, which ought to be a cosmetic because it beautifies the hair, is classed as a toiletry simply because it is mass-marketed. Pond's Cold Cream, basically no different from a cream coming from Estée Lauder, Revlon or Arden, is sold as a toiletry; the others as cosmetics. Some people do not even regard Avon as a cosmetics house at all because of the mass distribution of its products. And mass distribution does not always pay off. In the 1950s, Revlon increased the outlets for its basic line in the United Kingdom from 2,500 to 6,000 and sold fewer items as the products lost their exclusivity. The company then cut back to 1,400 outlets, and business improved markedly. The problem for the manufacturers is how to balance the cachet of exclusivity with the benefits that come by increasing outlets but not so much so that the public will turn to other products that seem more exclusive.

Those who are not wondering how to define their products are considering whether cosmetics should once again, after a lapse of centuries, become a branch of the medical industry. The basic cosmetics formulas have reamined unchanged for thousands of years; the new miracle ingredients are not miracles at all. They serve merely to soften the skin temporarily and protect it from the atmosphere. They cannot, by themselves, treat skin problems or make the skin more youthful. But if they were combined with drugs and medicines, it is possible that they could. There is no doubt that cosmetics are reaching the fringes of what is permissible under the various government regulations around the world. If further developments are to be made, it is likely that, in the future, dermatologists, who for many years have tended to treat cosmetics with disdain, will be looking at them more and more as if they were drugs. The point about this is that almost everywhere in the world the regulations controlling drugs are far more stringent than those for cosmetics.

Cosmetic companies are already suggesting that their products have therapeutic properties when they use words like "treatment" and "program" to describe them. The Erno Laszlo company has probably gone farthest in this regard. Once the diagnosis of the customer's skin is made, he or she is sold the various creams and lotions appropriate to that skin—and no others. There is no choice about it: the Laszlo representative decides exactly what is needed, and only those products are sold to the particular customer. In this process the company is getting as near to a medical diagnosis as is possible without using medicaments.

There is no doubt that there are drugs available today which do have effects on the skin, but none so far which slow down the aging process. The skin diseases of acne and seborrhea, for instance, which are directly related to hormone levels, can often be improved if women take high-dosage estrogen contraceptive pills. The amount of estrogen varies a great deal from one pill to another—it may be as high as 100 micrograms, but need only be 50 micrograms to prevent contraception. Acne and seborrhea are caused in different ways in men and women, and estrogen, a male hormone, raises the level of male hormones in the woman's body and has a beneficial effect on the skin of those women who suffer from the disease. It does not work for men, of course, as they already have all the estrogen they need. Unfortunately, as with all wonder cures, there is a snag. Women were not designed naturally to have high estrogen levels, and the high-dosage pill has been firmly linked with an increase in thrombosis, particularly in women who may already have a tendency toward it. There is a substantial level of research findings now available to show that women taking such pills run a much greater risk of death at all age levels than those who do not. For this reason, most doctors refuse to prescribe it, and the low-dosage pill which is preferred does not appear to have the same beneficial effect on the skin.

At this point, cosmetics work only on the surface of the skin. One claim that a cosmetics company must never make is that its product penetrates the skin: once it does that, the cosmetic will be reclassified as a drug and far more stringent tests must be applied before a drug can be marketed, including large-scale tests on human beings in some countries. It is doubtful whether any but the very biggest cosmetics companies have the resources to make such tests, which anyway are quite unnecessary in the case of cosmetics.

Today, however, more and more companies are making some limited tests on human beings before a cosmetic product is put on the market, after completing all the routine tests on animals. At Lancôme in 1979, a new skin program for oily skin was launched after being tested for six weeks on 100 volunteers aged between eighteen and forty-five. The results of the tests were reported factually to the public, which could then make up its mind. The assistance of dermatologists was sought, and they sponsored the product, stating quite firmly that in their view the women's skin looked and felt less greasy. Control was marketed on the basis of these claims.

Gone, probably forever, are the days when some people claimed that cosmetics were bad for the skin: the overriding question is whether they are any good. Many of the once-independent cosmetics companies are now allied with drug companies that have enormous research facilities, and it is logical that the development of the two products should go hand in hand. Companies are already stating that distinctions between the two are meaningless, claiming that anything that is put on the skin can have a beneficial effect, however temporary, even if it is classified simply as a cosmetic. It is now within the realm of possibility that products may be developed that can truly delay the aging process in the skin.

Whatever way it is looked at, the cosmetics industry can never be described as dull, uneventful or lacking in drama. In the psychology of cosmetics, it is important that the dream of a man or woman to become more attractive is never shattered. Cosmetics today are a science, but they are also an illusion, which it sees as vital to foster if the industry generally, and the individual companies in it, are to prosper. Some will inevitably fail, and as the industry becomes more and more polarized, not-always disinterested observers are watching struggling firms with some glee. The fate of Helena Rubinstein is now known, and the industry has turned its attention to other ailing companies, although it will still be interested to see what happens at Rubinstein under its new owners. It is not just the small companies that may go under, either. Helene Curtis is now showing distinct signs of senility, and even the giant Max Factor will have to show a sharp turnaround if it is not to face the ignominy of a fate like that of Madame Rubinstein's once proud company.

INDEX